Social Trust

With increasingly divergent views and commitments, and an all-or-nothing mindset in political life, it can seem hard to sustain the level of trust in other members of our society necessary to ensure our most basic institutions work. This book features interdisciplinary perspectives on social trust. The contributors address four main topics related to social trust. The first topic is empirical and formal work on norms and institutional trust, especially the relationships between trust and human behavior. The second topic concerns trust in particular institutions, notably the legal system, scientific community, and law enforcement. Third, the contributors address challenges posed by diversity and oppression in maintaining social trust. Finally, they discuss different forms of trust and social trust. *Social Trust* will be of interest to researchers in philosophy, political science, economics, law, psychology, and sociology.

Kevin Vallier is Associate Professor of Philosophy at Bowling Green State University and the author of four edited volumes, and 40 peer-reviewed articles. His books include *Liberal Politics and Public Faith* (Routledge 2014), *Must Politics Be War* (2019), and *Trust in a Polarized Age* (2020).

Michael Weber is Professor of Philosophy, and Department Chair, at Bowling Green State University. He has published on a wide variety of topics in ethics and political philosophy, including rational choice theory, ethics and the emotions, and egalitarianism. He has co-edited volumes on a variety of topics in applied ethics, including *Paternalism*, *Manipulation*, *The Ethics of Self-Defense*, and *Religious Exemptions*.

Routledge Studies in Contemporary Philosophy

The Philosophy and Psychology of Ambivalence
Being of Two Minds
Edited by Berit Brogaard and Dimitria Electra Gatzia

Concepts in Thought, Action, and Emotion
New Essays
Edited by Christoph Demmerling and Dirk Schröder

Towards a Philosophical Anthropology of Culture
Naturalism, Reflectivism, and Skepticism
Kevin M. Cahill

Examples and Their Role in Our Thinking
Ondřej Beran

Extimate Technology
Self-Formation in a Technological World
Ciano Aydin

Modes of Truth
The Unified Approach to Truth, Modality, and Paradox
Edited by Carlo Nicolai and Johannes Stern

Practices of Reason
Fusing the Inferentialist and Scientific Image
Ladislav Koreň

Social Trust
Edited by Kevin Vallier and Michael Weber

For more information about this series, please visit: https://www.routledge.com/Routledge-Studies-in-Contemporary-Philosophy/book-series/SE0720

Social Trust

Edited by Kevin Vallier
and Michael Weber

Routledge
Taylor & Francis Group
NEW YORK AND LONDON

First published 2021
by Routledge
52 Vanderbilt Avenue, New York, NY 10017

and by Routledge
2 Park Square, Milton Park, Abingdon, Oxon, OX14 4RN

Routledge is an imprint of the Taylor & Francis Group, an informa business

Library of Congress Cataloging-in-Publication Data
Names: Vallier, Kevin, editor.
Title: Social trust / edited by Kevin Vallier and Michael Weber.
Description: New York, NY : Routledge, an imprint of Taylor & Francis Group, 2021. | Series: Routledge studies in contemporary philosophy | Includes bibliographical references and index.
Identifiers: LCCN 2020058184 (print) | LCCN 2020058185 (ebook) |
Subjects: LCSH: Trust—Social aspects. | Trust—Political aspects. | Justice—Social aspects.
Classification: LCC HM1204 .S63 2021 (print) | LCC HM1204 (ebook) | DDC 158.2—dc23
LC record available at https://lccn.loc.gov/2020058184
LC ebook record available at https://lccn.loc.gov/2020058185

ISBN: 978-0-367-45845-4 (hbk)
ISBN: 978-0-367-76808-9 (pbk)
ISBN: 978-1-003-02978-6 (ebk)

Typeset in Sabon
by KnowledgeWorks Global Ltd.

Table of Contents

Social Trust Introduction

Kevin Vallier, Michael Weber

Our politics are polarizing and divisive, negative partisanship is on the rise, and people seem to be gradually retreating into their own information bubbles, only consuming information that reinforces their point of view. We are witnessing a global rise in populism, and liberal democracy is in retreat in some parts of the world, and under threat in others. Attempts to reduce polarization, including those carried out most prominently by former President Barack Obama, seem to have failed, or worse, backfired.

Many quite plausibly think these unfortunate events are at least in part the result of falling social and political trust. But there is surely significant complexity here, which is why it is important to develop research on the concepts, causes, and consequences of social trust in particular, and the ethical issues raised by social trust. That is the purpose of this volume.

0.1 What is Social Trust?

Social trust, often referred to as "generalized" trust, is trust in strangers—persons within one's society with whom one has little personal familiarity. Social trust can thus be understood broadly as trust in society. But trust to do what? Social trust is trust that persons will abide by social norms, which are publicly recognized, shared social rules that people both in fact expect one another to follow and think that everyone morally ought to follow. Social trust creates a climate of practical and strategic stability. Because people in trusting societies generally believe that others will follow these social norms, they can formulate projects and plans with relative confidence.

This understanding of social trust is well-grounded in the social-trust literature. Most scholars see trust as a product of durable mutual expectations about cooperative moral behavior. Some, such as Eric Uslaner, understand moralistic trust as trust that others share one's personal values. However, it is better to understand social trust as trust that people share and recognize an array of social rules that do not necessarily correspond to what persons consider of ultimate value in life. We do not need to know a person's ideology to know whether we expect them to stop at a red light, or to not steal your phone if you leave it in Starbucks by mistake. Social norms lie at the root of social trust, and norms and our personal ideals are not related in a straightforward way. Fortunately, that means we can socially trust persons with very different values than our own.

To be rational, social trust must be justified, and justified by trustworthiness, which we can understand as a disposition to comply with social norms. Social trust can only be rationally sustained if people think that those they trust merit that trust. In other words, it is rational to trust others only if we think they are trustworthy. And we can understand a socially trustworthy person as one who is disposed to follow shared social norms.

One ethical concern that arises is that, intuitively, we generally want social trust to be sustained for the right reasons. Pouring the "trust hormone" Oxytocin into the water supply might make people more trusting, but it is not a good way to promote social trust. More realistically, promoting trust by manufacturing a common enemy to create a bond between members of a community together seems unsatisfactory, and not just because it might be ineffective, leading to more division rather than cohesiveness. What we seek is to sustain social trust by giving persons morally appropriate incentives to be trustworthy, and then allowing social trust to form as a free cognitive and emotional response to observed trustworthy behavior.

A great deal of research on social trust is carried out by political scientists, indeed mostly by political scientists. Economists too research trust. But they study trust in different ways. Political scientists study trust mostly by way of surveys on how much people trust their government, each other, etc., while economists study trust in the laboratory, often running variations on the "trust game" in game theory to look at the circumstances in which people play cooperatively. One of us has written on the methods of measuring trust in some detail.[1] For the sake of the reader, the first essay in this volume reviews how trust is measured in some detail, so we will not review the measures here in the interests of brevity.

The present volume is divided into three parts: (1) empirical research on social trust, (2) concepts of social trust, and (3) the ethics and politics of social trust.

The empirical research on trust will likely be the most familiar to many readers, but each paper studies trust with different methods. Collectively, then, they should give the reader a sense for the breadth of ways in which trust is studied empirically. They should also provide the reader with an overview of how social trust is understood in different empirical literatures, setting up the next part of the book.

The concept of social trust is important for philosophical readers to have a clear sense for the topic of the book, given that social trust is often ill-defined or under-defined for the tastes of a philosophical audience. We end with essays on the ethical issues raised by or related to social trust. These include relationships with trust in the police, with trust in law enforcement more generally, and trust and parental care.

0.2 Chapter Summaries

0.2.1 Empirical Research on Social Trust

The volume begins with "Legal and Social Trust in Africa," which uses survey data to explore the relationship between social trust and trust in the legal system. Andreas Bergh, Christian Bjørnskov, and Kevin Vallier review how social trust is studied, and then draw on research on trust in Africa to argue that trust in the legal system is a function of social trust, and not necessarily the other way around. But social and legal trust are only connected when legal officials are seen as representative of most members of society. In the second piece, "Trustworthiness Is a Social Norm, but Trusting Is Not," Cristina Bicchieri, Erte Xiao, and Ryan Muldoon use a survey of strategic behavior in what are called "trust games" in game theory, which provides evidence for the claim that most people do not think they are obliged to trust one another, but that they are obliged to be trustworthy. This is because people do not ordinarily punish persons who fail to trust, but they do choose to punish those who fail to be trustworthy. In the third essay, "Trust, Diversity, and (Ir-)Rationality," Simon Scheller argues that we can explain out-group discrimination in trust situations as an emergent property of individually rational behavior, even when the collective behavior is irrational. Scheller uses a kind of computational model, known as an agent-based model, to make the case for his thesis. Each of these essays use distinct methods to measure trust—questionnaires, laboratory results, and computational models. The reader should come away with a sense for the breadth of methods used to measure trust.

0.2.2 Concepts of Social Trust

The next three articles explore how philosophers develop account of the nature of different kinds of trust, that is, analyses of the concept of trust and related extensions of the concept of trust, such as trust in science and social distrust. In the fourth article, "Disappointed Yet Unbetrayed," Edward Hinchman explores how to define trust and whether trusting someone involves more than merely relying on them, including whether trust is a two-place relation (A trusts B) or a three-place relation (A trusts B to X). Hinchman defends a new three-place model on which "A Xs through trust in B." This he calls the "Assurance View" of trust because, he claims, trusting B is to accept B's implicit invitation to truth—an assurance that B is trustworthy in the right way. This essay introduces readers to debates about how trust as a general concept is defined, which will have implications for how social trust should be conceptually defined. Marion Boulicault and S. Andrew Schroeder follow with "Public Trust in Science: Exploring the Idiosyncrasy-Free Ideal," which provides an account of the nature of public trust in the scientific process. The authors argue that the trustworthiness of science is partly based on the fact that it proceeds independently from the particular values, wishes, and goals of individual scientist. We can trust science when it would have reached the same conclusions, no matter which scientists were involved in the process. In this way, Boulicault and Schroeder defend an "idiosyncrasy-free ideal" of trust and trustworthiness in science. This essay develops a notion of trust appropriate for trust in the scientific community. Next, Lacey J. Davidson and Mark Satta argue in "Justified Social Distrust" that social *distrust*, namely distrust based on the belief that others in one's society are not trustworthy, is a concept worthy of analysis in its own right. They argue that members of oppressed groups are often epistemically justified in exhibiting social distrust under conditions of oppression. In some cases, oppressed groups are epistemically justified in distrusting their oppressors, but this distrust is harmful to the oppressed group. So, Davidson and Satta explore ways in which a community can build trust when social distrust is rational, in particular by structuring institutions to make the distrusted group more trustworthy. The articles in this section should give the reader a sense for how philosophers approach social trust, and some indication of how to formulate an account of trust and particular kinds of trust and distrust.

0.2.3 The Ethics and Politics of Social Trust

The third and final section of the volume focuses on the ethical and political issues relating to social trust, in particular how social trust and distrust play a role in evaluating personal behavior and institutions. In "I Feared For My Life: Police Killings, Epistemic Injustice, and Social Distrust" Alida Liberman argues that police violence is often excused on the grounds that the policeman feared for his life in committing a violent act against a suspect. Liberman argues that this is a new form of epistemic injustice, *ignorance bolstering*, where the excuse is used to create false beliefs in the dominant social group, which harms everyone, since it is now harder for them to learn the truth. Ignorance bolstering, Liberman contends, also undermines the basis for social trust between Black people and the police, and between Black people and the White majority.

In "Social Trust and Legal Interpretation," Ira Lindsay argues that trust between actors within the legal system helps legal theorists determine which method of constitutional interpretation to use. Lindsay claims that we should adopt legal methodologies that help officials increase agreement about what the law is and how to apply it. Thus, theories on how to interpret statutes should be chosen partly because of the degree of agreement they generate between conflicting interpreters. A textualist methodology would be appropriate in cases where moral disagreement creates differences in intuitions about how the law should be interpreted. But in cases where people agree about the underlying moral issues, a purposivist interpretative approach may be relevant. Lindsay ends by endorsing this "modest relativism" about legal interpretation.

In the next essay, "Social Trust and Mistrust of Parental Care," Amy Mullin addresses challenges to socially trusting parents to provide adequate care for their children. Children are often harmed by betrayed trust. Thus, trusters have a great responsibility to learn about factors that would lead them to reduce their confidence in the ability or motives of trusted parents. Mullin argues that there is no alternative, or no good alternative, to socially trusting parents to care for their children, but for trust to be apt, a community must develop a joint conception of the basic needs of children, the degree of care that they need, and the harm they suffer without that care. This includes practices of funding, monitoring, and making policy about childcare at different levels of government and in public–private partnerships.

Agnes Tam, in the final essay, "A Case for Political Epistemic Trust," begins with the observation that members of the public have to rely on the testimony of authorities. Trust of this kind involves a serious political risk, in part because authorities may abuse the trust the public places in them by providing the public with misinformation. One might think correcting misinformation means that defenders of liberal societies must cultivate *vigilant* trust, which helps monitor the trustworthiness of officials. But Tam argues that this is a mistake both because it over-intellectualizes trust, and because the risk of abuse from lost trust is often exaggerated. For officials often act on a social norm of providing trustworthy information, rather than acting purely from self-interest. A superior method of cultivating trustworthy epistemic authorities is to help them respond to the norm of epistemic trustworthiness, improving trust without making trust too intellectual. Tam then outlines how liberal democracy can pursue this strategy. Taken together, these four essays show how social trust and distrust can figure into normative arguments.

Our goal in putting these essays together in a volume is to help the reader look at the idea of social trust from different perspectives, helping to see how social trust is measured, defined, and used to make ethical and political arguments. Taken as a whole, they should help to lay the foundation for continued philosophical and interdisciplinary work on social trust.

Note

1. Vallier 2020.

Part I

Empirical Research on Social Trust

1 Social and Legal Trust

The Case of Africa

Andreas Bergh, Christian Bjørnskov, Kevin Vallier

We know a great deal about the effects of social trust, but much less about its causes, especially whether social trust is caused by any formal institutions as opposed to cultural forces. Effective, uncorrupted legal institutions are perhaps the most commonly cited institutional cause of social trust (Knack and Keefer 1997). This suggests that trust in legal institutions, what we will call *legal trust*, causes social trust to increase when legal institutions are trustworthy in enforcing formal social norms like laws, and perhaps many informal social norms as well (Rothstein and Stolle 2008). The data seems to bear this out. Trust in the legal system is higher than social trust in almost all countries. Thus, legal trust is *proportionately higher* than social trust in most countries. The main idea of several studies thus is that if you increase legal trust, or perhaps the basis of legal trust, then, perhaps you can increase social trust.

It is nonetheless unclear how social and legal trust are causally connected. Perhaps effective, uncorrupted legal institutions incentivize trustworthy behavior and punish untrustworthy behavior, creating more trust-building experiences in a society, and so increasing social trust all else equal. But the relationship between social and legal trust might be explained in other ways. Perhaps high-trust societies have high legal trust because higher trust leads to better functioning legal institutions and so more publicly observable legal trustworthiness (good behavior by courts and law enforcement), generating legal trust (cf. Bjørnskov 2010; Uslaner 2002). Alternatively, legal trust judgments may simply be a function of social trust judgments because citizens use social trust judgments plus the higher general reputation of police and courts to formulate a legal trust judgment, perhaps largely apart from real experiences with the legal system.

We hope to illuminate the relationship between social and legal trust by looking at cases where legal and social trust are poorly correlated, namely in many African countries. Our hypothesis is that the correlation between social and legal trust is conditional on whether people see legal officials as *exemplary representatives* of society as a whole. When legal officials are *not* seen as representative of society, whether exemplary or not, that loosens the connection between social and legal trust.

Interestingly, legal trust is still generally higher than social trust in countries where the correlation between the two is low. Accordingly, it looks like social trust judgments inform legal trust judgments when legal officials are seen as representing society, but when they are not seen as representative, legal trust judgments depend on other factors. What we feel confident in is that *when legal officials are seen as representative of society, legal trust depends on social trust, and otherwise not.*

We use data from the AfroBarometer to confirm our hypothesis. The AfroBarometer is a pan-African, non-partisan research network that conducts surveys on democracy, governance, economic conditions, and related issues, with six rounds conducted between 1999 and 2015, and 26 countries covered in the most recent wave. The survey method is face-to-face interviews in the language of the respondent's choice, and samples are nationally representative. For further details, see for example, Bratton and Gyimah-Boadi (2016).

As we have noted, in most countries social and legal trust are highly correlated, but this correlation does not exist in the countries included in the AfroBarometer. There is more variation in legal trust vis-à-vis social trust than in other countries around the world. One of the more interesting results is that in African countries with a legacy of French colonialism, people tend to have much less trust in courts, parliaments, and the ruling party (though not in the police), whereas there is no significant correlation for countries with a legacy of English colonialism. One reason for this may be that French colonial powers tended to staff institutions with their own citizens, whereas English colonial powers tended to use locals. If indeed this historical generalization holds, then that supports our hypothesis. When legal officials are not seen as representative of their society, then legal trust will be determined in other ways, perhaps by different causes than the causes of social trust. At the least, there is no *transferral* of social trust to legal trust in many African societies.

In this piece, intended for an audience that may not be familiar with the empirical literature on social trust, we begin by explaining and reviewing the trust measure that we appeal to and we discuss some potential challenges to that literature that we think can be overcome (1.1). We provide some historical background of the legacy of French and British colonialism in Africa, especially with respect to the staffing of legal institutions (1.2). We then discuss our data (1.3). The final section (1.4) provides some discussion of our hypothesis.

1.1 The Trust Measure

The standard measure of trust that arose in the 1960s is acquired through one simple question. Elisabeth Noelle-Neumann developed the standard trust question in the late 1940s and Morris Rosenberg introduced it into large US surveys in the 1950s (Rosenberg 1956). The question is this: "In general, do you think most people can be trusted or can't you be too careful in dealing with people?" The standard trust question has been asked in the General Social Survey (GSS) since the early 1960s, and also appears in the American National Election Studies (ANES) and other comparable surveys. The standard trust question first appears in the World Values Survey's first wave, gathered in the early 1980s. Nations, regions, and states are then assigned scores based on average trust levels within that nation, region, or state. We now have dozens of cross-national studies, beginning with Knack and Keefer's (1997) seminal work.

Some readers may worry about imperfections in the standard trust question, say whether it captures either who to trust or in which circumstances trust is appropriate. The question might also reflect different levels of risk aversion, which is distinct from trust. For instance, Fine (2001) claims that levels of social trust, as well as other aspects of social capital, depend on context and that the standard trust question appeals to different concepts in different countries. Further, Japan–US comparisons found in Yamagishi and Yamagishi (1994) as well as between Sweden and Tanzania (Holm and Danielson 2007) can be used to argue that the trust measures are polluted by character dispositions and worldview. These problems are often cited by scholars who reject cross-national trust questions.

Nonetheless, several findings show that we have reason to think that the WVS trust question aggregates are accurate proxies for a well-defined understanding of trust that is cross-national and even cross-cultural. Knack and Keefer (1997) offer a simple validity test through the exploration of the numbers of wallets dropped that are returned to their owners, based on an experiment that Reader's Digest performed around the world in 1995. The shares of wallet returns track the WVS social trust scores; and it conceptually corresponds to trust since wallet returns are not observed by police, the courts, government, or other formal institutions. Wallet returns thus is evidence of a moral action, one with an honest motive, which suggests a level of trustworthiness (Uslaner 2002). And this in turn suggests a way of measuring trust, specifically how many people believe that their wallets would be returned to them if lost (Felton 2001). In the 32 cases, the correlation between return share and social trust is .57, which improves when income differences are controlled for (Knack 2001). In two out of three high trust countries, Denmark and Norway, all wallets were returned, contents

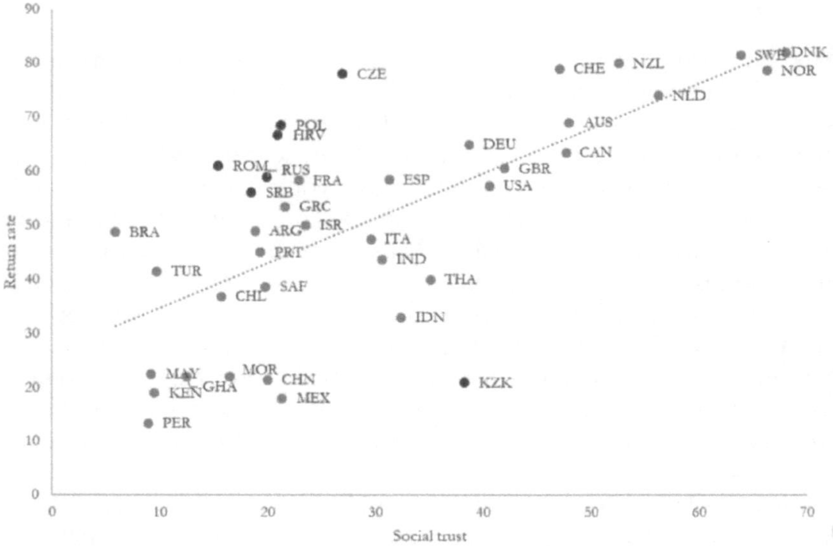

Figure 1.1 Return rates and social trust

unmolested. Similarly, as depicted in Figure 1.1, which we take from Bjørnskov (2019), when using return rates in the variant of the wallet drop experiment in Cohn et al. (2019), the correlation is .68 with a number of post-communist countries as clear outliers (red dots in the figure, excluding these increases the correlation to .85).

Uslaner (2002, 2016) offers more detailed information concerning what the scores measure at the level of individuals. The 2000 ANES pilot survey asked a series of questions where almost 75% of those who responded said that the trust question measured their moral attitude toward the world rather than their encounters with others. This type of trust does not appear to reflect any kind of reputation or Bayesian updating effect (Uslaner 2002, 141). The standard trust question then is "tied to people you do not know" such as those who work at your grocery store or doctor's office. Naef and Schupp (2009) find similar results in a large German survey that includes the standard trust question but adds three further questions about strangers. They find that questions about the behavior of strangers is highly correlated with the standard trust question, but not to trust in people respondents know. So the standard trust question appears to account for the trust people have in strangers. Consequently, there is only modest support in the individual-level data for the claim made by Rothstein (2003) and Beugelsdijk (2006) that the trust question measures the quality of formal institutions, such that people generalize from observing the behavior of civil servants.

There is further evidence favoring using the standard trust question, this time from trust games in the laboratory (Glaeser et al. 2000). The authors play a new version of the Berg, Dickhaut, and McCabe (1995) trust or "investment" game with students. In the original game, a sender receives some amount of funds (x) and can decide to offer a share s of her pot x to the receiver, who then acquires a multiple t of sx (often the amount sent is tripled, i.e. $t = 3$). In the next stage the receiver decides whether to return an amount y to the sender. The payoffs will thus be $(1 - s)x + y$ for the sender and $sxt - y$ for the receiver. The Nash equilibrium in the game is to return nothing and send nothing. Nonetheless, most people send a lot of their original pot and receive a large amount in return. These exchanges are a way to measure how much senders trust receivers, and how much they trust most people when experimenters anonymize receivers appropriately while return behavior represents trustworthiness and reciprocity. Importantly, when players are not anonymous, trust behavior and the standard trust question are more weakly correlated, but since anonymized sharing is arguably a better proxy for generalized trust, the anonymized experiments are more suited for verifying the validity of the standard trust question. There is further work demonstrating that actual trusting behavior is measured by the trust behavior as well (Capra, Lanier, and Meer 2008; Fehr et al. 2003). Cox et al. (2009) play both the ultimatum games and public goods games; they find that people who have not studied economics or strategic thinking act as the standard trust question predicts, and subject behavior is strongly correlated across the different games.

Sapienza, Toldra-Simats, and Zingales (2013) find similar results, namely a correlation between the WVS trust question and trust behavior, though only when the stakes of these games are sufficiently high. They say that "WVS-like questions are good at capturing the expectation component of trust" but subject preferences for fairness and equality provide a better account of their behavior with low stakes (Sapienza et al. 2013). People will act expressively when the costs of expressive behavior are low, but as costs increase, rational behavior begins to dominate expressive behavior (Hillman 2010). More recently, experimental approaches have confirmed the link between answers to the trust question and behavior. For example, Thöni, Tyran, and Wengström (2012) show, using a public good experiment, that answers are related to cooperation behavior and can be interpreted as a proxy for cooperation preferences. In sum, evidence supports the hypothesis that the GSS/WVS standard trust question actually captures a simple, yet socially relevant conception of trust.

Things are more complicated when social trust is measured cross-nationally, as they exhibit a lot of noise, and may pick up other attitudes (Capra et al. 2008). The fourth waves of the World Values Survey reveal some oddities, such as that Canadian trust seems to have fallen from

54% to 39% by the fourth wave in 2000, but three other surveys taken at the same time (Canadian National Election Study, Quebec Referendum Study, and University of British Columbia Social Capital Survey) all find a 54% trust level—perfectly stable across three different measures. A similar problem applies to British surveys, where a much-discussed drop in the 1990 and 1999 World Values Survey is nowhere to be seen in the contemporaneous British Social Attitudes Survey. Iran also appears to have a 60%+ Nordic level of trust in 1999 and a 10% trust level in 2005. China has WVS scores that are off of predicted values by two whole standard deviations. Belarus and Vietnam yield similar anomalies. Nonetheless, there is a strong correlation between different barometers in different regions of the world, namely Latin America, Africa, the Arab world, Asia and East Asia, and Europe: .85. The correlation between the Danish Social Capital Project and the WVS is .94.

Further, the cross-country and cross-state fluctuations in social trust levels can be predicted precisely by a small number of background variables (cf. Berggren and Jordahl 2006; Bjørnskov 2007; Brown and Uslaner 2005; Delhey and Newton 2005). This observation helps to back up the accuracy of the simple trust measures across countries and across time between those countries.

Critically for our purposes, trust in institutions is measured very similarly, and so the challenges and defensive strategies used to back up the social trust data back up the use of the legal and political trust data as well. Indeed, trust in other institutions is measured somewhat differently in terms of a four-point scale, but the trust questions are very similar. Surveyors don't try to elicit anything but simply ask basic trust questions targeted at particular institutions. However, a number of other factors play into institutional trust questions since people may have idiosyncratic knowledge of the behavior and the expectations of those institutions.

It is also important to understand that people really do have tailored trust opinions about different institutions. Trust in political parties can be far lower, for instance, than trust in the police or the military (in fact, this is extremely common). For our purposes, we are looking at the relationship between social trust and trust in what Rothstein and Stolle (2003) call order institutions, which as noted, we will call *legal trust*. So we do not need to provide a defense of the validity of trust scores for trust in democratic institutions or the civil service, just police and courts. There are some important differences between trust in the police and trust in the courts as well; people generally interact with the police far more, and police control more of their lives, but courts have greater power overall (Bradford, Jackson, and Hough 2018). Citizens must rely on the police more, and police much rely on citizens. People also arguably draw inferences about the trustworthiness of an institution based on taking an encounter with a police officer or judge as representative of that group as a whole (unlike trusting most people; trust in known others comes apart from trust in strangers).

Bradford et al. (2018), in a literature review on legal trust (more specifically the police and criminal courts), offer several claims about the nature and sources of legal trust, five of which are relevant for our purposes: (1) trust in legal authority is primarily cognitive, that is, based on beliefs, (2) trust is tied to beliefs about the ability and intentions of legal officials, (3) trust is based on direct and indirect experience with legal officials and their abilities and intentions, though (4) trust is still based on generalized motivations to trust; people often want to trust the legal system, (5) trust is partially generated by how legal officials act to reveal that they share values with trustors.

Brown and Benedict (2002) conclude that only three individual-level variables correlate with attitudes toward police—age, ethnicity, and contact with officers—though the levels vary across studies. Older people trust police more than younger people, people from the dominant ethnic group trust police more than ethnic minorities, and people who have recently interacted with police tend to have lower trust in them (Bradford et al. 2018). There is also some research on trust in courts based on US data, typically stressing procedural justice concerns as the strongest predictor of trust and confidence in the courts, also among offenders when controlling for their overall satisfaction of the outcome of their case (Sprott and Greene 2010; Tyler 2001) though trust in courts is measured in the same way as trust in police.

1.2 Historical Background: The Legacy of British and French Colonialism

Several authors have analyzed differences between British and French colonial strategies (Cohen 1970; Lee and Schultz 2012; Njoh 2008; Whittlesey 1937). An early account appeared in *Foreign Affairs* when Whittlesey (1937) described the British tendency toward governing Africans through their native rulers, the model of so-called indirect rule. The French, in contrast, typically put their own countrymen on important positions in the colony's administration.

The difference is described in more detail by Cohen (1970), who noted the French desire to "eradicate the political and social peculiarities of the colonial populations and pattern them after those existing in France" (430). Cohen emphasized that in the French colonies, indigenous societies and traditional leaders were distrusted, and the goal was to make colonies an integral part of France. In contrast, the British saw the end product of their colonial rule to be independence: "Instead of transforming the colonial societies into extensions of Britain the colonies were encouraged to develop along their own lines, thus preserving the best within traditional African and Asian society" (430).

Another difference that plausibly have had impact on institutional trust is the practice in French colonies to rely on forced labor, in the form of annual so-called "prestations" (Cordell and Gregory 1982). In practice, the prestations meant that colonial officials were able to divert laborers for work on private farms and plantations.

In all, it seems clear that the British typically left more traditional structures and institutions intact. There is also some evidence that the difference had both economic and social consequences. Lee and Schultz (2012) make use of the fact that a part of Cameroon was once colonized by Britain, with the border cutting across ethnic and religious boundaries. They show that rural areas on the British side have higher levels of wealth and better local public provision of piped water. To explain these results, they point to the British strategy of indirect rule described above and to the presence of forced labor on the French side, that arguably made it harder to generate institutional trust and overcome free rider problems when building small scale public works.

Another way in which French colonial rule may have had an impact on institutional trust is in colonial infra-structure. As discussed by Starostina (2010) the railroads that were built in French colonies (using forced labor) were often not completed. They were built primarily as a way to boost the spirit of the French nation.

In sum, the French staffed legal institutions with their own people, who were not seen as representatives of African societies controlled by the French, whereas the English staffed legal institutions with locals. These patterns seem to have continued somewhat even in the absence of French and English state control.

1.3 Data

We provide estimates of the association between social trust and legal trust at both the individual and country level in order to avoid committing an ecological fallacy (cf. Bjørnskov and Sønderskov 2013). In both cases, we use the AfroBarometer survey and dataset. As already mentioned, the AfroBarometer is a pan-African research network that conducts attitude surveys in African countries, and is similar to the World Values Surveys or the European Social Survey. The AfroBarometer is increasingly being used in research related to Africa (e.g. Eifert, Miguel, and Posner 2010; Nunn 2010). For each of the six currently available rounds of the survey, there are rarely fewer than 1,100 respondents per country and large countries such as Egypt and Nigeria typically include more than 2,000 respondents.

With a sample designed to be a representative cross-section of all citizens of voting age in a given country, the survey questions are focused on attitudes toward democracy but also cover socio-demographic information of the respondents. In rounds 1, 3, and 5, the questionnaire included the standard dichotomous question of social trust: "In general, do you think most people can be trusted or do you have to be very careful?"

In the individual-level analysis, we use round 5, which includes 34 countries. It offers us assessments of how much respondents trust five separate formal institutions. All respondents were asked "How much do you trust each of the following, or haven't you heard enough about them to say?" and given the answer categories "Not at all, just a little, somewhat, a lot and I don't know." We use the answers to the following formal institutions: courts of law, the police, the national electoral commission, the parliament, and the ruling party.

We add a set of control variables, all of which also derive from the AfroBarometer survey. We include a dummy for women, the respondent's age, and his or her self-perceived economic situation assessed as Fairly bad, Neither good nor bad, Fairly good, or Very good. We also include whether the respondent is unemployed, has part-time employment or is full-time employed; the comparison group is thus self-employed. We also include dummies for whether the respondent has only primary education, secondary education, or post-secondary education. For all control variables, we include a separate dummy if the respondent has answered "Don't know." Finally, we include a full set of fixed effects of self-assessed racial group.

In additional tests, we employ an additional feature of the AfroBarometer that was asked in all but one country (Swaziland) in round 5: which, if any, political parties the respondent supports. We use this information to code if respondents support the incumbent/ruling party, which provides us with a way to separate potentially informed trust in specific institutions with ideologically motivated—and therefore potentially expressive—declared support for whichever interest is in power.

In the cross-country application, we use the AfroBarometer to form an unbalanced panel of up to 62 observations from 34 countries. We combine the country-wave averages of the institutional variables and social trust available in rounds 1, 3, and 5, with six additional control variables. First, we use the dichotomous democracy indicator from Cheibub, Gandhi, and Vreeland (2010), as updated in Bjørnskov and Rode (2020). From the same dataset, we include dummies capturing whether countries have been either British or French colonies prior to independence. Second, we use the measure of (absence of) government repression from Fariss (2014). Additionally, we form a variable that captures the share of the last twenty years in which a country has been at war; our historical information is mainly from Encyclopædia Britannica (2018). Third, we include real purchasing-power adjusted GDP per capita, which we derive from the Penn World Tables, mark 9 (Feenstra, Inklaar, and Timmer 2015). Finally, we add fixed effects

Table 1.1a Descriptive statistics, individual-level data

Variable	*Mean*	*Standard deviation*	*Observations*
Trust in courts	2.144	1.837	51,122
Trust in the police	1.719	1.519	51,122
Trust in parliament	1.997	1.929	49,931
Trust in the elect commission	2.193	2.229	47,544
Trust in the ruling party	1.954	2.048	49,922
Age	37.182	14.606	51,157
Gender (female)	.500	.500	51,122
Fairly bad ec. situation	.298	.457	51,122
Neither good nor bad	.206	.404	51,122
Fairly good ec. situation	.259	.438	51,122
Very good ec. situation	.042	.199	51,122
Don't know situation	.003	.053	51,122
Unemployed	.286	.452	51,122
Part-time employed	.115	.319	51,122
Full-time employed	.216	.411	51,122
Don't know employment	.004	.060	51,122
Primary education	.319	.466	51,099
Secondary education	.351	.477	51,099
Post-secondary education	.127	.333	51,099
Don't know	.002	.044	51,099
Social trust	.186	.389	51,122
Don't know	.012	.111	51,122

Table 1.1b Descriptive statistics, individual-level data

Variable	*Mean*	*Standard deviation*	*Observations*
Trust in courts	2.796	.342	64
Trust in the police	2.613	.413	64
Trust in parliament	2.666	.410	51
Trust in the elect commission	2.691	.366	61
Trust in the ruling party	2.586	.414	51
Democracy	.392	.491	102
(Absence of) repression	–.140	.825	102
War (share of years)	.186	.285	102
Log GDP per capita	7.829	.934	102
Former British	.471	.502	102
Former French	.383	.488	102
Social trust	.188	.102	62

for rounds 1 and 3 in order to take out average changes from the different number of countries in each round. All individual level data are described in Table 1.1a while all cross-country data are described in Table 1.1b.

1.3.1 *A First Look at the Data*

When exploring the country averages, there is considerable variation across countries when it comes to institutional trust. For example, the population share with at least some trust in the courts of law is as low as 29 percent in Madagascar (an index of 1.31), but as high as 82 percent (2.35) in Niger, as indicated in Figure 1.1 below. Trust in other institutions also varies markedly across countries with the additional common feature that institutional trust tends to be substantially higher among respondents who support the incumbent, ruling party.

Similarly, the share of respondents stating that "most people can be trusted" varies from 5 percent in Lesotho to 55 percent in Burundi. Again, we observe that supporters of the ruling party tend to be more trusting than non-supporters. However, the association between social trust and legal trust, despite the similarities, appears to be fragile at best across Africa. As is visible in Figure 1.2, the cross-country correlation between social trust and trust in courts is positive, but it is entirely driven by the only two countries with high levels of social trust: Burundi (55 percent) and Niger (46 percent).

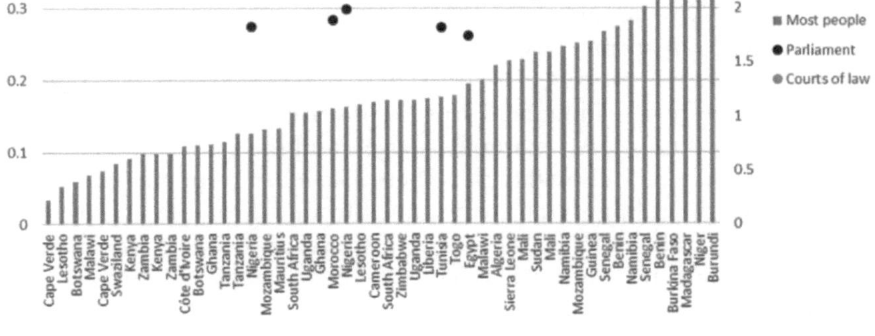

Figure 1.2 Social and legal trust in the AfroBarometer

1.3.2 *Empirical Results*

Analyzing survey data on individual characteristics uncovers some noteworthy patterns in trust in the five institutions of interest. Women are on average more prone to trusting all institutions, whereas education associates negatively with institutional trust. In other words, the better educated and presumably better informed are less likely to trust formal institutions in Africa. Conversely, there is a strong positive association between household income and trust in formal institutions with one notable exception: respondents who declare that they "don't know" their income—or more likely refuse to reveal it—are most trusting toward formal institutions. However, such refusals are often correlated with having particularly high incomes, which may resolve what otherwise appears as a puzzle.

Most importantly, controlling for individual characteristics, and including controls for race and country fixed effects, as reported in Table 1.2, we find a significant positive association between social trust and (all five types of) legal and political trust (political trust understood as trust in political institutions like parliament and the ruling party).

When we turn to the cross-country regressions in Table 1.3, we again find that social trust is positively associated with trust in formal institutions, although not significantly associated so for courts and the police. At first glance, the cross-country analysis thus corroborates the individual-level results. The analysis also reveals a highly intuitive positive association between absence of repression and institutional trust, and an interesting difference depending on colonial heritage such that former French colonies tend to have lower institutional trust.

The individual-level results nevertheless turn out to hide some interesting heterogeneity between countries. As we outline in Table 1.4, which summarizes the main results from a full set of jackknife tests, including tests in which we only include respondents who do *not* support the ruling party, the main results are not as robust as in other settings.[1] We further use the number of significant associations across the five types of formal institutions as the dependent in column 6 of Table 1.3.

In some countries, individual trust is positively associated with trust in all five institutions. An example is Niger, and the association between social trust and institutional trust is there also when respondents who do not support the ruling party are excluded from the sample. In contrast, there are several countries where the association between social trust and institutional trust is partly or completely driven by supporters of the ruling party, such as Burundi and Togo. In these cases, we cannot claim a general, robust association exists.

Table 1.2 Individual-level results

	1 Courts	2 Police	3 Parliament	4 Electoral com.	5 Ruling party
Female	.084***	.047***	.127***	.164***	.137***
	(.024)	(.017)	(.027)	(.039)	(.033)
Age	.001***	.000	.000	.001***	.000
	(.000)	(.000)	(.000)	(.000)	(.000)
Fairly bad ec.	.000	.055***	.079***	.019	.146***
situation	(.025)	(.019)	(.027)	(.048)	(.031)
Neither goor nor	.067**	.166***	.185***	.109*	.214***
bad	(.027)	(.034)	(.046)	(.063)	(.059)
Fairly good	.132***	.194***	.301***	.185***	.314***
	(.025)	(.027)	(.043)	(.066)	(.046)
Very good	.248***	.375***	.347***	.203*	.449***
	(.042)	(.080)	(.072)	(.103)	(.087)
Don't know	.597***	.583***	.863***	1.119***	.655***
	(.224)	(.167)	(.270)	(.307)	(.222)
Unemployed	-.089***	-.097***	-.164***	-.243***	-.177***
	(.021)	(.025)	(.029)	(.034)	(.034)
Part-time	-.185***	-.118***	-.158***	-.263***	-.178***
	(.026)	(.031)	(.039)	(.054)	(.043)
Full-time	-.125***	-.087***	-.124***	-.129***	-.127***
	(.021)	(.024)	(.035)	(.048)	(.048)
Don't know	.106	-.219	.179	-.032	.278
	(.198)	(.169)	(.202)	(.274)	(.212)
Primary	-.311***	-.219***	-.386***	-.452***	-.409***
education	(.028)	(.038)	(.062)	(.086)	(.077)
Secondary	-.576***	-.476***	-.679***	-.827***	-.706***
education	(.027)	(.051)	(.083)	(.108)	(.101)
Post-secondary	-.691***	-.621***	-.842***	-1.039***	-.924***
education	(.030)	(.070)	(.101)	(.129)	(.114)
Don't know	-.252	.024	.188	.062	.159
	(.253)	(.184)	(.252)	(.261)	(.455)
Social trust	.186***	.228***	.239***	.327***	.253***
	(.021)	(.035)	(.042)	(.071)	(.058)
Don't know	.614***	480***	.413***	.437**	.524***
	(.109)	(.174)	(.181)	(.215)	(.179)
Race FE	Yes	Yes	Yes	Yes	Yes
Country FE	Yes	Yes	Yes	Yes	Yes
Observations	51,099	51,099	49,908	47,526	49,899
R squared	.069	.103	.089	.086	.089
Root MSE	1.773	1.440	1.849	2.133	1.955
Excluding supports of the ruling party					
Social trust	.178***	.211***	.252***	.370***	.304***
	(.039)	(.036)	(.053)	(.087)	(.074)
Don't know	.589***	.555***	.427**	.495**	.587***
	(.207)	(.207)	(.172)	(.222)	(.199)

Note: *** (**) [*] denote significance at p<.01 (p<.05) [p<.10]. Numbers in parentheses are standard errors clustered at the country level.

Overall, our findings suggest that the strength of the otherwise well-known association between social trust and trust in formal institutions is not as general in Africa as in the developed world. The summary in Table 1.4 suggests that the association particularly often breaks down when we focus on respondents' trust in courts.

As a final test, we separate former French and British colonies. This additional test shows that the five different trust-institutions associations are generally significant in 65 percent of cases in the 13 French colonies while it is only significant in 27 percent of cases in the latter 15 countries. As we outline in the discussion in the last section, we interpret this as a partial confirmation of our hypothesis that part of the reason that

Table 1.3 Cross-country results

	1 Courts	2 Police	3 Parliament	4 Electoral com.	5 Ruling party	6 # sign.
Democracy	-.126	-.204*	-.218**	-.093	.154	.532*
	(.099)	(.110)	(.110)	(.117)	(.108)	(.323)
(Absence of)	.226***	.334***	.302***	.218***	.243***	-.599***
repression	(.071)	(.080)	(.078)	(.084)	(.079)	(.233)
War (share of	.286	.601***	.265	.098	.226	-.187
years)	(.179)	(.204)	(.215)	(.214)	(.217)	(.529)
Log GDP per	-.058	-.071	-.219***	-.094	-.163***	-.143
capita	(.056)	(.062)	(.061)	(.067)	(.061)	(.157)
Former	.038	-.138	.030	.041	-.001	2.095***
British	(.143)	(.157)	(.152)	(.159)	(.153)	(575)
Former	-.344**	-.109	-.349**	-.227	-.442***	3.466***
French	(.142)	(.156)	(.148)	(.162)	(.148)	(.558)
Social trust	.491	.654	1.466**	1.007*	1.359**	2.109
	(.426)	(.503)	(.623)	(.538)	(.638)	(1.799)
Round FE	Yes	Yes	Yes	Yes	Yes	Yes
Observations	62	62	50	59	50	62
Countries	34	34	34	32	33	34
R squared	.444	.473	.534	.262	.509	.216
F Statistic	33.90	35.96	41.23	15.90	38.93	55.36

Note: *** (**) [*] denote significance at p<.01 (p<.05) [p<.10]. Numbers in parentheses are robust standard errors. Results in column 6 derive from ordered probit.

Table 1.4 Countries driving results

Country	No. sign	Which not trusted	No. sign	Which not trusted
	All observations		No ruling party supporters	
Algeria	4	Pol.	3	Cou., pol.
Burundi	3	Elec., rule.	0	All
Benin	5	None	5	None
Burkina Faso	2	Cou., pol., rul.	2	Cou., pol., rul.
Botswana	0	All	0	All
Cameroon	1	Cou., par., elec., rul.	0	All
Côte d'Ivoire	3	Par., rul.	2	Cou., par., rul.
Cape Verda	0	All	0	All
Egypt	2	Cou., par., elec.	2	Cou., par., elec.
Ghana	2	Cou., pol., rul.	2	Cou., pol., rul.
Guinea	4	Par.	2	Pol., par., rul.
Kenya	1	Pol., par., elec., rul.	0	All
Lesotho	1	Cou., pol., par., rul.	0	All
Liberia	0	All	0	All
Madagascar	3	Cou., rul.	3	Cou., rul.
Mauritius	0	All	0	All
Mali	5	None	5	None
Malawi	1	Cou., pol., par., rul.	1	Cou., pol., par., rul.
Mozambique	0	All	0	All
Morocco	0	None	0	None
Namibia	0	All	0	All
Niger	5	None	5	None
Nigeria	4	Elec.	3	Par., elec.
South Africa	3	Par., elec.	2	Cou., par., elec.
Senegal	1	Cou., par., elec., rul.	0	All
Sierra Leone	0	All	0	All
Sudan	1	Cou., par., elec., rul.	0	All
Swaziland	0	All	-	-
Tanzania	0	All	0	All
Togo	5	None	2	Pol., par., rul.
Tunisia	3	Cou., rul.	4	Cou.
Uganda	2	Cou., par., rul.	3	Cou., par.,
Zambia	0	All	0	All
Zimbabwe	4	Cou.	4	Cou.

Note: countries in italics did not ask all questions; Swaziland did not ask question about party support.

the correlation between social and legal trust comes apart in Africa is because of the legacy of colonialism.

1.4 Discussion

We have here explored the association between social trust and trust in formal institutions: the courts, the police, parliament, the electoral commission, and the ruling party. In general, we find the association is positive at both the cross-country and individual level. However, we find very substantial heterogeneity across African countries such that it is difficult to make general claims.

Overall, the data nevertheless appear to be consistent with our hypothesis about how legal trust judgments change in accord with judgments about the representativeness of legal officials. However, do these results tell us how legal trust is formed and whether it affects social trust? There are three questions we might ask about the significance of our findings.

1 Why is legal trust usually higher than social trust when legal officials are seen as representative of society, that is, when current legal systems are not likely to be the remnants of the former colonial institutions?
2 Why is legal trust more proportionate to social trust when legal officials are seen as representative of society?
3 What are the causal relationships between social and legal trust that are consistent with the answers to 1 and 2?

Regarding question 1, let's first note that legal trust is almost always higher than social trust *even when* legal and social trust are weakly correlated, as we have seen above. This may be because police and courts, among other legal institutions, are seen as more trustworthy in general because of the importance and visibility of their occupations, the fact that they are seen as neutral and treating citizens similarly, especially in contrast to political officials, and that they may be subject to effective checks and balances on the behavior of judges and bureaucrats.

We wonder whether this effect is sensitive to whether police and judges are in fact more trustworthy, such that legal trust is at least partially a response to the observation or seeming observation of trustworthy behavior. One possibility is that legal officials tend to act in a trustworthy fashion on balance, and they do so in very visible and important ways, such as keeping people safe or helping them redress wrongs at critical points in their lives. This suggests that legal trust is higher when individuals have positive experiences with legal officials. However, in further tests, we find that quasi-objective indicators of quality, such as the rule of law indicator from the World Governance Indicators (Kaufmann, Kraay, and Zoido-Lobatón 1999), don't correlate with social trust in our African sample. So this possibility seems less likely.

Regarding question 2, when legal officials are seen as representative of their society, people may form legal trust judgments by first consulting their social trust judgments and then combine it with their belief in the greater relative trustworthiness of legal officials to generate a legal trust judgment. Thus, when legal officials are seen as representative, people believe that social trust judgments are helpful for determining the trustworthiness of legal officials. But when legal officials are not seen as representative, people will rely more on other judgments about legal officials. Our main argument here is that legal officials in former French colonies are much more likely to be representative, as France transplanted its own institutions with French civil servants in its colonies, and most civil servants and legal officials consequently also left when these colonies gained their independence. Conversely, former British colonies are substantially more likely to have legal institutions—most visibly in Botswana—that are the direct descendants of the colonial institutions and thus *unlikely* to be representative (Acemoglu, Johnson, and Robinson 2003).

Perhaps, then, legal trust in non-representative officials is largely a function of beliefs about legal trustworthiness *unmediated* by a social trust judgment, such that legal trust is determined by reputation effects and personal experience, and perhaps a general desirability belief that the police and courts can keep one safe. However, if legal officials are representative, then social trust judgments *mediate* legal trust judgments, allowing people to develop more precise legal trust judgments based on more information, and this tends to yield higher legal trust judgments.

Regarding question 3, it appears that individuals formulate legal trust judgments by drawing on a number of antecedent beliefs, and that if a person believes that legal officials are representative of society, this goes into the mix of beliefs that determine legal trust. So social trust leads to legal trust by providing proxy information for legal trust judgments.

There are some claims in the empirical literature that legal trust and trustworthiness impact social trust. One reason for this is that good police and courts enforce formal and informal social norms, which gives people additional motivation to be trustworthy, which will generate social trust judgments in turn. Thus, on the one hand, legal trust should cause at least some portion of social trust because it increases the observational basis for trust. This might help explain why legal trust judgments are higher than social trust judgments, because legal officials are seen as keeping most people honest and well-behaved. On the other hand, such mechanisms only make logical sense if social trust is effectively an individual risk assessment. If trust is instead driven by emotions that are independent of the consequences of trusting (as argued in e.g. Schlösser et al. 2016 and Dunning et al. 2012), institutions might not matter at all, and trust would be explained by cultural factors such as upbringing.

Legal trust may be higher in countries where social and legal trust are correlated than in countries where they are not correlated. This would be the case, for example, if legal institutions are populated in a fair and meritocratic way, such that legal officials will be representative of "most people." However, such an explanation is inconsistent with our finding that trust in institutions is generally lower in former French colonies and that the association between social and institutional trust is weaker in these countries. We also note that if only a relatively small minority of people can be trusted, as appears to be the case in a number of African countries, most ordinary citizens would be interested in legal institutions with officials that are emphatically *not* representative of most people.

A main observation is that legal officials can still enforce formal and informal norms when they are not representative. It may indeed well be that unrepresentative legal officials may still be effective, such that they are seen as trustworthy and keeping others trustworthy. Strictly speaking, then, our findings are compatible with the claim that legal trust and trustworthiness causes social trust in some cases. But if the relevance of representativeness judgments works as we hypothesize, then it seems to provide a bit more support for the hypothesis that legal trust is a function of social trust and not as much the other way around because it reveals that social trust judgments are consulted in making legal trust judgments.

Note

1. Our jackknife consists of running all analyses excluding one country at a time. We repeat all analyses excluding respondents who support the ruling party in order to avoid that our individual-level results are due to reflection. This could be the case if respondents who support the ruling party generally declare themselves to be more positive toward all aspects of society.

References

Acemoglu, Daron, Simon Johnson, and James Robinson. (2003). An African Success Story: Botswana. In Dani Rodrik (Ed.), In *Search of Prosperity: Analytic Narratives on Economic Growth*. Princeton, Princeton University Press, 80–122.

Berg, Joyce, John Dickhaut, and Kevin McCabe. (1995). Trust, Reciprocity and Social History. *Games and Economic Behavior* 10, 122–42.

Berggren, Niclas, and Henrik Jordahl. (2006). Free to Trust? Economic Freedom and Social Capital. *Kyklos* 59, 141–69.

Beugelsdijk, Sjoerd. (2006). A Note on the Theory and Measurement of Trust in Explaining Differences in Economic Growth. *Cambridge Journal of Economics* 30, 371–87.

Bjørnskov, Christian. (2007). Determinants of Generalized Trust. A Cross-Country Comparison. *Public Choice* 130, 1–21.

Bjørnskov, Christian. (2010). How Does Social Trust Lead to Better Governance? An Attempt to Separate Electoral and Bureaucratic Mechanisms. *Public Choice* 144, 323–46.

Bjørnskov, Christian. (2019). Civic Honesty and Cultures of Trust. Working paper, Aarhus, Aarhus University.

Bjørnskov, Christian, and Kim Mannemar Sønderskov. (2013). Is Social Capital a Good Concept? *Social Indicators Research* 114, 1225–42.

Bjørnskov, Christian, and Martin Rode. (2020). Regimes and Regime Transitions: A New Dataset on Democracy, Coups, and Political Institutions. *Review of International Organizations* 15, 531–51. Data available at http://www.christianbjoernskov.com/bjoernskovrodedata/ (accessed September 2018).

Bradford, Ben, Jonathan Jackson, and Mike Hough. (2018). Trust in Justice. In Eric M. Uslaner (Ed.), *Oxford Handbook of Social and Political Trust*. Oxford, Oxford University Press, 633–53.

Bratton, Michael, and E. Gyimah-Boadi. (2016). Do trustworthy institutions matter for development? Corruption, trust, and government performance in Africa. Afrobarometer Dispatch No. 112.

Encyclopædia Britannica. (2018). *Censorship*. Online encyclopedia, data available at https://www.britannica.com/topic/censorship#ref358885 (accessed July 2018).

Brown, Ben and William Reed Benedict. (2002). Perceptions of the Police: Past Findings, Methodological Issues, Conceptual Issues and Policy Implications. *Policing* 25, 543–80.

Brown, Mitchell, and Eric M. Uslaner. (2005). Inequality, Trust, and Civic Engagement. *American Political Research* 31, 1–27.

Capra, C. Mónica, Kelli Lanier, and Shireen Meer. (2008). *Attitudinal and Behavioral Measures of Trust: A New Comparison. Working Paper*, Atlanta, Emory University.

Cheibub, José A., Jennifer Gandhi, and James R. Vreeland. (2010). Democracy and Dictatorship Revisited. *Public Choice* 143, 67–101.

Cohen, W. B. (1970). The Colonized as Child: British and French Colonial Rule. *African Historical Studies*, 3 (2), 427–31.

Cohn, Alain, Michel André Maréchal, David Tannenbaum, and Christian Lukas Zünd. (2019). Civic Honesty Around the Globe. *Science* 365, 70–73.

Cordell, D. D., and Gregory, J. W. (1982). Labour Reservoirs and Population: French Colonial Strategies in Koudougou, Upper Volta, 1914 to 1939. *Journal of African History* 23 (2), 205–24.

Cox, James C., Elinor Ostrom, James M. Walker, Antonio Jaime Castillo, Eric Coleman, Robert Holahan, Michael Schoon, and Brian Steed. (2009). Trust in Private and Common Property Experiments. *Southern Economic Journal* 75, 957–75.

Delhey, Jan, and Kenneth Newton. (2005). Predicting Cross-National Levels of Social Trust: Global Pattern or Nordic Exceptionalism? *European Sociological Review* 21, 311–27.

Dunning, David, Detlef Fetchenhauer and Thomas Schlösser. (2012). Trust as a social and emotional act: Noneconomic considerations in trust behavior. *Journal of Economic Psychology* 33, 686–694.

Eifert, Benn, Edward Miguel, and Daniel N. Posner. (2010). Political Competition and Ethnic Identification in Africa. *American Journal of Political Science* 54, 494–510.

Fariss, Christopher J. (2014). Respect for Human Rights Has Improved Over Time: Modeling the Changing Standard of Accountability. *American Political Science Review* 108, 297–318.

Feenstra, Robert C., Inklaar, Robert, and Timmer, Marcel P. (2015). The Next Generation of the Penn World Table. *American Economic Review* 105, 3150–82.

Fehr, Ernst, Urs Fischbacher, Bernhard von Rosenbladt, Jürgen Schupp, and Gert Wagner. (2003). A Nation-Wide Laboratory. Examining Trust and Trustworthiness by Integrating Behavioral Experiments into Representative Surveys. CESIfo working paper 866. Munich, CESIfo.

Felton, Eric. (2001). Finders Keepers? *Reader's Digest* April, 103–107.

Fine, Ben. (2001). *Social Capital versus Social Theory*. Routledge: London.

Glaeser, Edward, David Laibson, J, Scheinkman, and C. Soutter. (2000). Measuring Trust. *Quarterly Journal of Economics* 115, 811–46.

Hillman, Arye. (2010). Expressive Behavior in Economics and Politics. *European Journal of Political Economy* 26, 404–19.

Holm, Hakan, and Anders Danielson. (2007). Tropic Trust versus Nordic Trust: Experimental Evidence from Tanzania and Sweden. *The Economic Journal* 115, 505–32.

Kaufmann, Daniel, Aart Kraay, and Pablo Zoido-Lobatón. (1999). Aggregating Governance Indicators. World Bank Policy Research Working Paper #2195. Washington DC, World Bank.

Knack, Stephen. (2001). Trust, Associational Life and Economic Performance. In John F. Helliwell (Ed.), *In The Contribution of Human and Social Capital to Sustained Economic Growth and Well-Being*. Quebec, Canada: Human Resources Development, 171–202.

Knack, Stephen, and Philip Keefer. (1997). Does Social Capital Have an Economic Pay-Off? A Cross-Country Investigation. *Quarterly Journal of Economics* 112, 1251–88.

Lee, A., and Schultz, K. A. (2012). Comparing British and French Colonial Legacies: A Discontinuity Analysis of Cameroon. *Quarterly Journal of Political Science* 7 (4), 365–410.

Naef, Michael, and Jürgen Schupp. (2009). Measuring Trust: Experiments and Surveys in Contrast and Combination. *SOEP working paper 167*, DIW Berlin.

Njoh, A. J. (2008). Colonial Philosophies, Urban Space, and Racial Segregation in British and French Colonial Africa. *Journal of Black Studies* 38 (4), 579–99.

Nunn, Nathan. (2010). Religious Conversion in Colonial Africa. *American Economic Review Papers and Proceedings* 100, 147–52.

Rosenberg, M. (1956). Misanthropy and Political Ideology. *American Sociological Review* 21, 690–5.

Rothstein, Bo. (2003). Social Capital, Economic Growth and Quality of Government. *New Political Economy* 4, 9–72.

Rothstein, Bo, and Dietlind Stolle. (2003). Introduction: Social Capital in Scandinavia. *Scandinavian Political Studies* 26, 1–26.

Rothstein Bo, and Dietlind Stolle. (2008). Political Institutions and Generalized Trust. In Dario Castiglione, Jan W. van Deth, and Guglielmo Wolleb (Eds.), In *The Handbook of Social Capital*. Oxford, Oxford University Press.

Sapienza Paola, Anna Toldra-Simats, and Luigi Zingales. (2013). Understanding Trust. *The Economic Journal* 123, 1313–32.

Schlösser, Thomas, Detlef Fetchenhauer and David Dunning. (2016). Trust against all odds? Emotional dynamics in trust behavior. *Decision* 3 (3), 216–230.

Sprott, Jane B., and Carolyn Greene. (2010). Trust and Confidence in the Courts. *Crime & Delinquency* 56 (2), 269–89. Sprott, Jane B., and Carolyn Greene. (2010). Trust and Confidence in the Courts. *Crime & Delinquency* 56 (2), 269–89.

Starostina, Natalia. (2010). Ambiguous Modernity: Representations of French Colonial Railways in the Third Republic. *Journal of the Western Society for French History* 38, 179–200.

Thöni, Christian, Jean Robert Tyran, and Erik Wengström. (2012). Microfoundations of Social Capital. *Journal of Public Economics* 96 (7–8): 635–43.

Tyler, T. R. (2001). Public Trust and Confidence in Legal Authorities: What Do Majority and Minority Group Members Want from the Law and Legal Institutions? *Behavioral Sciences & the Law* 19, 215–35.

Uslaner, Eric M. (2002). *The Moral Foundations of Trust*. Cambridge: Cambridge University Press.

Uslaner, Eric M. (2016). Measuring Generalized Trust: In Defense of the "Standard" Question. In Fergus Lyon, Guido Möllering, Mark Sanders, and Tally Hatzakis (Eds.), In *Handbook of Research Methods on Trust*. London, Edward Elgar, 97–106.

Whittlesey, D. (1937). British and French Colonial Technique in West Africa. *Foreign Affairs* 15 (2), 362.

Yamagishi, Toshio, and Midori Yamagishi. (1994). Trust and Commitment in the United States and Japan. *Motivation and Emotion* 18, 129–66.

2 Trustworthiness Is a Social Norm, but Trusting Is Not

Cristina Bicchieri, Erte Xiao, Ryan Muldoon

It is impossible to go through life without trust: that is to be imprisoned in the worst cell of all, oneself.

—*Graham Greene*

2.1 Introduction

The purpose of this article is to distinguish between trusting as a behavior that is norm driven versus trusting as a behavior that is predicated on the anticipation of profit through reciprocation. This distinction is particularly important since trust and trustworthiness are important elements in personal, social, and economic exchanges. Without trust neither markets nor social relations could function and thrive, as nobody would willingly give something of value, be it money, goods, time, or sensitive information, if not for the expectation that the exchange will bear some fruit and will not leave the giver poorer or otherwise injured. The placement of trust allows actions that would not otherwise be possible and, depending upon the performance of the trustee, the truster may be better off or worse off than if he had not trusted. Trusting someone means making a choice that can either benefit both the truster and the trustee or benefit the trustee to a greater extent, but at the truster's expense.

According to Hardin's (2006) view of trust as encapsulated self-interest, if A trusts B, she must have good reasons to do so. In other words, A trusts B to do x because it is in B's interest to fulfill A's trust. Being trustworthy in this context means not having an incentive to exploit A's trust. According to this view, when such incentives are absent, trusting makes no sense and is patently irrational. This view of trust draws a wedge between personal and *generalized* trust,[1] since someone who is embedded in a thick network of trusting relationships and experiences the trustworthiness of people around them may not have the propensity to extend trust to strangers. Trust as encapsulated self-interest may work in close, repeated interactions, or in any case in which one's actions are observable by others who may become partners in future interactions. But what about anonymous encounters or any situation in which the link between truster and trustee is not close, there is no transparency, and the possibility of sanctions is remote or just unfeasible?

An answer favored by some (Putnam, 1993) is that there is continuity between personal and generalized trust; those who are embedded in a thick network of trusting relationships and experience the trustworthiness of people around them will have the propensity to extend trust even to strangers. In this light, it would be expected that a person who is accustomed to particularistic trust would be disposed to generalize and invest resources even when faced with anonymous partners. The breeding ground of trust, cooperative habits, and solidarity is always the small group, and the move to generalized trust is something that happens almost by default, as a habit one does not shed just because the situation is unusual or different. There are, however, many examples of discontinuity between personal and generalized trust, and examples abound of societies in which individuals display high levels of trust or reciprocation among family members and small networks, but show complete mistrust of strangers, institutions, and other beneficiaries of generalized trust. There is even evidence that in countries with widespread corruption, impersonal trust is a scarce good, whereas personal trust may flourish (Ensminger, 2001).

Yamagishi (2001) made an important distinction between trust and assurance that captures the discontinuity discussed earlier. People within committed relations or stable groups feel safe with insiders because formal and informal sanctions (including ostracism) against a betrayer are strong enough. Assurance is precisely an expectation of trustworthiness of others based on an assessment of their interests and incentives. Assurance does not generalize to interactions or situations that are not "guaranteed" by existing incentive structures. Trust, on the contrary, is meaningful only in situations characterized by a high level of social uncertainty, in which there are incentives to act dishonestly, and the consequences of being the target of dishonesty are costly. Trust, in Yamagishi's view, is independent of an assessment of trustworthiness and is, rather, a generalized expectation about human benevolence.

Another way to detach trust from trustworthiness is to treat trust as a heuristic (Messick and Kramer, 2001). The idea is that we have developed simple rules to deal with specific classes of situations, and these rules, in general, produce satisfactory results. Thus, a default rule of trusting may be almost automatically applied in many situations in which a less automatic decision would require a significant expenditure of time and resources to gather information on one's partner, if that were at all possible. In this view, trusting occurs irrespective of one's expectations of others' trustworthiness, and thus is uncoupled from self-interest, and more generally from a consequentialist assessment of its potential outcomes. In a similar vein, Elster (1979: 146) says that "trust and solidarity are genuine phenomena that cannot be dissolved into ultra-subtle forms of self-interest". Trust, in this case, may mean having a personal disposition to follow a social or even a moral norm, without a thought to the potentially negative effects that one's trusting actions may bring about.

We agree with Yamagishi in linking trust with unavoidable social uncertainty. That is, an agent faces social uncertainty when she believes her interaction partner has an incentive to act in a way that imposes costs (or harm) on her and she does not have enough information to predict if the partner will in fact act in such a way (Yamagishi and Yamagishi, 1994). In other words, when we trust, we know that the trustee's choice is unconstrained by such mechanisms as formal contracts, verbal commitments that can affect reputation, and explicit or implicit promises of future rewards or punishments. If any such mechanism were in place, then we would have good reasons to expect trustworthiness, but in this case, it would make little sense to talk of "trust." Yet, if people are willing to trust even when they know the potential trustee has an incentive to behave opportunistically, are they behaving rationally?

Though we accept the distinction between assurance (or encapsulated self-interest) and trust, we want to claim that trusting can be rational, insofar as trusting acts as a signal, whose intended effect is to focus the recipient on a reciprocity norm. If such a norm exists and is shared, then it is rational to trust insofar as one believes that in so doing one will trigger reciprocation even when the material incentives to reciprocate are absent. Thus, Hardin's view that trusting is rational is vindicated only insofar as the truster's expectation of reciprocity plays a role in the decision to trust; however, this expectation is not necessarily generated by previous experience or interaction with the trustee or by assessing the trustee's self-interest. If, indeed, a reciprocity norm exists and is commonly shared, then it makes sense for the truster to try to focus the trustee on it, in the expectation that he will reciprocate and thus benefit the truster. Though trust may not be a social norm or a default rule, the existence of a strong reciprocity norm could be enough to support generalized trust.

Generalized trust is exemplified by a game that is meant to study behavioral trust, that is, the willingness to bet that another party will reciprocate (at a cost) a risky move. In most experiments with trust games, trusters invest around 50 percent of their money, contrary to game-theoretic predictions. Trustees on average repay close to the original investment. This behavior is difficult to explain within the usual game-theoretic models, as they all make the auxiliary hypothesis that agents are selfish and only care about their material payoffs. Reciprocal altruism has been advanced as a possible alternative explanation. According to this hypothesis, people will send money to the extent that they believe doing so will elicit reciprocity on the part of the other person. While reciprocal altruism would account for the fact that experimental participants frequently send and send back positive amounts of money, it also implies that there should be a correlation between the proportion of the investor's endowment that is sent and the return rate—but there is none. Moreover, reciprocal altruism would predict no sending (or sending back) in instances in which the person you send to (or received from) is not the same as the person deciding whether (or who decided) to send money. Yet, in treatments in which this was the case, there was some sending (and sending back) although willingness to do either clearly declines when the tie between senders and receivers is indirect.

These results have led some behavioral scientists to claim that trust is norm driven (Dawes, 1991; Orbell and Dawes, 1991). This means that either (1) the act of trusting is an almost automatic response to a situation that, though different from the typical ones in which trust is normally bestowed, is perceived as similar enough to induce trusting behavior or (2) in a more conscious way, people believe that they are expected to trust and that not trusting is a form of behavior that is reproachable. Be that as it may, if trusting were a social norm, then we would expect a general agreement that lack of trust, unless justified by the situation, is blameworthy.

As we said at the outset, the goal of this article is precisely to distinguish between trusting as a behavior that is norm driven versus trusting as grounded on the anticipation of profit through reciprocation. If trusting were a social norm, then we would expect a general agreement that lack of trust would be punished. That is, individuals would expect non-trusting behavior to be penalized, even when they themselves would not be inclined to punish a transgressor. This is because a social norm, as opposed to a personal value, does not require one's allegiance; for a norm to exist, there must be a collective belief that the behavior dictated by the norm is widespread, as well as a shared belief that one is expected to engage in such behavior when appropriate and that transgressions might be punished. This means one may follow a norm of trust without a personal value or disposition to be trusting, simply because one expects others to follow it and one believes others think one ought to follow it. A social norm only requires a conditional preference for following it, a preference grounded on the right kind of expectations, not an unwavering commitment. It is therefore important, in order to determine whether a norm exists and applies to a particular situation, to elicit individuals' expectations about what *others* would do or expect one to do in that situation (Bicchieri, 2006). *Empirical expectations* about what most people similarly situated will or would do are important, since any norm (once it is in place) has a coordination function, and believing that none or very few follow it would deprive the norm of its power. Yet empirical expectations alone are not sufficient to induce compliance. Typically, pro-social norms do not reflect the immediate self-interest of their followers, and thus we also need a *normative expectation* that others think we should conform to the norm, and are prepared to punish us if we do not. Since compliance with a social norm depends upon the individual's expectations, even a person who would normally obey a trust norm may shirk it in anonymous encounters, where the weight of normative expectations is greatly diluted. Just observing behavior in such situations does not allow us to conclude that a norm does or does not exist, but there are other ways to explore this issue.

Asking people whether a specific behavior elicits condemnation or punishment is a better way to determine whether that behavior is dictated by a norm. Yet we cannot establish that there is a norm of trust only by asking people whether *they* would punish non-trusting behavior. Depending upon their personal values, some would punish no matter what and others would not. Some may feel a deep personal allegiance to a trust norm, whereas others may just abide by it in the right circumstances, but evade it whenever possible, and thus look upon transgressors with great indulgence. If we instead ask people what they expect others to do, then we have a clearer picture of what sort of behavior is socially required, provided individuals' expectations are in agreement. Only when there is such a consensus are we justified in claiming that a norm exists.

Note that a norm of trust may be contingent upon the relationship existing between the parties. It is entirely possible that, whereas there is no norm telling us to trust strangers, there exists a strong norm about trusting friends and family. In this case, lack of generalized trust may not be considered negative, but failing to trust a friend may elicit punishment. We thus designed an experiment aimed at eliciting participants' expectations about which behaviors, in the context of a trust game, bring about punishment, and as we shall see, lack of trust (either of a friend or of a stranger) is not one of them, but lack of reciprocity is.

2.2 Experiment

2.2.1 *Experimental Design*

To determine the normative status of trust, we designed a survey with salient rewards to elicit participants' attitudes regarding the punishment of untrusting behavior. We began by supposing that if trust is a social norm, then participants should expect that untrusting behavior would be punished, following the account of social norms developed in Bicchieri (2006). Thus, our experimental aim was to elicit individuals' expectations about punishment so as to inform our understanding of whether trust is a norm.

To elicit the relevant expectations, we first described to the participants a previously conducted standard trust game (Berg et al., 1995). The standard trust game creates a situation in which one player must decide whether to trust another, who must then decide whether to honor or abuse this trust. Specifically, in the trust game, both investor and trustee receive an endowment of, for example, US$10. The investor transfers some, all, or none of his endowment to the trustee and the experimenter triples any amount sent. After observing the tripled amount, the trustee transfers back some, all, or none of the tripled amount to the investor. The investor earns his endowment of US$10, minus the transfer amount and plus any amount transferred back. The trustee earns the endowment of US$10, plus the tripled transfer amount and less any amount transferred back.

Trust is interpreted here as the willingness to bet that another player will reciprocate a risky move at a cost to themselves. Thus, a zero-transfer amount suggests the investor does not trust the trustee at all and, similarly, a zero-return amount suggests the trustee is not trustworthy.[2] Though economic theory predicts that in a one-shot, anonymous trust game, there will be no trust and reciprocation, experimental data tell otherwise. In most experiments, participants do trust by investing around half of their endowment, but trustees' repayments are usually equal to or less than the original investment (Camerer, 2003). An interesting question is thus why so many individuals, when in the role of truster or investor, tend to "trust" their counterpart when in fact it appears that trusting is costly. In particular, we test whether trust is a norm and thus people trust to obey the norm.

To test this, we described to the participants instances of the standard trust game in which the investor did not transfer any money and also instances in which the investor transferred some positive amount of money to the trustee. In these latter instances, we also described cases in which trustees did not return any money as well as cases in which the trustees returned some positive amount of money to the investor. For each scenario considered, we asked the participants two questions: whether they would impose a fine on either the investor or the trustee and what their expectations were about what the other participants would choose to do.

As noted before, we wished to consider whether the relationship between the investor and the trustee matters to the normative status of trust: it may be the case that trust among friends has a different status than trust among strangers. To investigate this possibility, we conducted both a "stranger" treatment and "friend" treatment of the full experiment. The only difference between these two treatments is that in the former, the participants were told that the investor and the trustee are strangers, whereas in the friend treatment, participants were told that the investor and the trustee are friends. By supplying this additional

Table 2.1 Scenarios to consider when making punishment decisions

Punishment target	*Scenario to be considered*	*Denotation*
Investor	The investor transferred US$0 to the trustee	*I(0)*
	The investor transferred US$5 to the trustee	*I(1/2)*
	The investor transferred US$10 to the trustee	*I(1)*
Trustee	The investor transferred US$5 and the trustee returned US$0	*R(0)*
	The investor transferred US$5 and the trustee returned US$5	*R(1/3)*
	The investor transferred US$5 and the trustee returned US$10	*R(2/3)*
	The investor transferred US$5 and the trustee returned US$15	*R(1)*

context about the relationship of the two parties, we aimed to activate any context-sensitive norms that may not have been triggered without such specification.

In both treatments, participants were first familiarized with the trust game, and then were asked to make judgments about whether they wanted to punish one of the actors in seven different scenarios, three of which focused on an investor's decision while the other four focused on a trustee's decision. The participants did not have to pay anything to punish the actors in the trust game. The details of the seven scenarios are listed in Table 2.1.

Each subject answered three questions within each scenario. First, participants were asked what fine (called a "payoff cut" in the instructions) they would like to impose on the decision-maker described in the scenario. Possible options were 0 percent, 10 percent, 30 percent, 50 percent, 70 percent, 90 percent, and 100 percent of the actor's earnings. It was made clear to the subject that the fine's amount would not go either to the subject herself or to the punished individual's counterpart. The money was taken away, but not redistributed.

The second question asked the subject to estimate how many participants in her session chose not to fine the decision-maker (that is, chose a fine of 0 percent). Participants were reminded that they would earn a point for giving a correct estimate. A third, related question was also asked: participants were asked to choose the punishment amount that most participants would choose in the subjects' session. As with the second question, the participants were made aware that correct choices would earn them one point. Each subject earned US$3 by completing all seven questions. At the end of the experiment, two questions were randomly selected from those for which participants could earn points. Participants earned US$3 per point on those two questions only (the Appendix provides details).

2.2.2 *Experimental Procedure*

The participants were recruited at the University of Pennsylvania through the web-based "Experiments @ Penn" recruitment system. They were given instructions for the trust experiment and were told that they would be asked to answer several questions regarding the participants' decisions in that experiment. Participants were given a short quiz to make sure that they understood the trust game. After each participant correctly completed the quiz, the experimenter handed out the punishment surveys. After all participants finished the surveys, two questions were randomly selected and participants were paid according to their answers to those questions. Each participant received a US$5 attendance bonus in addition to the money earned in the game and the survey (US$4 on average). Participants were in the laboratory for less than one hour.

2.3 Results

We obtained observations on 62 participants: 30 in the stranger treatment and 32 in the friend treatment. In each treatment *k* (with "*f*" designating the friend treatment and "*s*" designating the stranger treatment), participant *j* indicated the amount of the fine to impose on the investor in each of the three scenarios *I(.)* or the trustees in each of the four scenarios *R(.)* (see Table 2.1). We obtained data on participant *j*'s expectation regarding the percentage of participants who imposed no punishment on the decision-maker (investor or trustee) in each scenario. We denote this as $S_{j,I(.),k}$, and $S_{j,R(.),k}$, respectively. We also obtained the participants' expectations regarding the most frequently chosen fine amount, denoted as $P_{j,I(.),k}$ for the investor scenario and $P_{j,R(.),k}$ for the trustee scenario. For each scenario in each treatment, we calculated the average of each expectation across the participants: $\bar{S}_{I(.),k}$, $\bar{S}_{R(.),k}$, $\bar{P}_{I(.),k}$, and $\bar{P}_{R(.),k}$.

Previous research has shown that reciprocity is a social norm and third parties are often willing to punish violators (for example, Fehr and Fischbacher, 2004; Kurzban et al., 2006). Here, we compare punishment expectations between cases in which the investor is completely untrusting (that is, *I(0)*) and in which the trustee is completely untrustworthy (that is, *R(0)*). In addition, we compare results between the friend and stranger treatments to determine how a trust norm might vary according to the relationship between the investor and the trustee.

We begin with an analysis of the stranger treatment. We report participants' answers to questions regarding how many other participants they think will choose "no punishment" in each of our several hypothetical investments and returns. If trust were a norm, then we would expect that, on average, individuals believe that a majority (more than 50 percent) will punish a completely untrusting investor (that is, $\bar{S}_{I(0),k}$ 50 percent). In fact, we find that, on average, participants believed that 60 percent of participants in their session would *not* impose any punishment on an investor who transferred zero (this is not statistically different from 50 percent, one-tail *t*-test $p = 0.944$). In contrast, only 24 percent (significantly less than 50 percent, one-tail *t*-test $p < 0.01$) of participants were expected not to impose a fine on a trustee who returned zero. The difference between these two mean expectations (60 percent and 24 percent) is significant (two-tail paired *t*-test, $p < 0.01$).

Figure 2.1A plots the distribution of $\bar{S}_{j,I(0),s}$ and $\bar{S}_{j,R(0),s}$. Significantly more participants expect at least 50 percent of participants to choose no punishment in the untrusting investor case than in the untrustworthy trustee case (60 percent versus 17 percent, two- tail paired *t*-test, $p < 0.01$). Moreover, 20 percent of participants (6 out of 30[3]) expected nobody to impose a fine on untrusting investors (that is, $\bar{S}_{j,I(0),s}$ 100), but only 3 percent of participants (1 out of 30) believed nobody would punish an untrustworthy trustee. On the other hand, while 30 percent (9 out of 30) believed at least some people would fine untrustworthy participants (that is, $\bar{S}_{j,R(0),s}$ 0), only 3 percent (1 out of 30) believed so for the untrusting investor. This evidence runs counter to the view that trust is a social norm.

Another way to measure whether trust is a norm is to ask how much punishment participants think most people would impose on an untrusting action. We next report data on the expectations that participants hold regarding the punishment level that most participants would choose. We plot the distribution of $\bar{P}_{j,I(0),s}$ or $\bar{P}_{j,R(0),s}$ in 53 percent of participants expected zero punishment to be the most popular choice when an investor transfers zero. However, when the trustee returns nothing, only about 17 percent of participants expected that most participants would choose no punishment. The average expected magnitude of the fine is also lower in the zero investment case than in the zero return case (21 percent versus 58 percent, respectively, two-tail paired *t*-test $p < 0.01$). This provides convergent evidence that choosing not to trust is not a norm violation.

As we argued earlier, whether trust is a norm might vary with the relationship between the investor and trustee. In particular, a trust norm might generally exist among friends even if it does not exist among strangers. We were surprised to find that this does not seem to be the case. In particular, we conducted the same analysis in the friend treatment as in the stranger treatment discussed above. First, when the

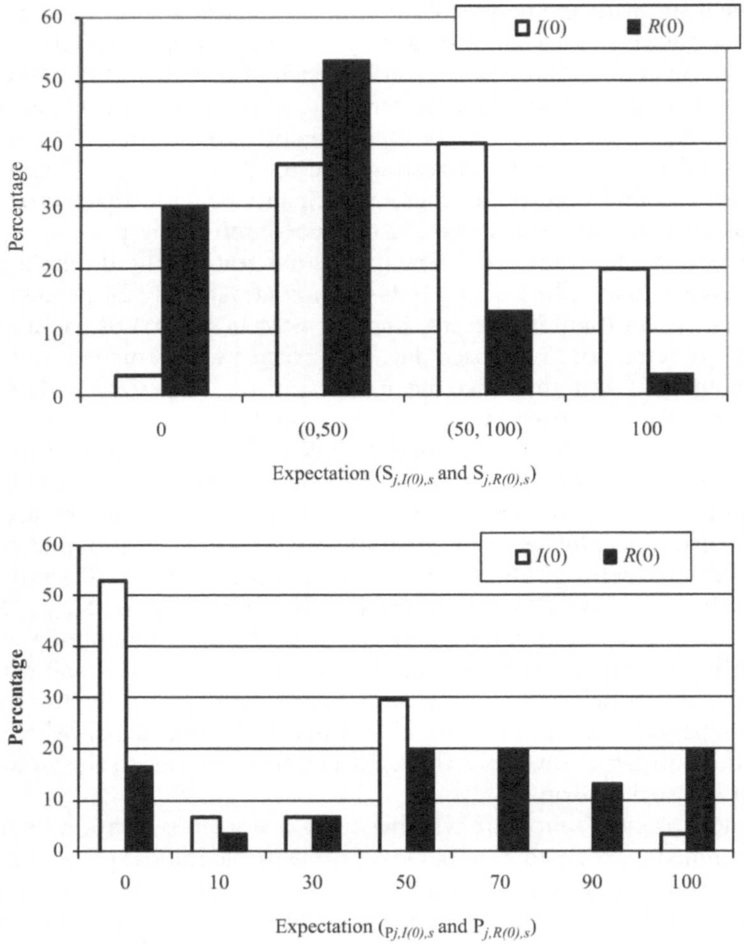

Figure 2.1 (A) Expectations of punishment in the stranger treatment: the distribution of expectations regarding the percentage of people who imposed no punishment on the investor when the investment amount is zero ($S_{j,I(0),s}$) or on the trustee when the amount returned is zero ($S_{j,R(0),s}$). (B) Expectations of punishment in the stranger treatment: the distribution of expectations regarding the most frequently chosen fine amount imposed on the investor when the investment amount is zero ($P_{j,I(0),s}$) and the amount imposed on the trustee when the amount returned is zero ($P_{j,R(0),s}$)

trustee and the investor are friends, on average, participants expected that 47 percent of the participants would not punish the investor at all if she transferred zero to her friend (this is not statistically significantly less than 50 percent (one-tail *t*-test $p = 0.342$) nor is it significantly different from 60 percent in the corresponding stranger treatment (two-tail *t*-test $p = 0.17$)). On the other hand, only 20 percent of participants were expected not to fine the trustee if she returned nothing to her friend (significantly less than 50 percent (one-tail *t*-test $p < 0.01$) and not significantly different from 24 percent in the corresponding stranger treatment (two-tail *t*-test $p = 0.50$)). The difference between these two expectations is significant (47 percent versus 20 percent, two-tail paired *t*-test, $p < 0.01$).

The distribution of $\bar{S}_{j,I(0),f}$ and $\bar{S}_{j,R(0),f}$ is plotted in Figure 2.2A. Significantly more participants expect at least 50 percent of participants to choose no punishment in the untrusting investor case than in the case of an untrustworthy trustee (53 percent versus 16 percent, two-tail paired *t*-test, $p < 0.01$).

Figure 2.2B plots the distribution of $\bar{P}_{j,I(0),f}$ or $\bar{P}_{j,R(0),f}$ in the friend treatment. About 47 percent of participants expected that most participants would choose not to punish an untrusting investor at all. However, if the trustee returns nothing, only about 19 percent of participants expected most participants would choose not to punish the trustee. The average magnitude of the fine that most participants expected to be imposed is also lower in the zero investment case than that in the zero return case (30 percent versus 57 percent, two-tail pair *t*-test $p < 0.01$). Again, we do not find statistically significant differences between the stranger and friend treatments.

These results suggest that even when the trustee is the investor's friend, people do not expect that others would punish a decision not to trust the trustee. Thus, people do not seem to believe trust is a norm that people should obey, regardless of whether or not the investor and the trustee are friends.

We have discussed expectations regarding punishment decisions in cases in which either the investor shows no trust at all (sends nothing) or the trustee is completely untrustworthy (returns nothing). We next address how people expect punishment decisions to be made when the investor shows some degree of trust or the trustee is trustworthy to some degree. In our experiment, the investor in scenario *I(1/2)* signals some degree of trust, but not full trust, and in scenario *I(1)*, the investor signals complete trust. In both cases, we found that, on average, about 90 percent of participants expected others not to punish the investor in the stranger treatment. About 80 percent of participants expected no punishment in the corresponding friend treatment.

Figure 2.3 plots $\bar{P}_{I(.),k}$ in all three investor cases *I(0)*, *I(1/2)*, and *I(1)* as well as in the four trustee cases *R(0)*, *R(1/3)*, *R(2/3)*, and *R(1)* in both treatments. Note that there is no apparent difference between the stranger and the friend treatments. If the investor transferred half of the endowment (scenario *I(1/2)*), the average expected fine amount chosen by most participants was close to zero. This was true regardless of whether the investor and trustee were friends or strangers. In particular, more

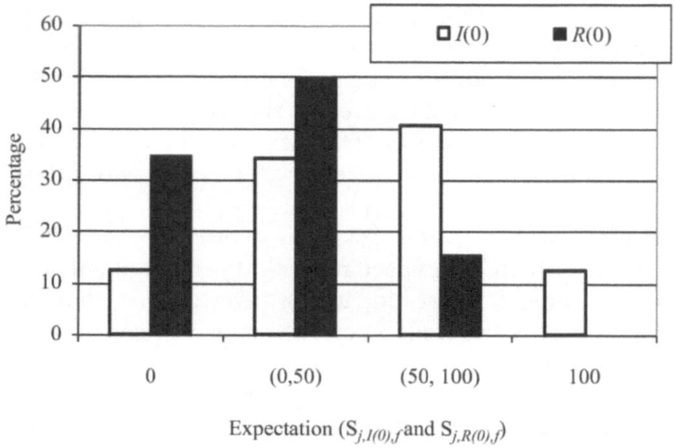

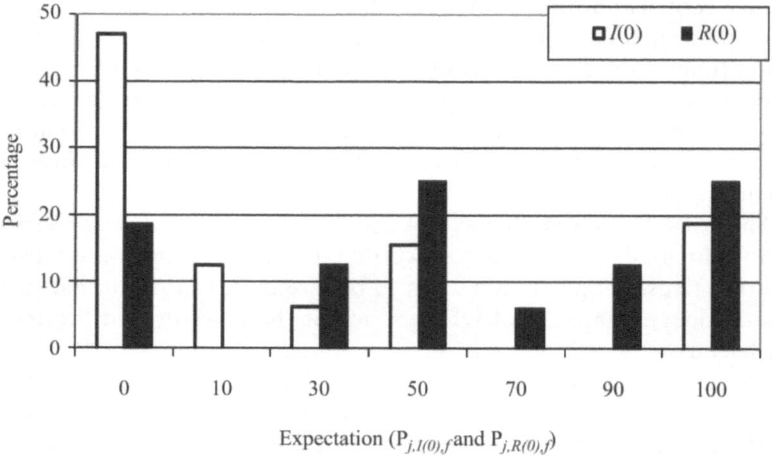

Figure 2.2 (A) Expectations of punishment in the friend treatment: the distribution of expectations regarding the percentage of participants who imposed no punishment on the investor when the investment amount is zero ($S_{j,I(0),f}$) or on the trustee when the amount returned is zero ($S_{j,R(0),f}$). (B) Expectations of punishment in the friend treatment: the distribution of expectations regarding the most frequently chosen fine amount imposed on the investor when the investment amount is zero ($P_{j,I(0),f}$) and the amount imposed on the trustee when the amount returned is zero ($P_{j,R(0),f}$)

than 90 percent of participants expected a zero fine to be chosen by most participants in both treatments. When the trustee returned the transfer amount (that is, *R(1/3)*), the expected fine was significantly lower than when the return amount was zero (28 percent versus 58 percent, two-tail paired *t*-test $p < 0.01$ in the stranger treatment and 30 percent versus

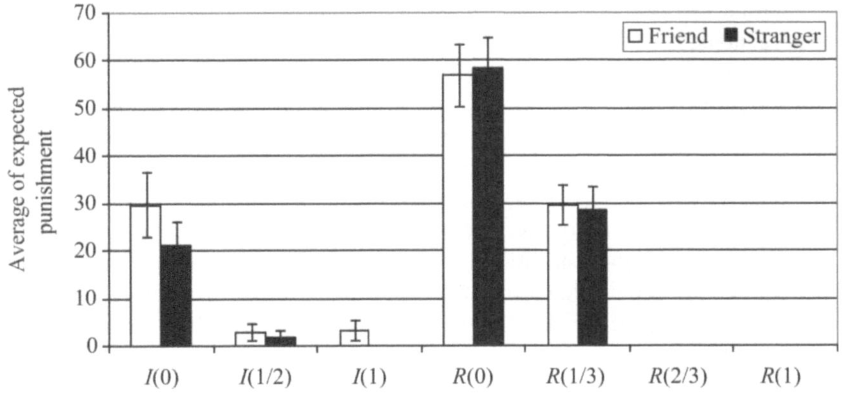

Figure 2.3 Average expected punishment amount imposed on the investor $\bar{P}_I(.)_{,k}$ and the trustee $\bar{P}_R(.)_{,k}$ in all seven scenarios in the stranger treatment and friend treatment

57 percent, two-tail paired *t*-test $p < 0.01$ in the friend treatment). It is also interesting to notice that $\bar{P}_{R(1/3),s}$ is not significantly different from $\bar{P}I(0)_{,s}$ (28 percent versus 21 percent, two-tail paired *t*-test $p = 0.29$) and that the same is true for $\bar{P}_{R(1/3),f}$ versus $\bar{P}_{I(0),f}$ in the friend treatment (both 30 percent). This suggests that returning the original investment amount, so that the investor is made whole, is not viewed as a norm violation. Finally, in both treatments nobody expected any punishment to occur when the trustee returned the fair amount.

In sum, we obtained convergent evidence that people do not believe that to trust is a norm. Our participants expected that most people would not punish untrusting investors, regardless of whether the potential trustee was a friend or stranger. On the other hand, our participants behaved as though behaving in a trustworthy manner is a social norm: most of the participants believed that most people would punish someone who failed to reciprocate a stranger's or a friend's trust.

2.4 Discussion

Our results provide no evidence about the existence of a norm of trust. Interestingly, our data suggest that there is no difference in people's normative beliefs regarding trusting friends and trusting strangers. Often norms are contextual, in that they only cover a specific class of situations. So, for example, it may be the case that there is a general obligation to trust friends, but not strangers. What we observed, however, is that, even in close relationships, trusting does not seem to be normatively required. In contrast, punishment expectations show that there is a norm of reciprocity. This is not surprising. In every society, such norms define certain actions and obligations as repayment for benefits received.

Trust is grounded upon reciprocity norms. Their very existence provides grounds for the expectation of being reciprocated. We expect people to help those who have helped them, and therefore we expect those whom we trust to have an obligation to honor our trust. This is the reason why we have argued that trusting can be rational, insofar as the truster expects, by her action, to focus the trustee on a reciprocity norm and thus trigger an adequate response. Nobody would trust without expecting to be at least made whole, but this expectation is a general one, not one specific to a particular party one knows has an interest in reciprocating.

Though our experiment only aimed to assess whether there is a trust norm, our results suggest that it is the presence of a norm of reciprocity that elicits trusting behavior in impersonal contexts. Interestingly, the fact that trustees usually return an amount equal to or less than the original investment may also be explained by a theory of norm compliance in which compliance is conditional upon having the right sort of expectations (Bicchieri, 2006). In the anonymous environment, there is no risk of being punished, and thus the pull of the norm, though present, is less strong.

Appendix: Instructions of the Stranger Treatment

Thank you for coming! You've earned \$5 for showing up on time, and the instructions explain how you can make decisions and earn more money.

In today's session, every participant will be given a questionnaire. You will be asked to make decisions in several questions regarding participants' decisions in another experiment (Experiment A). Your payoff depends on your decisions in the questionnaire. To answer the questionnaire, you need to first understand Experiment A. The next page describes the experiment. Please read it carefully.

Description of Experiment A

In this experiment, two participants are paired up. One plays as Actor 1 and the other plays as Actor 2.

> *Actor 1 and Actor 2 are randomly and anonymously paired up. They will never be informed of each other's identity.*

At the beginning of the experiment, *both actors* receive an initial endowment of \$10. First, Actor 1, can transfer, from his/her endowment, any amount from \$0 to \$10 to Actor 2. The experimenters will *triple* this transferred amount so that Actor 2 receives three times the number of dollars Actor 1 transferred.

Then, after Actor 1's decision, Actor 2 can transfer back to Actor 1 any amount of the tripled number of dollar bills he/she received.

Final payoffs. Actor 1 receives: $10—transfer to Actor 2 back-transfer from Actor 2.

Actor 2 receives: $10 3 transfer from Actor 1—back-transfer to Actor 1. To ensure you understand Experiment A, please complete the following exercise:

1 At the beginning of the experiment, _________ receive an initial endowment of $10.

a) Actor 1 b) Actor 2 c) Actor 1 and Actor 2 d) No one

2 If Actor 1 transfers $5 and Actor 2 transfers $10 back to Actor 1, then Actor 1's final payoff $_________

Actor 2's final payoff $_________

3 In Question 2, if Actor 2 transfers $1 back to Actor 1, then Actor 1's final payoff ¼ $_________

Actor 2's final payoff ¼ $_________

Note: Both Actor 1 and Actor 2 receive an initial endowment of $10.
Final payoffs. Actor 1 receives: $10—transfer to Actor 2 þ back-transfer from Actor 2.
Actor 2 receives: $10 þ 3 x transfer from Actor 1—back-transfer to Actor 1.

Questionnaire

Please read the following questions carefully, you will earn $3 by finishing all the questions. You will earn points from some of the questions. At the end of the experiment, two questions will be randomly selected from those for which you can earn points. You will earn $3 for each point you earned.

In order to answer the following questions, you need to know there are participants in total in today's session.

ID: In the following questions, you will decide whether to impose a payoff cut to *Actor 1*'s final payoff in each scenario. The payoff cut amount is the number of *cents* you would deduct from *each dollar* of Actor 1's earnings. The payoff cut amount does *NOT* go to either Actor 2 or you.

In order to answer the following questions, you need to know there are participants in total in today's session.

Scenario: Actor 1 transferred $0 to Actor 2.

I would choose ___________.

a no payoff cut to Actor 1
b to deduct 10 cents from each dollar of Actor 1's earnings
c to deduct 30 cents from each dollar of Actor 1's earnings
d to deduct 50 cents from each dollar of Actor 1's earnings
e to deduct 70 cents from each dollar of Actor 1's earnings
f to deduct 90 cents from each dollar of Actor 1's earnings
g to deduct all the earnings from Actor 1

Please Briefly Explain Your Decision Here

- How many participants in today's session do you think chose "a) no payoff cut to Actor 1"?
(If your answer is right, you will get one point.)
- What is the option that you think most participants chose today?
(If your answer is right, you will get one point.)

Scenario: Actor 1 transferred $5 to Actor 2.

I would choose ___________.

a no payoff cut to Actor 1
b to deduct 10 cents from each dollar of Actor 1's earnings
c to deduct 30 cents from each dollar of Actor 1's earnings
d to deduct 50 cents from each dollar of Actor 1's earnings
e to deduct 70 cents from each dollar of Actor 1's earnings
f to deduct 90 cents from each dollar of Actor 1's earnings
g to deduct all the earnings from Actor 1

Please Briefly Explain Your Decision Here

- How many participants in today's session do you think chose "a) no payoff cut to Actor 1"?
(If your answer is right, you will get one point.)
- What is the option that you think most participants chose today?
(If your answer is right, you will get one point.)

Scenario: Actor 1 transferred $10 to Actor 2.

I would choose ___________.

a no payoff cut to Actor 1
b to deduct 10 cents from each dollar of Actor 1's earnings
c to deduct 30 cents from each dollar of Actor 1's earnings
d to deduct 50 cents from each dollar of Actor 1's earnings
e to deduct 70 cents from each dollar of Actor 1's earnings
f to deduct 90 cents from each dollar of Actor 1's earnings
g to deduct all the earnings from Actor 1

Please Briefly Explain Your Decision Here

- How many participants in today's session do you think chose "a) no payoff cut to Actor 1"?
  (If your answer is right, you will get one point.)
- What is the option that you think most participants chose today?
  (If your answer is right, you will get one point.)

ID: In the following questions, you will decide whether to impose a payoff cut to *Actor 2*'s final payoff in each scenario. The payoff cut amount is the number of *cents* you would deduct from *each dollar* of Actor 2's earnings. The payoff cut amount does *NOT* go to either Actor 1 or you.

In order to answer the following questions, you need to know there are participants in total in today's session.

Scenario: Actor 1 transferred $5 and so Actor 2 received $15. Then Actor 2 transferred back $0. Therefore, at the end of the experiment, Actor 1 received $5 and Actor 2 received $25.

I would choose ___________.

a no payoff cut to Actor 2
b to deduct 10 cents from each dollar of Actor 2's earnings
c to deduct 30 cents from each dollar of Actor 2's earnings
d to deduct 50 cents from each dollar of Actor 2's earnings
e to deduct 70 cents from each dollar of Actor 2's earnings
f to deduct 90 cents from each dollar of Actor 2's earnings
g to deduct all the earnings from Actor 2

Please Briefly Explain Your Decision Here

- How many participants in today's session do you think chose "a) no payoff cut to Actor 2"?
  (If your answer is right, you will get one point.)
- What is the option that you think most participants chose today?
  (If your answer is right, you will get one point.)

Scenario: Actor 1 transferred $5 and so Actor 2 received $15. Then Actor 2 transferred back $5. Therefore, at the end of the experiment, Actor 1 received $10 and Actor 2 received $20.

I would choose ___________.

a no payoff cut to Actor 2
b to deduct 10 cents from each dollar of Actor 2's earnings
c to deduct 30 cents from each dollar of Actor 2's earnings
d to deduct 50 cents from each dollar of Actor 2's earnings
e to deduct 70 cents from each dollar of Actor 2's earnings
f to deduct 90 cents from each dollar of Actor 2's earnings
g to deduct all the earnings from Actor 2

Please Briefly Explain Your Decision Here

- How many participants in today's session do you think chose "a) no payoff cut to Actor 2"?
  (If your answer is right, you will get one point.)
- What is the option that you think most participants chose today?
  (If your answer is right, you will get one point.)

Scenario: Actor 1 transferred $5 and so Actor 2 received $15. Then Actor 2 transferred back $10. Therefore, at the end of the experiment, Actor 1 received $20 and Actor 2 received $10.

I would choose ___________.

a no payoff cut to Actor 2
b to deduct 10 cents from each dollar of Actor 2's earnings
c to deduct 30 cents from each dollar of Actor 2's earnings
d to deduct 50 cents from each dollar of Actor 2's earnings
e to deduct 70 cents from each dollar of Actor 2's earnings
f to deduct 90 cents from each dollar of Actor 2's earnings
g to deduct all the earnings from Actor 2

Please Briefly Explain Your Decision Here

- How many participants in today's session do you think chose "a) no payoff cut to Actor 2"?
  (If your answer is right, you will get one point.)
- What is the option that you think most participants chose today?
  (If your answer is right, you will get one point.)

Scenario: Actor 1 transferred $5 and so Actor 2 received $15. Then Actor 2 transferred back $15. Therefore, at the end of the experiment, Actor 1 received $20 and Actor 2 received $10.

I would choose ___________.

a no payoff cut to Actor 2
b to deduct 10 cents from each dollar of Actor 2's earnings
c to deduct 30 cents from each dollar of Actor 2's earnings
d to deduct 50 cents from each dollar of Actor 2's earnings
e to deduct 70 cents from each dollar of Actor 2's earnings
f to deduct 90 cents from each dollar of Actor 2's earnings
g to deduct all the earnings from Actor 2

Please Briefly Explain Your Decision Here

- How many participants in today's session do you think chose "a) no payoff cut to Actor 2"?
  (If your answer is right, you will get one point.)
- What is the option that you think most participants chose today?
  (If your answer is right, you will get one point.)

Acknowledgment

We wish to thank Alex Chavez and Gerry Mackie for comments.

Notes

1. What is meant by "generalized trust" is not just trust extended to random others, but also trust extended to impersonal actors such as social institutions, without grounding such trust in prior relationships or in the possibility of monitoring and sanctioning lack of trustworthiness.
2. Cox (2004) designed a triadic game to sort out the motivations of investors and trustees in the trust game. He found that part of the reason that investors transfer a positive amount may be due to altruistic motivation and that trustees may also return a positive amount due to inequality aversion. Nevertheless, we may still assume that a zero transfer amount signals no trust and that a zero return signals no reciprocity. Our conclusions are thus drawn from the data for the cases of zero transfer and zero return.
3. Of these six participants, two believed nobody would choose to impose zero punishment on the trustee when she returned zero.

References

Berg J, Dickhaut J and McCabe K (1995) Trust, reciprocity, and social history. *Games and Economic Behavior* 10: 122–42.

Bicchieri C (2006) *The Grammar of Society: The Nature and Dynamics of Social Norms*. Cambridge: Cambridge University Press.

Camerer C (2003) *Behavioral Game Theory*. New York: Russell Sage Foundation.

Cox J (2004) How to identify trust and reciprocity. *Games and Economic Behavior* 46: 260–81.

Dawes R (1991) Social dilemmas, economic self-interest and evolutionary theory. In: Brown DR, Smith JEK (eds.) *Recent Research in Psychology: Frontiers of Mathematical Psychology: Essays in Honor of Clyde Coombs*. New York: Springer-Verlag, 53–79.

Elster J (1979) *Ulysses and the Sirens: Studies in Rationality and Irrationality*. New York and Cambridge: Cambridge University Press.

Ensminger J (2001) Reputations, trust, and the principal-agent problem. In: Cook K. (ed.) *Trust and Society*. New York: Russell Sage Foundation.

Fehr E and Fischbacher U (2004) Third-party punishment and social norms. *Evolution and Human Behavior* 25: 63–87.

Hardin R (2006) *Trust*. New York: Wiley.

Kurzban R, DeScioli P and O'Brien E (2006) Audience effects on moralistic punishment. *Evolution and Human Behavior* 28: 75–84.

Messick D and Kramer R (2001) Trust as a form of shallow morality. In: Cook K. (ed.) *Trust in Society*. New York: Russell Sage Foundation.

Orbell J and Dawes R (1991) A "cognitive miser" theory of cooperators' advantage. *American Political Science Review* 85(2): 515–28.

Putnam R (1993) *Making Democracy Work: Civic Traditions in Modern Italy*. Princeton, NJ: Princeton University Press.

Yamagishi T (2001) Trust as a form of social intelligence. In: Cook Karen S. (ed.) *Trust in Society*. New York: Russell Sage Foundation.

Yamagishi T and Yamagishi M (1994) Trust and commitment in the United States and Japan. *Motivation and Emotion* 18: 129–66.

3 Trust, Diversity, and (Ir-)Rationality

How Categorization Can Lead to Discrimination

Simon Scheller

3.1 Introduction

Trust constitutes an essential component of social interaction. Trust enables peaceful coexistence, simplifies and stimulates economic exchange, and fosters economic growth (Asongu and Kodila-Tedika, 2017; Bjørnskov, 2017; Coleman, 1994; Cox, 2008; Güth et al., 2008; Kappmeier, 2016; Knack and Keefer, 1997; Zak and Knack, 2001).

Recently however, increasing population heterogeneity (e.g. through refugee- or labor migration) has posed a challenge to societal trust. Some empirical studies show a tendency toward lower trust in foreigners (Alesina and La Ferrara, 2000a,b; van der Meer and Tolsma, 2014), while people are more likely to trust others with similar characteristics (Tanis and Postmes, 2005) or engage with them in cooperative activities (Balliet et al., 2014). Somewhat contrastingly, Dinesen and Sønderskov (2018) found that many of these results are context sensitive and overall mixed. However, group-based distrust constitutes a serious problem for both minority and majority groups, as this potentially leaves opportunities untaken, hampers progress in many areas and contributes to a climate of deteriorating social cohesion. These problems necessitate inquiry into the causal roots of group-based distrust. Such an analysis is warranted and justified despite the complexity of empirical results—or maybe even more so.

Why do people sometimes trust outsiders less than people "from their own group"? A common and immediate answer points to people's cultural sentiments and their feeling of group belonging that lead to group-based discrimination in matters of trust. While this paper does not dispute or excuse the persistence of any form of such sentiments, it identifies an alternative explanation for different trust-levels based on individually rational considerations.

By means of an agent-based model (ABM), this paper explores the dynamics of trust within and between different societal groups. ABMs provide formal computational representations of social systems, allowing researchers to study complex dynamic interactions by means of simulation analysis. In our case, simulation results suggest that out-group trust is harder to establish as soon as people distinguish between members of their own group and the out-group—even if trustworthiness is constant across groups, and no other biases are present. As will be explained, the result is driven by a seemingly minor asymmetry in learning when people conditionalize their beliefs about trustworthiness on group membership.

These simulation results point empirical researchers toward a phenomenon of great importance. While the employed model is simplistic in its build-up, this does not undermine the results' credibility. Instead, it may be the case that rather sparse conditions are sufficient to generate discriminatory beliefs. Hence, the presumed process might work parallel to other mechanisms that foster out-group distrust. This should invite further empirical investigations concerning structurally discriminating features in trust situations and for situations with salient groups more generally.

To elaborate these issues, the rest of this paper proceeds as follows: after briefly summarizing some empirical findings on out-group distrust, Section 2 reviews the most common explanations for out-group discrimination in trust situations. In Section 3, I outline a formal model of trust, which allows us to set up a scenario where all of the previously introduced explanations are ruled out. Section 4 reports the results of systematically carried out model analyses that show how out-group discrimination emerges nonetheless in this setting, and explains how they come about. Finally, Section 5 concludes by discussing the status of these results, their limitations and potential implications.

3.2 Out-Group Discrimination and Its Potential Causes

Empirical evidence from survey studies suggests that population homogeneity favors societal trust, while trust is weaker in ethnically, linguistically, and economically heterogeneous neighborhoods (Alesina and La Ferrara, 2000a,b; Glaeser et al., 1999; Leigh, 2006; Rothstein and Uslaner, 2005; Zak and Knack, 2001). In a laboratory experiment, Tanis and Postmes (2005) find that participants placed significantly higher trust in in-group members compared to out-group members, and more so if group membership was emphasized. Similar findings are obtained by Brewer and Silver (1978); Brewer (1979); Platow et al. (1990); De Cremer and Van Vugt (1998); Kramer and Brewer (1984). While Yuki et al. (2005) find some cultural differences between Western and Asian cultures, Platow et al. (2012) emphasizes the importance of common knowledge of group membership, and Williams (2001) further analyzes motivational factors for trust-discrimination. At the same time, out-group members are judged as less trustworthy in organizational and other contexts (B. Brewer and Brown, 1998; Kramer, 1994; Kramer and Messick, 1998). Balliet et al. (2014) and Dinesen and Sønderskov

(2018) provide extensive meta-analyses of the issue, shedding light on the impact of various influencing factors of in-group-favoritism, such as mutual interdependence, common knowledge of group membership, or group composition. The bottom line of this literature is that there exists ample evidence that, at least in certain circumstances, people place more trust in members of their own group, and less trust in out-group-members. This highly troubling phenomenon, which is also in accordance with many people's intuitions, constitutes the point of departure for this paper.

What explains this trust-discrimination of outsiders? In what follows, I outline three major explanations for this phenomenon's occurrence: (1) the rational-and-justified explanation, (2) the explanation based on group identification or social norms, and (3) the explanation based on individually irrational behavior. It seems natural and reasonable to suggest that no out-group discrimination should emerge in case neither of those factors are present. This means: if there exists no factual basis for discriminating between groups, if people act individually rational, and if people's actions and beliefs are not driven by any feelings of group sentiment or other forms of in-group favoritism, then the existence of groups should not matter for trust. As the subsequently presented model will show, this is not the case.

3.2.1 *Rational and Justified Out-Group Distrust*

Bicchieri et al. (2004) define trust as "the disposition to engage in social exchanges that involve uncertainty and vulnerability, but that are also potentially rewarding." Crucially, this view captures a rationalistic notion of trust: whether or not to trust someone constitutes a decision under uncertainty, and thus, as Hardin (1993, p. 516) puts it, "my estimation of the risk is my degree of trust in you." As a result, people need to distinguish between trustworthy and untrustworthy others. This renders trust essentially an individualistic epistemic problem (Hardin, 1993).

When specific individuals are personally identifiable, trustworthiness is usually established through repeated interaction. These constitute instances of "thick" trust, which, in the literature on social capital (Coleman, 2000; Newton, 1997; Putnam et al., 1994; Uslaner, 2002), are distinguished from instances of "thin" trust. Thin trust concerns potential interactions with unknown strangers, about whom no personal experiences regarding their trustworthiness are available. As thin trust is much more relevant for trust on a society-wide level, this will be our focus henceforth.

If no personal track record of trustworthiness is available to an individual, she can generalize from previous interactions with others. Such past encounters may provide at least a rough estimate of a current partner's trustworthiness through generalization from the entire population—or parts thereof. To improve one's estimate's accuracy, individuals may consider additional cues, such as visible group membership. If, for example, my past encounters have given me reason to believe that members of group *X* are trustworthy, it may be reasonable to use this as an indicator for judging the trustworthiness of other members of group *X*.

Under the assumption that people make judgements in a fully rational way when using such group-membership cues, what would explain the aforementioned empirical findings? Certainly, if groups were to actually differ concerning their trustworthiness, group-based discrimination would be rational from a cost-benefit point-of-view. This paper makes no claim about when (or if ever) this is the case in the real world. It only claims that out-group distrust would be explained if group *A* would be overall less trustworthy than group *B* in principle on the basis of such a rationalistic standpoint. In such a case, there would simply exist a factual basis for discrimination. Then, a collectively rational attitude can be said to emerge from individually rational behavior.

However, while this argument might explain collective distrust against certain groups in particular, it fails to provide a reason for why lack of trust would structurally always be toward the *out-group*. Given that people are equally trustworthy toward everyone, it is logically impossible for two distinct groups to be both less trustworthy than the other at the same time. Instead, members of the less trustworthy group should rationally exhibit a stronger out-group than in-group trust. Hence, the only possible explanation for mutual out-group distrust based on individually rationality and factual group-differences would require some form of reciprocity when it comes being trustworthy in the first place.

3.2.2 *The Explanation from Social Identity*

Such reciprocity norms, as well as plainly discriminatory beliefs more generally, could stem from social preferences and in-group favoritism. The supposition that people easily and strongly associate with social groups and exhibit in-group favoritism even under rather minimal conditions was first theorized by Tajfel (1970) under the label "Social Identity Theory." Since then, it has been employed to explain a large number of phenomena, such as intergroup-aggression (Markus et al., 2008), sentiments of prejudice (Klein et al., 2003), or rapid mass mobilization (Klein et al., 2007). Furthermore, in accordance with the above findings, in-group homogeneity has been found to increase group identification (Leach et al., 2008).

This framework stands in contrast to the rationalistic setting from before, and instead highlights trust's character as a social norm. As Tanis and Postmes (2005) contrasts these two views: "In certain group contexts, trust is not so much based on the economic calculation of what happens if the other individual preserves or violates the trust (so called calculus-based trust) but is based on common membership of a salient social group—i.e. *identification based trust*" (Tanis and Postmes, 2005, p. 414, emphasis in original).

Under this paradigm, some have argued that trust and cooperation in groups increases because people distinguish less between their own benefit and that of the group (Kramer and Brewer, 1984; Turner, 2014). Others have added to that an evolutionary explanation, according to which social identity's purpose is to establish communities of trust, as this is favorable for all group members. Accordingly, Brewer (1999, p. 433) defines "in-group communities as bounded communities of mutual trust," and a similar argument is provided by Takagi (1996).

In order to explain out-group trust discrimination based on social identity, one could argue that lower trust against out-group members could stem from the blind following of social trust norms. The collective behavior that emerges from social identity cannot be said to be individually rational in the sense of the previous explanation. However, they might be rational in an evolutionary sense, meaning that a certain group benefits from the aggregate outcome of such norms in the long run. Hence, this would constitute a case where distrust against out-groups would emerge based on social trust norms prescribing actions that are individually irrational in the short term, yet potentially leading to collectively rational outcomes—at least for some groups.

Reciprocity, in particular, may be the strongest norm inducing trusting behavior toward in-group members (Anderson et al., 2006; Berg et al., 1995; Güth et al., 2008; Simpson, 2006). Yet, in clearly identifiable one-shot scenarios, it is questionable under which conditions these explanations hold and when reciprocity norms can arise, and if so under what circumstances they would be resilient to exploitation. Hence, while discriminatory norms may be present in some cases, there may be still be others where (a large majority of) people do not discriminate based on group sentiment and social norms.

3.2.3 *Other Forms of Individual Irrationality*

Finally, discriminatory beliefs could emerge based on other forms of individually irrational or biased behavior. For instance, people may hold false initial beliefs about a certain group and do not manage to abandon these false beliefs due to their initial prejudice, which may have been inherited or otherwise socially acquired (Hadler, 2012).

Another form of irrationality could be located in the way with which individuals process information about other's trustworthiness: a person might, for example, follow a biased pattern of associating blame for untrustworthy behavior in the sense that they will attribute blame for betrayal to someone's out-group-membership, but would not associate blame to people from the in-group in turn (Rodin et al., 1990).

Plenty of other forms of individual irrationality are imaginable in principle, for instance individuals that do not learn at all from the evidence they receive, or individuals that are biased toward accepting information which is in accordance with the views they currently hold, a phenomenon commonly known as confirmation bias (Nickerson, 1998). Given the appropriate circumstances, all these forms of individual irrationality could explain why individuals discriminate out-group members when it comes to trust interactions. In general, these would be instances where collectively irrational behavior emerges from individually irrational actions.

3.2.4 *Collective Irrationality and Individually Rationality*

As the previous elaborations have shown, trust discrimination is sometimes explained as (a) a rational collective attitude based on individually rational decisions, (b) as the result of (individually irrational) group-sentiments that may turn out to be collectively rational or not, and (c) as the result of individually irrational beliefs or belief-formation processes that lead to collectively suboptimal outcomes. This suggests that the links between collective and individual (ir-)rationality are potentially complicated, as depicted in Figure 3.1.

However, none of the previous considerations suggests the emergence of collective irrationality from individually rational behavior. It is intuitive to think that if everyone acts rationally, the aggregate outcome should not be irrational. For the case at hand: if no factual basis for discrimination exists, if people act rationally, and if their behavior is not driven by any kind of group sentiments, then one should expect equal treatment of others within and across groups, and no irrational out-group trust discrimination.

Other cases exist where (ir-)rationally on the individual and collective level need not be monotonically connected. For example, as in cases of wisdom of crowds (Hong and Page, 2001, 2004; Mayo-Wilson et al., 2013) or the functioning of ant colonies (Schelling, 2006), individually

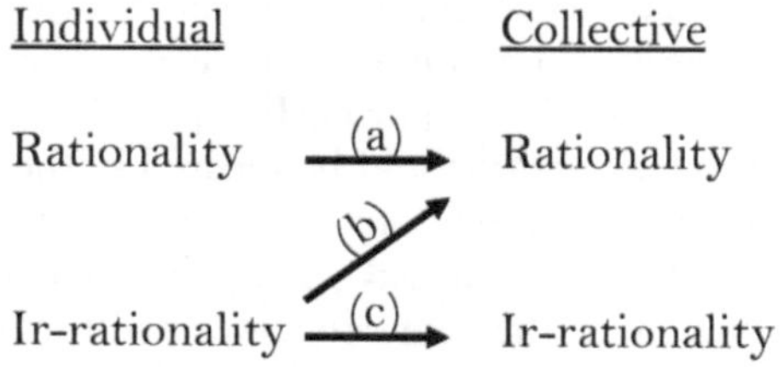

Figure 3.1 Possible relations between Individual and collective (ir-)rationality

irrational behavior can lead to collectively rational outcomes. On the other hand, phenomena like herding on financial markets (Devenow and Welch, 1996) or binge-drinking as a social norm on campus (Prentice and Miller, 1993) illustrate that collectively irrational norms can emerge even if individuals act rationally in a classic decision theoretic sense (Merdes, 2017).

Given that a lack of out-group trust is collectively irrational (since it results collectively inefficient) if actual trustworthiness is equal between groups, the previous considerations invite the question if out-group trust-discrimination can be explained solely based on individually rational behavior. This paper explores the emergence of trust by asking: is it possible for out-group distrust to emerge even if individuals act rationally and there exists no factual basis for discrimination?

3.3 Modeling the Dynamics of Trust

The previous sections have outlined competing explanations as to why out-group trust may be hampered relative to in-group trust. These explanations may be more or less applicable to different cases and situations, and there is clearly no one-fits-all explanation. One major reason why these explanations are hard to distinguish in reality is that an empirical analysis must evaluate individual motives for decisions. These motives are very hard to assess directly. People may not know the reasons for their decisions, they may fall prey to ex-post rationalization, or may not want to state their motives truthfully. It is even harder to assess complex social interactions of individuals that are based on these hard-to-assess motives. As a result, most approaches either focus on micro-level motives *or* aggregate level outcomes, and, therefore, they do not specify potential links between these two levels of analysis.

One approach that has been fruitfully applied to studying the emergence of trust is agent-based modeling. In contrast to standard empirical approaches, agent-based modeling explains the emergence of social phenomena—in this case the (non-)emergence of trust—in a fundamentally different way than most empirical approaches: ABMs start by stipulating individual behavioral rules. Then, a society interacting on the basis of these rules is simulated. From such simulations, macro-phenomena can be derived based on the dynamic interactions of individual agents. By explicitly modeling individual behavior and group interactions, one is able to causally connect the outcomes emerging on the societal level with individual behavior. This allows researchers to identify and analyze potential connections between micro-level behavior and macro-level outcomes.

Agent-based modeling and simulation have been frequently used to study interactive systems, and in particular also for studying the *emergence of trust*. In their seminal paper, Bicchieri et al. (2004) analyze how trust can emerge as a stable norm in a community of conditional co-operators. Kreps (1990) uses a similar argument based on the notion of reputation in repeated games.

Macy and Skvoretz (1998) model how local interactions enable the spread of trust throughout society, given that individuals have a chance to walk away from an interaction partners. Similarly, Fang et al. (2002) show how repeated trial-and-error learning can lead to the emergence of trust under rather broad conditions. Klein and Marx (2018a) analyze how individual mobility influences the emergence of trust in spatial scenarios.

Falcone and Castelfranchi (2004) look at the importance of attribution of behavior in trust encounters; Birk (2001) shows how realistically modeled learning rules can result in the emergence of trust, as they argue that genetic arguments are less suitable to fast-changing social environments; Jonker and Treur (1999) further envisage how different learning rules foster or hamper the emergence of trust.

As this short (and certainly selective) literature overview illustrates, plenty of contributions analyze the emergence of trust using ABMs. At the same time, some authors have addressed the dynamics of in-group favoritism. With an evolutionary perspective in a spatial model, Hammond and Axelrod (2006) show that in-group favoritism can develop because in-group cooperation provides fertile soil for spatial expansion of one group. Cohen (2012) analyzes this argument for the case of accents as an evolving linguistic group marker. With a mathematical model, Fu et al. (2012) analyze the conditions for in-group favoritism to emerge, while at the same time allowing for the possibility of out-group-cooperation.

The subsequent modeling approach aims to contribute to the literature on the emergence of trust by considering the role of visible group characteristics. As the analysis focuses on agents that act rationally in all considerable ways, the setting aims to inquire how even individually rational behavior may lead to collectively irrational outcomes such as out-group-distrust.

3.4 Model Description

To address the previously formulated question "Is it possible for out-group distrust to emerge even if individuals act rationally and there exists no factual basis for discrimination?," let us first consider how to capture the essential features of intergroup trust relations. For this purpose, consider the following baseline trust game between two players, a trustor and a trustee: the trustor decides whether or not to engage in a cooperative endeavor with the trustee. If the trustor decides to place trust in the trustee, the trustee subsequently decides whether to reward the trustor's trust, or to betray the trustor's trust. If the trustor does not

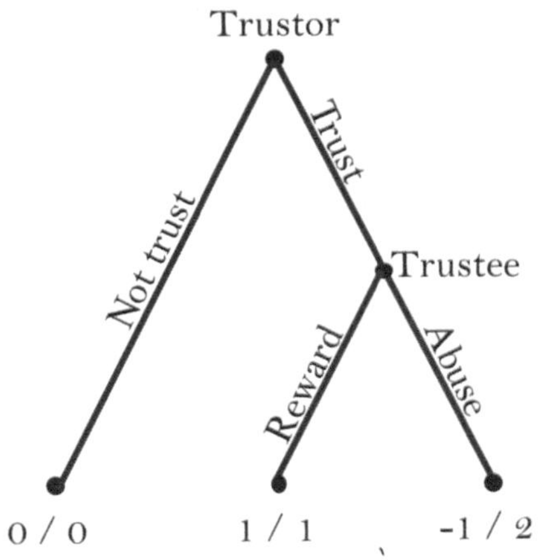

Figure 3.2 Sequential form of the baseline trust game

place trust in the trustee, the game ends without any further decisions and actions.

An illustrative example of such a situation would be a simple investment decision. The trustor as the investor needs to decide whether or not to give $1 to the trustee. The trustee, in turn, either rewards the investor's trust by re-paying her an amount of $2, or to keep all the gains to herself. Accordingly, the trustee's payoffs are 0 if no trust is placed in her, 2 if she betrays the trustor's trust, and 1 if she shares gains with the trustor equally. This sequential situation is depicted in Figure 3.2. Investment games of this type have been frequently used in studies of trust (Berg et al., 1995; Bicchieri and Fukui, 1999; Güth et al., 2008; Kreps, 1990).

In a population of 100 agents, we stipulate that players are matched in pairs randomly. Player roles (trustor or trustee) are assigned randomly for each game. In order to start with a maximally sparse model that captures only the essential features of the described situation, further assume that a player's behavior as a trustee is fixed over the whole history of the model. Hence, each agent starts out as either a trustworthy or a non-trustworthy type, and remains so forever. The share of trustworthy agents from the total populations later constitutes one crucial model parameter, as it constitutes the variable of interest according to which a rational agent should decide whether or not to place trust in an unknown trustee.

There are multiple reasons for assuming fixed trustworthiness-types for the purpose of this model. First, the decision by the agents that we want to focus on is whether or not to place trust in an anonymous trustee. Hence, fixing trustee-actions simplifies the situation. Furthermore, this also excludes any forms of potential reciprocity effects, as our goal

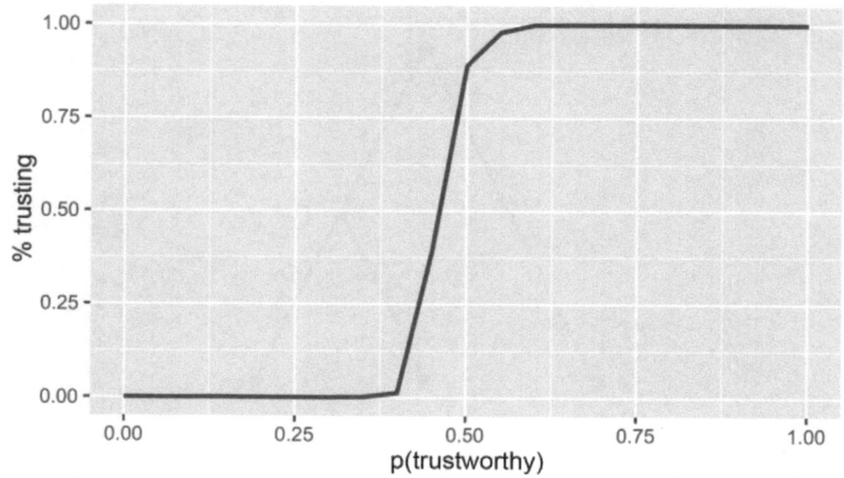

Figure 3.3 Trust in a homogeneous population

is to see if discrimination can emerge without reciprocity. Finally, as empirically observed in a series of experiments by Bicchieri et al. (2011), there exists a social norm concerning trustworthiness, but not for trusting. Our model specifications match this empirical observation.

In the simple game depicted in Figure 3.3, a trustee maximizes expected utility for each individual game through the following choice rule: if she believes that it is more likely that her partner is trustworthy than not, that is, $p(trustworthy) \geq p(not\ trustworthy)$, or $p(trustworthy) > 0.5$ then she should place trust in the trustee; else she should not place trust. Importantly, this setup is reflective of a rational choice conception of trusting, as the paper aims to show how distrust can emerge from individually *rational* choices.

As payoffs are fixed and known, the decision about trusting or not trusting boils down to a trustor's evaluation of *p(trustworthy)*. To estimate this value, individuals can learn from previous trust-interactions with other agents in different ways, depending on their role and behavior. A *trustor* who places trust learns about the trustee's type by observing the trustee's behavior, that is, whether or not the trustee rewards or betrays the trust placed in her. A trustor who does not place trust cannot learn anything about the partner's trustworthiness.

Additionally, players can learn from games as *trustees* by making an indirect inference: if the trustor decides to place trust, her assessment of *p(trustworthy)* must be larger than or equal to 0.5, or else she would not have placed trust.[1] If the trustor does not place trust, then the trustee can infer that her opponent must hold $p(trustworthy) < 0.5$.

These observations are factored into an agent's assessment of p by means of Bayesian updating. As it is mathematically impossible to compute a precise value for processing indirect social information, we assume that social information is treated with the same weight as direct information.[2] In the literature, Bayesian updating is generally seen as the archetype for rational updating of one's beliefs (Bovens et al., 2003).[3]

Note that these learning mechanisms are asymmetric in a way that will turn out to be important later on: direct learning as a trustor occurs only if one places trust in others. On the other hand, social learning as a trustee, that is, making an inference from whether or not the trustor places trust in oneself, occurs regardless of anyone's decisions and hence in all cases. Hence, one's belief updating concerning other's trustworthiness depends on one's current beliefs in a very specific and systematic way.

Figure 3.3 depicts the percentage of agents that are trusting after 100 trust encounters (y-axis), given different shares of trustworthy agents in the society (x-axis). As can be implied from the figure, agents are relatively well able to learn about the occurring trustworthiness levels in society, since almost all agents learn to make the right choice in most situations: when the average trustworthiness-level is at least 0.5, agents learn to trust; if the level is below 0.5, agents learn to distrust others. In the close proximity of the threshold value of 0.5, the share of trusting agents increases rapidly for increasing average trustworthiness. We can take these results as a consistency check for the baseline model and observe that it behaves as expected for rational agents.

3.5 Trust within and between Groups

In order to address the initially stated research question, we now introduce group membership. For this, agents are allocated to the blue or the red group. Each group contains exactly 50 agents to exclude potential effects from group size. Also, the share of trustworthy agents in both groups is exactly the same. In other words, blue agents are just as trustworthy as red agents on aggregate, and there is no rational basis for discriminating between groups. Also, no rules for reciprocity are implemented: whether or not an agent rewards or exploits trustworthiness is independent from the opponent's group affiliation—as before, trustworthiness-types are fixed. Together with the rationality of the agents' learning, this setup guarantees that all the necessary conditions to address our research question are met: agents choose rationally whether or not to trust, they update their beliefs rationally and in an unbiased fashion. There is no factual basis for discrimination, as neither reciprocity norms nor group differences are present. As before, agent pairings and roles are allocated randomly.

Crucially, we assume that agents recognize their current partner's group membership and can therefore conditionalize their beliefs of trustworthiness and their strategy choice on it. In simple terms, agents treat their peer group and the out-group as separate entities with independent probability estimates of trustworthiness. For an agent's decision rule, this implies that she will place trust in a blue agent if she beliefs the share of trustworthy blue agents to be at least 0.5, that is, $p_{blue}(trustworthy) \geq 0.5$, and distrusts otherwise; the same is true for red agents.

The fact that agents make this distinction has implications for their belief-updating. Agents in the role of *trustors* potentially gather information about their current *partner*'s group: If an agent places trust in a blue agent, she will learn about the trustworthiness of blue agents (namely by observing her partner's behavior), and the same is true for when she places trust in a red agent. Recall that a trustor does not learn if she does not place trust.

In contrast, for agents in the role of the *trustee*, a second asymmetry occurs: no matter what color the current trustor-partner, the trustee will always gather information about *her own group*, and never about members of the other group. This is because the inference always traces back to the trustee's own group membership, as she assesses what others think about her own group. In other words, a *blue* trustee infers about other's beliefs about *blue* trustees. Vice versa, a red agent can never observe a game from the point of view of a blue trustee, and hence she will never be able to socially learn about what others believe the trustworthiness of red agents to be. This framework allows addressing the fundamental research question of this paper. Formulated in a different way, we ask: *How does the sole fact that individuals distinguish between groups influence the emergence and persistence of trust?* Intuitively, one should expect that the model specifications guarantee that out-group-discrimination does not emerge. To scrutinize this intuition, we conducted simulations of the model and measure the levels of trust after 100 trust-interactions per agent as in the baseline model.[4]

Under ideal circumstances, a group should be trusted if a majority of its members are trustworthy, since this results in positive expected utility for the deciding individual. Since red and blue agents are equally trustworthy, trusting levels should not differ with regards to group membership on a rational basis. Ideally, individuals will learn to trust others (regardless of their color) if overall trustworthiness is 0.5 or above, and they should learn to distrust strangers if the average trustworthiness is below 0.5. This would maximize their expected utility, which is what rational (risk-neutral) actors should choose to do. To what extent can they form correct beliefs about these properties? In the simulation experiments, the aggregate trustworthiness varies between 0 percent and 100 percent. To measure trust levels within and across groups, we report the

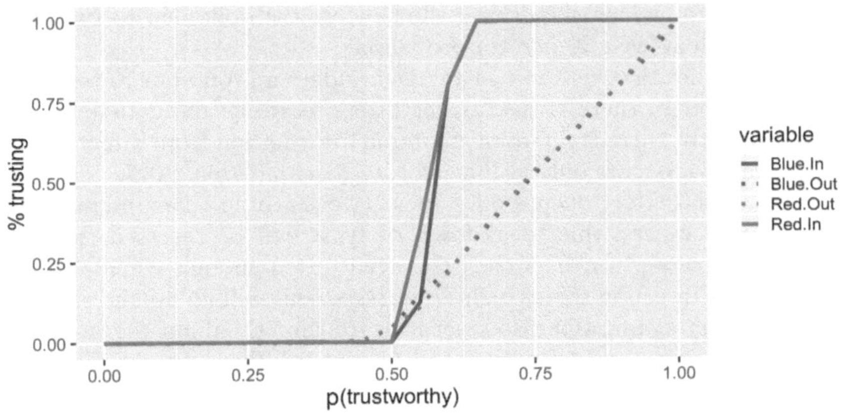

Figure 3.4 Trust with two equally sized groups

share of agents from each group that trusts each group, respectively; that is, for example: "What share of blue agents trusts red agents?" (= "blue. trust.red"), "What share of red agents trusts red agents?," and so on. These results are displayed in Figure 3.4.

As Figure 3.4 shows, for both groups, in-group trust is significantly higher than out-group trust. Apparently, in this situation, out-group discrimination in trust emerges *even if* individuals act rationally in any considerable way and there exists no factual basis for discriminatory treatments. Or with regards to the other formulation of our research question: the sheer fact that individuals make a distinction according to visible group membership is sufficient for out-group-discrimination to emerge. How come?

3.6 An Explanation Based on Asymmetric Learning

To understand this phenomenon, consider again the two structural asymmetries in learning. Recall that an agent in the role of a trustee can *always* learn socially by inferring the trustor's beliefs about her own group, with the reasoning: "An agent that trusts me must think that my kind is trustworthy. Hence, I should increase my trustworthiness-estimate of my in-group." As roles are assigned randomly, every agent is a trustee in about half of all exchanges, and hence at least half of an agent's knowledge stems from indirect learning. This has the straightforward implication that the amount of knowledge about one's own group is usually larger than that about the out-group.

Now recall the second learning asymmetry: *Indirect* learning occurs unconditionally whenever the agent functions as trustee. In contrast, *direct* learning as a trustor occurs only if the individual herself decides to place trust, which she does if she believes the opponent to be trustworthy with at least 50 percent probability.

This implies that, as soon as an agent judges a group not to be trustworthy enough, there is no further direct learning about that group. Consequently, there is no more incoming information from direct learning because it occurs only as long as $p_{group}(trustworthy) \geq 0.5$.

The crucial effect occurs once these two learning rules interact: for in-group-members, this breakdown of trust can be reversed through indirect learning: if others trust the agent often enough when she is a trustee, her in-group trustworthiness assessment will go up and she will start to trust again, and also start to learn directly about the in-group again. For exchanges with out-group members, this reversal is impossible because direct learning is the only way to learn about out-group-members. In short, if an individual mistrusts her in-group at a certain point in time, indirect learning may resuscitate her in-group trust. If an individual mistrusts the out-group, there is no going back to trusting the out-group.

This explains the significantly higher levels of in-group-trust in the simulation results: for the in-group, continuous social learning ensures correct belief convergence even after a relatively short time. For the out-group, there will always be a share of agents with initially bad experiences, who will then never go on to receive positive information that could change their mind about the out-group. This lock-in constitutes the decisive feature in the agents' learning process. Hence, rational learning appears to contain an in-built in-group advantage—or, negatively put, an out-group disadvantage.

3.7 Conclusion

As the previous analysis has shown, the emergence and persistence of out-group trust can be systematically hindered even when the only discriminatory behavior that individuals exhibit is to distinguish according to group membership. Surprisingly, this effect can occur even if individuals act rationally and do not form beliefs or act based on group sentiments. The occurrence of this effect has been traced back to structural asymmetries in direct and indirect learning. As such, the outlined simulation of trust in heterogeneous societies constitutes an exemplary case where collective irrationality emerges based on individually rational behavior: even though agents base their choices on all information available to them, update beliefs rationally and make their choices based on an expected utility calculus, the collective outcome is both discriminatory and inefficient.

Potentially, these findings carry far-reaching implications. On the one hand, even seemingly neutral group membership categorizations might by themselves turn out to be problematic for the emergence of trust.

Categorization itself can be problematic. On the other hand, some cases of perceived non-trustworthiness of out-groups may be unjustified, even if the agents making the judgments manage to adhere to highest standards of rationality. Mistrust and discrimination based on group membership may arise from rational individual choices even if there exists no factual basis for such discrimination. Vice versa, the occurrence of unjustified discrimination need not necessarily be the product of genuine discriminatory sentiment. This could challenge persisting assessments of discriminatory behavior, and suggest alternative means to overcome them. At the same time, the described process also illustrates how easily unjustified distrust can arise even among people who have no tendency for genuine discrimination.

Importantly, however, the proposed mechanism has been shown *in theory only*, and constitutes merely one of many possible explanations for lower out-group distrust. Reduced out-group trust *may* be an instance of collective irrationality, but may also very well be caused by real differences in trustworthiness, individual irrationality or group sentiments and social identity. The proposed mechanism does not exclude these possibilities, but merely extends the realm of possible scenarios—for a case, however, that many would prematurely rule out intuitively.

The argument of this paper aims to show that out-group discrimination *need not necessarily* imply either of the initially described causes, but *can* also emerge *even if* people behave individually rationally (in terms of how they form their believes about trustworthiness). The described model outlines how asymmetric learning biases rationally formed collective beliefs in the direction of lower out-group trust. As such, the presented analysis constitutes an archetypical instance of a "how-possibly" explanation, which is a characterization frequently attributed to ABM projects of this kind (Reutlinger et al., 2017). Only corroborating empirical evidence suggesting that the described mechanism *actually* impacts intergroup trust relations would change the status of the presented results.

However, more than this standard "how-possibly" explanation can be said in the specific case we are considering here. The described mechanism requires only a very sparse set of assumptions, namely a reasonable learning rule and visible group characteristics that are taken into account by the agents. Agents distinguishing between groups is something that is required for all possible (and actual) explanations of discriminatory behavior, as it is unclear how any form of discrimination could emerge without group membership being visible. Similarly, some form of belief-updating should be ascribed to agents, and the case that is considered here should be seen as the hardest case for discrimination to emerge. Hence, the simplicity of the setup and the sparsity of required assumptions suggests that the described asymmetry mechanism might be inherent to other explanations for out-group discrimination if they incorporate the factors that are sufficient to generate this effect here. Interestingly, in order to argue for this point, the simplicity of the model setup constitutes a crucial factor—contrary to frequent criticism of such ABMs of being overly simplistic.

For some cases like racial profiling, there is a particularly hard-fought discussion about the motives behind group-conditional distrust, which once again highlights the political relevance of the questions at the heart of this paper. As direct inquiries into individuals' motives face severe empirical difficulties, the simulation approach taken in this paper provides an important contribution toward understanding the possible mechanisms behind the phenomenon of out-group discrimination in trust-interactions.

The identified structural bias toward less out-group trust must thereby not be used to excuse existing discriminatory sentiments, but rather as a device to pinpoint, where hidden structural problems might be buried. What remains to be done, then, is to assess empirically by what individual motives people are driven. Ideally, this theoretical approach supports such an endeavor by providing a firm theoretical model and by outlining an explanatory pattern that is easily overlooked and neglected in practice.

Interestingly, similar discriminatory effects of learning asymmetries have also been discovered elsewhere. One class of papers, for example (O'Connor, 2017), Rubin and O'Connor (2018), or Bruner (2019) identify disadvantages that arise through the sheer minority status of certain groups. In the presented model, these effects should be expected to even increase discrimination against a group if it is in the minority, and hence needs to interact more frequently with the majority group through sheer group size. Comparable learning asymmetries have also been shown to influence outcomes in bargaining situations, even if bargaining mechanisms are structurally symmetric (Klein et al., 2018a,b; Klein and Marx, 2018b). In these cases and the one in this paper, the common explanatory factor seems to be that what an agent knows at a given time structurally influences what she will learn in the future. Future research should aim at uncovering the general nature of such processes, what they have in common and in what kinds of social situations they are most likely to occur.

From a normative point of view, however, categorization of individuals itself should be questioned based on the presented findings: while it may seem rational at first to use group-membership as a seemingly neutral source of information, it has been shown that categorization of individuals is problematic not just on moral grounds, but also because it can divide societies even in the absence of any intentional discriminatory behavior or sentiments. Hopefully, the understanding that categorization on its own can lead to discrimination will help (re-)build trust regardless of group membership, and will not be used as a cover-up for other discriminatory practices.

Notes

1. This of course assumes that all agents behave according to the simple (rational) choice rule from above, and that every agent takes this assumption for granted.
2. Technically, there are two factors to consider for factoring in social information: On the one hand, the information from direct observation provides certain knowledge about one (and only one) individual, namely whether or not she is trustworthy. On the other hand, social information is less precise since the inferring agent does not know the exact value of the trustee's estimated p, but only whether it is above or below 0.5. Yet, social knowledge of this kind is richer because it was formed based on a potentially large number of observations, and may thus be more reliable than a single direct observation.
3. Other updating rules have been shown to result in qualitatively similar results. The same is true for varying the relative weighting of indirect information.
4. This timeframe turned out to be sufficient for the analysis, as group beliefs already converge at this point and no further changes occur afterwards.

References

Alesina, A. and La Ferrara, E. (2000a). *The Determinants of Trust.* Technical report, National Bureau of Economic Research.

Alesina, A. and La Ferrara, E. (2000b). Participation in heterogeneous communities. *The Quarterly Journal of Economics*, 115(3):847–904.

Anderson, L. R., Mellor, J. M., and Milyo, J. (2006). Induced heterogeneity in trust experiments. *Experimental Economics*, 9(3):223–35.

Asongu, S. and Kodila-Tedika, O. (2017). Trust and growth revisited. *Economics Bulletin*, 37(4):2951–61.

B. Brewer, M. and Brown, R. (1998). Intergroup relations. In D. T. Gilbert, S. T. Fiske, G. L., editor, *The Handbook of Social Psychology*, pages 554–94. New York, NY, US: McGraw-Hill.

Balliet, D., Wu, J., and De Dreu, C. K. (2014). In-group favoritism in cooperation: A meta-analysis. *Psychological Bulletin*, 140(6):1556.

Berg, J., Dickhaut, J., and McCabe, K. (1995). Trust, reciprocity, and social history. *Games and Economic Behaviour*, 10(1):122–42.

Bicchieri, C., Duffy, J., and Tolle, G. (2004). Trust among strangers. *Philosophy of Science*, 71(3):286–319.

Bicchieri, C. and Fukui, Y. (1999). The great illusion: Ignorance, informational cascades, and the persistence of unpopular norms. *Business Ethics Quarterly*, 9(1):127–55.

Bicchieri, C., Xiao, E., and Muldoon, R. (2011). Trustworthiness is a social norm, but trusting is not. *Politics, Philosophy & Economics*, 10(2):170–87.

Birk, A. (2001). Learning to trust. In Falcone, R., Singh, M., and Tan, Y-H., editors, *Trust in Cyber-societies, pages* 133–44. Berlin and elsewhere, Springer.

Bjørnskov, C. (2018). Social trust and economic growth. In Uslaner, E., editor, *The Oxford Handbook of Social and Political Trust*. New York, Oxford University Press.

Bovens, L., Hartmann, S., et al. (2003). *Bayesian Epistemology*. Oxford, Oxford University Press on Demand.

Brewer, M. B. (1979). In-group bias in the minimal intergroup situation: A cognitive-motivational analysis. *Psychological Bulletin*, 86(2):307.

Brewer, M. B. (1999). The psychology of prejudice: In-group love and out-group hate? *Journal of Social Issues*, 55(3):429–44.

Brewer, M. B. and Silver, M. (1978). In-group bias as a function of task characteristics. *European Journal of Social Psychology*, 8(3):393–400.

Bruner, J. P. (2019). Minority (dis)advantage in population games. *Synthese*, 196(1):413–27.

Cohen, E. (2012). The evolution of tag-based cooperation in humans: The case for accent. *Current Anthropology*, 53(5):588–616.

Coleman, J. (1994). *Foundations of Social Theory*. Cambridge (Massachusets) and London, Belknap Press.

Coleman, J. S. (2000). Social capital in the creation of human capital. In Lesser, E., editor, *Knowledge and Social Capital, pages* 17–41. USA, Elsevier.

Cox, M. (2009). *Social Capital and Peace-building: Creating and Resolving Conflict with Trust and Social Networks*. London and New York, Routledge.

De Cremer, D. and Van Vugt, M. (1998). Collective identity and cooperation in a public goods dilemma: A matter of trust or self-efficacy. *Current Research in Social Psychology*, 3(1):1–11.

Devenow, A. and Welch, I. (1996). Rational herding in financial economics. *European Economic Review*, 40(3-5):603–15.

Dinesen, P. T. and Sønderskov, K. M. (2018). Ethnic diversity and social trust: a critical review of the literature and suggestions for a research agenda. In Uslaner, E., editor, *The Oxford Handbook on Social and Political Trust*, pages 175–204. New York, Oxford University Press.

Falcone, R. and Castelfranchi, C. (2004). Trust dynamics: How trust is influenced by direct experiences and by trust itself. In *Autonomous Agents and Multiagent Systems, 2004. AAMAS 2004. Proceedings of the Third International Joint Conference on Autonomous Agents and Multiagent Systems,* pages 740–7. Washington DC, IEEE.

Fang, C., Kimbrough, S. O., Pace, S., Valluri, A., and Zheng, Z. (2002). On adaptive emergence of trust behaviour in the game of stag hunt. *Group Decision and Negotiation*, 11(6):449–67.

Fu, F., Tarnita, C. E., Christakis, N. A., Wang, L., Rand, D. G., and Nowak, M. A. (2012). Evolution of in-group favoritism. *Scientific Reports*, 2:460.

Glaeser, E. L., Laibson, D., Scheinkman, J. A., and Soutter, C. L. (1999). *What Is Social Capital? The Determinants of Trust and Trustworthiness*. Technical report, National Bureau of Economic Research.

Güth, W., Levati, M. V., and Ploner, M. (2008). Social identity and trust—an experimental investigation. *The Journal of Socio-Economics*, 37(4):1293–308.

Hadler, M. (2012). The influence of world societal forces on social tolerance. A time comparative study of prejudices in 32 countries. *The Sociological Quarterly*, 53(2):211–37.

Hammond, R. A. and Axelrod, R. (2006). The evolution of ethnocentrism. *Journal of Conflict Resolution*, 50(6):926–36.
Hardin, R. (1993). The street-level epistemology of trust. *Politics & Society*, 21(4):505–29.
Hong, L. and Page, S. E. (2001). Problem solving by heterogeneous agents. *Journal of Economic Theory*, 97(1):123–63.
Hong, L. and Page, S. E. (2004). Groups of diverse problem solvers can outperform groups of high-ability problem solvers. *Proceedings of the National Academy of Sciences of the United States of America*, 101(46):16385–9.
Jonker, C. M. and Treur, J. (1999). Formal analysis of models for the dynamics of trust based on experiences. In Garijo, F. J. and Magnus Boman, M., editors, *European Workshop on Modelling Autonomous Agents in a Multi-Agent World,* pages 221–31. Berlin and Heidelberg, Springer.
Kappmeier, M. (2016). Trusting the enemy—towards a comprehensive understanding of trust in intergroup conflict. *Peace and Conflict: Journal of Peace Psychology*, 22(2):134.
Kemmelmeier, M., Broadus, A. D., and Padilla, J. B. (2008). Inter-group aggression in New Orleans in the immediate aftermath of hurricane Katrina. *Analyses of Social Issues and Public Policy*, 8(1):211–245.
Klein, D. and Marx, J. (2018). Generalized trust in the mirror: An agent-based model on the dynamics of trust. *Historical Social Research*, 43(1):234–58.
Klein, D., Marx, J., and Scheller, S. (2018a). Rational choice and asymmetric learning in iterated social interactions — some lessons from agent-based modelling. In Marker, K., Schmitt, A., and Sirsch, J., editors, *Demokratie und Entscheidung Beiträge zur Analytischen Politischen Theorie*, pages 277–94. Wiesbaden, Springer.
Klein, D., Marx, J., and Scheller, S. (2020). Rationality in context. *Synthese.*
Klein, O., Licata, L., Azzi, A. E., and Durala, I. (2003). "How European am I?": Prejudice expression and the presentation of social identity. *Self and Identity*, 2(3):251–64.
Klein, O., Spears, R., and Reicher, S. (2007). Social identity performance: Extending the strategic side of side. *Personality and Social Psychology Review*, 11(1):28–45. PMID: 18453454.
Knack, S. and Keefer, P. (1997). Does social capital have an economic payoff? A cross-country investigation. *The Quarterly Journal of Economics*, 112(4):1251–88.
Kramer, R. M. (1994). The sinister attribution error: Paranoid cognition and collective distrust in organizations. *Motivation and Emotion*, 18(2):199–230.
Kramer, R. M. and Brewer, M. B. (1984). Effects of group identity on resource use in a simulated commons dilemma. *Journal of Personality and Social Psychology*, 46(5):1044.
Kramer, R. M. and Messick, D. M. (1998). Getting by with a little help from our enemies: Collective paranoia and its role in intergroup relations. In C. Sedikides, J. Schopler, C. A. I., editor, *Intergroup Cognition and Intergroup Behaviour*, pages 233–55. Mahwah, NJ, US: Lawrence Erlbaum Associates Publishers.
Kreps, D. (1990). Corporate culture and economic theory. In Alt, J. and Shepsle, K., editors, *Perspectives on Political Economy*, pages 90–143. Cambridge University Press.

Leach, C. W., van Zomeren, M., Zebel, S., Vliek, M. L. W., Pennekamp, S. F., Doosje, B., Ouwerkerk, J. W., and Spears, R. (2008). Group-level self-definition and self-investment: A hierarchical (multicomponent) model of in-group identification. *Journal of Personality and Social Psychology*, 95(1):144–65.

Leigh, A. (2006). Trust, inequality and ethnic heterogeneity. *Economic Record*, 82(258):268–80.

Macy, M. W. and Skvoretz, J. (1998). The evolution of trust and cooperation between strangers: A computational model. *American Sociological Review*, 63(5):638–60.

Mayo-Wilson, C., Zollman, K., and Danks, D. (2013). Wisdom of crowds versus groupthink: Learning in groups and in isolation. *International Journal of Game Theory*, 42(3):695–723.

Merdes, C. (2017). Growing unpopular norms. *Journal of Artificial Societies and Social Simulation*, 20(3):5.

Newton, K. (1997). Social capital and democracy. *American Behavioural Scientist*, 40(5):575–86.

Nickerson, R. S. (1998). Confirmation bias: A ubiquitous phenomenon in many guises. *Review of General Psychology*, 2(2):175–220.

O'Connor, C. (2017). The cultural red king effect. *The Journal of Mathematical Sociology*, 41(3):155–71.

Platow, M. J., Foddy, M., Yamagishi, T., Lim, L., and Chow, A. (2012). Two experimental tests of trust in in-group strangers: The moderating role of common knowledge of group membership. *European Journal of Social Psychology*, 42(1):30–35.

Platow, M. J., McClintock, C. G., and Liebrand, W. B. (1990). Predicting intergroup fairness and in-group bias in the minimal group paradigm. *European Journal of Social Psychology*, 20(3):221–39.

Prentice, D. A. and Miller, D. T. (1993). Pluralistic ignorance and alcohol use on campus: Some consequences of misperceiving the social norm. *Journal of Personality and Social Psychology*, 64(2):243.

Putnam, R. D., Leonardi, R., and Nanetti, R. Y. (1994). *Making Democracy Work: Civic Traditions in Modern Italy*. Princeton, NJ, Princeton University Press.

Reutlinger, A., Hangleiter, D., and Hartmann, S. (2017). Understanding (with) toy models. *The British Journal for the Philosophy of Science*, 69(4):1069–99.

Rodin, M. J., Price, J. M., Bryson, J. B., and Sanchez, F. J. (1990). Asymmetry in prejudice attribution. *Journal of Experimental Social Psychology*, 26(6):481–504.

Rothstein, B. and Uslaner, E. M. (2005). All for all: Equality, corruption, and social trust. *World Politics*, 58(1):41–72.

Rubin, H. and O'Connor, C. (2018). Discrimination and collaboration in science. *Philosophy of Science*, 85(3):380–402.

Schelling, T. C. (2006). *Micromotives and Macrobehaviour*. New York and London, WW Norton & Company.

Simpson, B. (2006). Social identity and cooperation in social dilemmas. *Rationality and Society*, 18(4):443–70.

Tajfel, H. (1970). Experiments in intergroup discrimination. *Scientific American*, 223(5):96–103.

Takagi, E. (1996). The generalized exchange perspective on the evolution of altruism. In Liebrand, W. B. G. and Messick, D. M., editors, *Frontiers in Social Dilemmas Research*, pages 311–36. Berlin, Heidelberg: Springer.

Tanis, M. and Postmes, T. (2005). A social identity approach to trust: Interpersonal perception, group membership and trusting behaviour. *European Journal of Social Psychology*, 35(3):413–24.

Turner, M. (2014). *Groups at Work: Theory and Research. Applied Social Research Series*. New York and London, Taylor & Francis.

Uslaner, E. M. (2002). *The Moral Foundations of Trust*. Cambridge (UK), Cambridge University Press.

van der Meer, T. and Tolsma, J. (2014). Ethnic diversity and its effects on social cohesion. *Annual Review of Sociology*, 40(1):459–78.

Williams, M. (2001). In whom we trust: Group membership as an affective context for trust development. *Academy of Management Review*, 26(3):377–96.

Yuki, M., Maddux, W. W., Brewer, M. B., and Takemura, K. (2005). Crosscultural differences in relationship-and group-based trust. *Personality and Social Psychology Bulletin*, 31(1):48–62.

Zak, P. J. and Knack, S. (2001). Trust and growth. *The Economic Journal*, 111(470):295–321.

Part II

Concepts of Social Trust

4 Disappointed Yet Unbetrayed

A New Three-Place Analysis of Trust

Edward Hinchman

Simple observations reveal an obvious difference between betrayed trust and disappointed trust. Say A trusts B to perform some action, ϕ. And say B does ϕ and thereby does not disappoint A's trust. Could B somehow nonetheless betray A's trust? If A's trust in B to ϕ amounts to something more than his merely relying on B to ϕ, then it is easy to see how B might betray A's trust even though she does not disappoint it—since she does, at least, ϕ. Perhaps B ϕs only because someone—perhaps A himself—coerces her into ϕing. Or perhaps B ϕs with no memory of A's trust and with a firm disposition not to ϕ were she to remember it. In each case, B betrays A's trust in her to ϕ, though B does ϕ and thereby does not disappoint A's trust. Such cases lead many—as we'll see—to assume that trust builds on mere reliance, that the fundamental normative structure of trust is "A trusts B to ϕ," and that the task for defining trust, by contrast with mere reliance, lies in explaining how the necessary condition imposed by this structure falls short of sufficiency—as revealed when trust is undisappointed yet betrayed. I aim to question that assumption—that trust builds on mere reliance—by investigating a more complex case. What if the relation between disappointment and betrayal works the other way round? What if, instead of being undisappointed but betrayed, A's trust is disappointed yet unbetrayed?

To set up the more complex case, let's ask why it seemed that trust builds on mere reliance. We were gripped, it seems, by two more specific assumptions: (i) that there are two conditions in play—one of *fidelity* (B does not omit to do what A trusts her to do), another of *concern* (B shows the right attitude toward A)—and (ii) that we can answer our initial question about betrayal by seeing how the condition of concern builds on the condition of fidelity. When B disappoints A's trust in her to ϕ, she thereby betrays that trust, we assumed, because B cannot show appropriate concern for A if she omits to do what A is trusting her to do. I argue that this assumption is false, not because B can show concern without fidelity but because there are contexts in which B cannot show fidelity without concern. On some occasions for trust—I focus on interpersonal trust in a promise and intrapersonal trust in an intention—the condition of fidelity builds on the condition of concern: nothing that fails to show appropriate concern could count as fidelity to the normative understanding that informs the trust.

That possibility explains the more complex possibility that we'll explore: trust disappointed yet unbetrayed. Here B does not ϕ, disappointing A's trust in her to ϕ. Is A's trust thereby betrayed? To take the question seriously, we must work from a suitably sharp contrast between the concepts in play of disappointment and betrayal. Toward that end, I stipulate that someone trusted to ϕ who does not ϕ thereby disappoints that trust, even if (perhaps) she does not betray it, and that someone trusted to ϕ who does ϕ does not disappoint that trust, even if she does betray it. This concept of disappointment is not, as such, psychological or moral. It is a concept whose application is governed entirely by the single question: did you perform the action that you were trusted to perform? Given that the concepts are distinct, my question is whether our understanding of betrayed trust builds on this understanding of disappointed trust, in a way that parallels our initial assumption that trust builds on mere reliance. I argue that it does not.

Since there are two contrasts in play—fidelity versus concern, disappointment versus betrayal—we'll naturally wonder how they compare. Note first that the question of fidelity arises only when trust manifests a normative understanding that responds to an assurance: when you trust B to ϕ though B has not promised to ϕ, there is, strictly speaking, nothing for B to show fidelity to. (I discuss this issue in Section VII.) I argue that one who has promised to ϕ can meet the fidelity condition, not omitting to do what her promisee trusts her to do, even when that trust is disappointed, since she fails to ϕ. It follows that not omitting to do what your promisee trusts you to do is not the same as doing what you have promised to do. Colloquially, what your promisee trusts you to do is to "keep" your promise. I argue that keeping your promise—remaining "true" to it—does not reduce to doing what you've promised to do. Promissory trust is disappointed yet unbetrayed when the promisor remains true to her promise despite not doing what she has promised to do. My approach aims to explain how that is possible. I pursue the parallel with intention to help develop that explanation.

We need a new analysis of trust because the possibility of trust disappointed yet unbetrayed undermines the core rationale for the traditional three-place analysis, "A trusts B to ϕ." I argue that trust most fundamentally has this different normative structure: "A ϕs through trust in B." We do, of course, trust people to do things. But its more fundamental normative structure articulates how trust puts us in touch with reasons to do or plan to do other things on the basis of the trusted's worthiness of that trust—whether to act on trusted advice, to believe on trusted testimony, or to plan through trusting a promise or intention. I call this an Assurance View of trust because it treats trusting as accepting an invitation to trust—in effect, an assurance that the other (perhaps your own earlier self) is relevantly trustworthy. We need an emphasis on assurance to explain how trust can be disappointed yet unbetrayed—as, for example, when a promisor remains faithful to her promise despite, in unexpected circumstances, failing to do what she has promised to do. And an emphasis on assurance explains key instances of trust undisappointed yet betrayed—as, for example, when following through on your intention betrays the self-trust informing that commitment. We'll discuss both kinds of case in detail.

The commitments—promises and intentions—on which we'll focus mark a contrast between faithful and rigid execution, between fidelity to A's normative expectation and a rigid adherence to it that violates the understanding that gives normative content to A's trust. Even when A does not accept an explicit invitation to trust—I discuss such cases in Section VII—A's trust rests on implicit assumptions about how B's doing what A trusts B to do serves A's planning needs or interests. When B does it without appropriate regard for those needs or interests, A's trust may prove betrayed though undisappointed. And when B refrains from doing it from concern that doing it violates those needs or interests, A's trust may prove disappointed yet unbetrayed. When A ϕs through trust in B in these cases, A relies on B to provide a planning reason to ϕ. That reliance ensures that A's trust is not a mere extension of reliance on B to act.[1]

4.1 Toward a New Three-Place Analysis of Trust

Let me begin by presenting my approach systematically within the broad dialectic that informs it. In this section, I explain how it provides an alternative to standard approaches to the nature of trust. In the next section, I begin my argument by explaining the core issue driving my alternative. These stage-setting discussions are, perhaps unfortunately, rather abstract and schematic. Having clarified what I think and roughly why I think it, I develop my argument with rich examples in Section III. (Readers who need examples to motivate their intuitions could skip directly to Section III and only later return to the overviews presented in the first two sections.)

My approach engages two philosophical debates about trust, deriving from two distinct questions about the nature of trust. The first asks how to define trust. Does trusting B to φ involve anything more than relying on B to φ? Over the past three decades, debate on this question has revolved around three positions. Reductionism answers no: trusting B is just believing B relevantly reliable.[2] The Affective Attitude View answers yes; trust manifests felt optimism about B's goodwill.[3] The Reactive Attitude View also answers yes, though for a different reason: the expectation informing trust is not merely predictive but normative, backed by a disposition to resent B for not φing (among other possible reactive attitudes).[4] I argue for a fourth view, the Assurance View, by pairing the definitional question with a second question.

This second question addresses the normative structure of trust. Does trust most fundamentally embody a two-place or a three-place relation? On the standard three-place model, "A trusts B to φ" is most fundamental.[5] On the two-place model, "A trusts B to φ" is less fundamental than "A trusts B": what is fundamental is the relation between A and B.[6] In the recent literature, this second debate comprises challenges to the standard three-place model meant to motivate a shift to the two-pace model, but my challenge pushes in a different direction. toward a new three-place model, on which "A trusts B to φ" is less fundamental than "A φs through trust in B." Though we trust people to do things, trust more fundamentally lies in doing something through trust in a person: believing through trust in someone's testimony, acting through trust in someone's advice, and engaging in mutual activity through trust in someone's invitation to share an intention—along with the cases of promising and intending that I highlight. Though I agree with proponents of the standard three-place model that trust in a person most fundamentally makes reference to an action, I agree with proponents of the two-place model that the question whether to perform that action makes fundamental reference to the trust relation.

This new position on the second debate yields an equally new position on the first. I vindicate my new three-place model of trust by vindicating an affirmative alternative to the Affective Attitude and Reactive Attitude Views which more effectively counters the argument for Reductionism. The Assurance View thus yields a new account of the normative structure of trust and a new explanation of how trust differs from mere reliance. Trust differs from mere reliance through how it gives access to a reason to rely on the trusted. In mere reliance, your reason to rely on B is exogenous to the reliance relation: these reasons are typically grounded in B's track record of relevant reliability. When you trust B, by contrast, you take yourself to have a reason to rely on B that is endogenous to this interpersonal relation: you take yourself to have a reason grounded not merely in B's reliability but in B's responsiveness to your relevant needs.

There we have an outline of my position. Let me now offer an outline of my argument. I defend my three-place model by agreeing with defenders of the two-place model up to a point. A simple dialectic generates the two-place view. If trust does not reduce to mere reliance, how do they differ? Two-placers explain how trust differs from mere reliance by viewing three-place trust as informed by a deeper two-place trust relation. I too aim to explain how trust differs from mere reliance by viewing the three-place trust relation "A trusts B to φ" as informed by deeper trust. But I do not regard the deeper trust as two-place trust. This deeper trust, which explains how trust differs from mere reliance, has a three-place structure: "A φs through trust in B."

What exactly is this three-place relation? Here's one thing I do not mean—though my shorthand formula may suggest it. Say A trusts B to do some particular thing. Must that trust lead A to perform some *action*, φ, through trust in B? Obviously not. Say you trust B to make plans for a picnic; there need be no action that you perform, or even plan to perform, in trusting B to make those plans. When I say that A φs through trust in B, I do not mean that A takes some positive step to express his trust in B. A may merely rest assured that B will act. In our schema, "A ϕs through trust in B," ϕing may merely amount to resting assured. What's important is that A regards himself as having a reason to adopt that stance: a reason to rest assured through trust in B. In our example, you presume that you have a reason to take B's picnic planning for granted—a reason to rest assured that B will plan competently—without seeing any reason to perform any further action to express that trust in B. On my Assurance View, that's part of the point of trust: to reap this rational reward of trust—the right to leave positive action up to the trusted—while undergoing trust's distinctive risk of betrayal. My thesis is that we can explain how trust differs from mere reliance not only by focusing on the risk of betrayal but also by viewing trust and trustworthiness as a source of reasons irreducible to mere reliance or reliability.

Why prefer my three-place model to the two-place? The key contrast between my three-place model and a two-place model derives from the contrast between rationality and morality. On a two-place model, given its explanatory aims, the trust relation is broadly moral. In trusting B, A brings himself into a moral relation with B either (along the lines of an Affective Attitude View) by making himself morally vulnerable to B's will or (along the lines of a Reactive Attitude View) by holding B morally accountable for her will. On my three-place model, the trust relation need not be moral, and in Section VI we'll consider one explanation why: B's betrayal of A's trust need express nothing like ill will toward A, or make B an appropriate target for reactive attitudes such as resentment. In the cases on which we'll ultimately focus, B betrays A's trust through misinterpreting what the promissory agreement between them requires of her—an error that need not be moral or call out for reactive-attitudinal response. In φing through trust in B, A treats B's trustworthiness primarily as a source of reasons. Reductionists are right to oppose the Affective and Reactive Attitude Views: trust is not moral *as such*. But I say that as an anti-reductionist: what distinguishes trust from mere reliance is the distinctive way that trust gives reasons, in this key dimension of interpersonal (and, I later argue, intrapersonal) rationality. Assuming B worthy of A's trust, the reason B makes available is A's *reward* in trust. To receive that reward, A must make himself vulnerable to betrayal, the distinctive *risk* in trust.

4.2 On the Risks and Rewards of Trust

I now begin my argument by motivating my emphasis on reason-giving rather than morality. This section, like the last, is rather abstract. I begin working from examples in Section III.

Any anti-reductive view of trust must explain how trust risks betrayal, not merely disappointment. It is clear enough how trust risks betrayal on the two established anti-reductive views. On the Affective Attitude View, B betrays A's trust if she fails to vindicate A's optimism about her goodwill toward him. On the Reactive Attitudes View, B betrays A's trust if she fails to live up to the normative expectation that informs his trust, a normative expectation backed by appropriate reactive attitudes toward B. My alternative approach begins from the hypothesis that what distinguishes trust from mere reliance lies not in either party's attitude toward the other but in the point of trusting someone—in what trust does for the one trusting. The hypothesis leads me to focus on B's act of assurance, and on what trusting B insofar as B assures A does for A. Though trust need not respond to an assurance (more on that in Section VII), the normative structure of trust is clearest when A responds to B's invitation to trust. I argue that the normative structure of the trust relation takes this form: B represents herself as giving A a reason in offering her assurance, and A responds by coming to regard himself as acquiring that reason. If betrayal is what A risks in trusting, this reason is A's reward in trusting—if B proves appropriately trustworthy. B betrays A's trust if she fails to provide the reason—if she is not thus trustworthy.

My approach engages a background issue about the role of assurance in a trust relation. In her defense of the Affective Attitude View, Annette Baier characterizes that role as follows:

> The assurance typically given (implicitly or explicitly) by the person who invites our trust ... is not assurance of some very specific action or set of actions, but assurance simply that the trusting's welfare is, and will one day be seen to have been, in good hands. (1994, 137)
> Baier develops a contrast on this point between an invitation to trust and a promise, which she calls "that peculiar case of assurance." I disagree that promises are peculiar instances of trust, but I more fundamentally disagree with her moral emphasis. Baier is on the right track, but the assurance at the core of an invitation to trust targets the trusting's rationality—his responsiveness to reasons—not the trusting's welfare. When we grasp how assurance works we'll grasp why a promise is not a peculiar case of assurance: in a key respect, it is the purest case.

The difference between my approach and Baier's arises from my emphasis on rationality and reason-giving, which I intend as a corrective to Baier's moral emphasis. In arguing that the risks of trust track the rewards of trust, I make two claims. First, it does not follow from how trust risks betrayal that trust is a moral relation. Second, it does follow from how trust risks betrayal that trust is a rational relation. Trust is a rational relation, I argue, because to invite trust, as opposed to mere reliance, is to represent yourself as a source of planning reasons, both interpersonally for a promisee to do things that depend on your promise and intrapersonally for your later self to do things that depend on your intention. Betrayal can derive from a rational norm, because when you invite A's trust, by offering a propositional assurance, you represent yourself as taking responsibility for A's status as rational in letting himself be guided by your assurance. We thereby work our way up from rational considerations to moral ones. The obligation not to betray another's trust manifests a kind of normative power: you undertake this obligation when you give your assurance. On my approach, we best understand this normative power from the inside out: just as you undertake an obligation to be worthy of your own trust when you invite your own trust by forming a judgment or intention, so you undertake an obligation to be worthy of A's trust when you invite A's trust by giving A "your word."

On my Assurance View of trust, the distinction between trust and mere reliance mirrors Paul Grice's distinction between natural and non-natural meaning.[7] Grice drew that distinction by contrasting an evidential mechanism—"Those clouds mean rain," "Those spots mean measles"—with a mechanism that works through recognition of the speaker's intentions. In non-natural meaning, Grice argued, a speaker intends to give her addressee a reason to produce a certain response grounded not in evidence of her reliability or in any other evidential basis but specifically in the addressee's recognition of her intention to give him this reason.

What my approach inherits from Grice's is an emphasis on the distinctive way in which speech acts aim to give reasons: not through an evidential mechanism but through a structure of mutual recognition and understanding. To observe that such assurances aim to give a reason *simply* through the addressee's recognition of that aim is to observe that the speaker invites the addressee's trust. Such an assurance is an invitation to trust in this respect: B invites A to regard himself as having a reason to act or believe grounded, in part, in how B undertakes an obligation in issuing the invitation. I call such an invitation to trust a *propositional assurance*. Generally speaking, reliance is mere reliance unless thus invited by a propositional assurance; thus invited, however, it grounds an obligation, on B's side, and reasons, on A's side. Because the speaker's obligation derives from her claim to relevant reliability, the reasons are grounded in her status as relevantly reliable (not, as we'll see, in the trust relation itself). While both "natural" and "non-natural" reason-giving depend on B's reliability, there is a crucial difference in how they depend on reliability, and a correlative difference in what counts as relevant reliability.

We can understand the distinctive element in each species of propositional assurance—whether testimony, advice or a promise—by contrasting how it makes reasons available with the evidential mechanism that makes reasons available through mere assertion. Some common cases rest on this evidential mechanism: A treats B's assertion as reason-giving through his assessment of evidence that B is relevantly reliable. But the equally common cases that my approach highlights rest on a quasi-Gricean mechanism: A treats B's speech act as reason-giving through his trusting receptivity to B's influence, as governed by his exercise of a counterfactual sensitivity to evidence that B is *not* relevantly reliable. The contrast illustrates a key distinction between two forms of uptake. Sometimes you rely on someone because you have positive evidence that the person is relevantly reliable, but other times you lack such evidence. When you lack evidence that someone is relevantly reliable, you can let your reliance on her be guided by your sensitivity to evidence that she is not relevantly reliable: if you get such evidence, you'll cease to rely on her; and (counterfactually) if you had such evidence you would not have relied on her. This second species of reliance is trust, and the species of reliability at issue is trustworthiness—worthiness of reliance not governed by positive evidence of relevant reliability.

Framing the contrast between forms of uptake now from the speaker's perspective, you give an assurance that invites your addressee to rely on *you* as a source of reasons, not merely on the reason-giving force of evidence of your reliability, and you present yourself as worthy of precisely that species of reliance. What grounds the reason is what would vindicate the presumption at the core of your invitation: your presumption to do justice to your addressee's needs in respects relevant to the shared understanding at the core of the invited trust relation. Mere reliance can be disappointed, but interpersonal trust can also be betrayed, I'm arguing, because betrayal taps into the normative role played by this shared understanding.

Here, then, is how the risks and rewards of trust fit together into a single normative structure. If you uphold your end of the trust relation by being relevantly trustworthy, your addressee gets a reason. If your addressee upholds his end of the trust relation, by trusting you in appropriate ways as determined by the understanding that you invite him to share in trusting you, you count as undertaking an obligation to be thus trustworthy. A trust relation can be betrayed because this shared understanding can be betrayed. In the next section, I treat two forms such a shared understanding can take: the implicit agreement at the normative core of a promise, and the ongoing understanding of what you're up to at the normative core of an intention. Just as a trustworthy promise makes available reasons for the promisee to do things that depend on the promisor's remaining true to the promise, so your trustworthy intention makes available reasons to do things that depend on your following through on the intention. The understanding that is betrayed when trust is betrayed plays this normative role because it plays a more fundamental normative role in interpersonal and intrapersonal reason-giving.

4.3 The Crux: Trust Disappointed Yet Unbetrayed

Let me now illustrate my approach with a detailed case—a case in which trust is disappointed yet unbetrayed. On the three-place model that I reject, a trust relation most fundamentally takes this form: A trusts B to ϕ. Within that normative structure, B's failure to ϕ suffices for her to count as betraying A's trust. I reject that model because I deny this claim of sufficiency. How, then, might B thus disappoint A's trust without betraying it? As I'll use the case to show, B does not betray A's trust when disappointing it manifests appropriate concern for A's planning needs.

One complexity is that I do not see how there can be such a case without a propositional assurance. Another is that, among interpersonal propositional assurances, it is plausible that only promissory assurances permit this possibility, since it appears to depend on the temporal articulation of a promise. I'll explain these complexities as we proceed, but let's first consider a case of promissory trust disappointed yet unbetrayed.

I'll use up-to-date examples in later sections, but let's first work from a case modeled on Hume's famous farmers whose corn ripens on different days (1978, 520).

> *Three Farmers.* Ben owns a large farm and needs help in harvesting his crops next month. To get that help, he has promised to harvest this month the crops of two friends, Albert and Andrew, who own smaller farms, given that these friends are traveling for urgent personal reasons and the crops they've planted need to be harvested this month rather than next. Albert and Andrew are depending on Ben; each is planning in concrete ways (rescheduling other commitments, committing to rent necessary equipment for those dates, etc.) that depend on Ben's remaining faithful to his promise. But as Ben makes preparations to harvest these crops, a swarm of locusts descends on his and his nearest neighbor's farm, preventing him from acting on these promises, since he is too busy fending off the locusts. Should he apologize? Well, of course he should—to Andrew. As it happens, Ben's closest neighbor is Albert, whose crops are equally threatened by these locusts, and given this background it does not appear to make sense for Ben to apologize to Albert. The threat to Ben's crops is also a threat to Albert's crops—though not to Andrew's crops, since Andrew lives farther away. Ben *could* harvest Albert's crops, but let's stipulate the assessment that harvesting them under these conditions would damage them more, in ways that matter, than leaving them unharvested and instead fending off the

> locusts. However we imagine the details, this is key: not harvesting better serves not just Albert's interests but his *planning* interests; if Ben does not fend off the locusts, Albert will have to hire others to do so and perhaps to return from his urgent travels, thereby thwarting many planning needs, including the very needs that informed Ben's promise. It therefore does not make sense for Ben to apologize to Albert, and it equally would be wrong for Albert to hold Ben's non-performance against him when he decides whether to help Ben harvest his own crops next month. What grounds the intuitions about accountability and apology is our grasp on what is at stake in the promissory agreement: Albert trusts Ben to do justice to Albert's ongoing needs in respects relevant to the point of Albert's reliance on Ben's promise, which is determined not by Albert's expectation the Ben will rigidly execute the promise but the implicit agreement that informs it. Our intuitions about accountability and apology derive from this difference between Ben's promises. Ben owes Andrew an apology because he violates that promissory agreement, though with an excuse that makes the violation forgivable. But Ben need not offer Albert any excuse or ask for his forgiveness. All he owes Albert is an explanation that makes it clear how fidelity to his promise does not require acting in these unexpected circumstances. I'll say more about this distinctive element in the case in Section IV, using less canonical but more realistic examples.[8]

This distinctive element in the case focuses the crux of my argument. When A trusts B to keep her promise to φ, A need not engage in contingency planning for fear that B will φ *rigidly*—that is, without being guided by their shared grasp of the point of the promise. The planning reasons that B's promise gives A derive from B's aretaic concern to do justice to the promise, to remain faithful to it. In gaining access to these reasons, A does not trust B simply to φ. Again, if A trusts B simply to φ, then A will have to plan for the contingency that B φs rigidly, without regard to their promissory agreement—an absurdity illustrated if Albert had to plan for the off-chance that Ben would harvest the crops amidst the locust swarms, thereby damaging them more than if he had left them be. As we'll see in Sections IV and VI, a promise thereby resembles an intention. Neither, as such, rationalizes contingency planning for counter-normative rigidity.

We can now see how in promissory trust, at least, the condition of fidelity serves the condition of concern. Here again are the two conditions, formulated generally:

> *Condition of fidelity*: B does not omit to do what A is trusting her to do.
> *Condition of concern*: B shows the right attitude toward A.

In testimony and advice, these conditions appear to apply separately, the second building on the first. A trusts B's testimony to give him the truth, but it betrays that trust if B does so through a lucky guess, or in some other way that shows no concern for his epistemic needs—including his need to meet the epistemic standard that applies in his context of inquiry. A trusts B's advice to tell him what he has reason to do, but it betrays that trust if self-absorbed B does so because she happens at the moment to have practical needs that resemble A's, with no responsiveness to A's needs conceived as such.[9] But, as Three Farmers illustrates, B as promisor does what A as promisee is trusting her to do *by* thereby manifesting appropriate responsiveness to a subset of A's needs, conceived as such: those that inform the promissory agreement. B keeps the promise, thereby vindicating A's trust, not simply by doing what she promised to do but by remaining faithful to this promissory agreement. Unlike a testifier or advisor, a promisor cannot meet the condition of fidelity without also, and thereby, meeting the condition of concern. Disappointed trust need not be betrayed trust because disappointing your promisee's expectations, by failing to do what you have promised to do, need not amount to infidelity to your promise.

We must therefore be careful how we describe the simpler case from which we began—trust undisappointed yet betrayed—when the trust in question is promissory trust. In such a case, A trusts B to keep her promise to ϕ, B does not disappoint A's trust (as we're using the term) because she does ϕ, yet B betrays A's trust because she does not ϕ with the right attitude toward A. In failing to meet the condition of concern, B also fails to meet the condition of fidelity. Trust can be undisappointed and yet betrayed when it is trust in testimony or advice, or when there is no propositional assurance. A testifier or advisor who speaks truthfully but without appropriate concern for your other relevant needs may count as relevantly faithful—as we might say, "to the truth"—but as nonetheless betraying your trust. And someone whom you trust to ϕ, with no promissory agreement that she ϕ, may faithfully do what you're trusting her to do but betray your trust through her attitudes toward you. In promissory trust, however, what you trust the promisor to do is to remain faithful to her promise by being appropriately responsive to needs of yours—planning needs—that the promise itself makes a condition of her fidelity. If she is not thus responsive, she fails both conditions, not merely the condition of concern.

4.4 The Crucial Parallel between Promises and Intentions

When we see this difference between promissory and these other forms of trust, our next question is why the former should have this feature. The answer lies in grasping how a promise resembles an intention. If we try to view an intention as a promise made "to yourself," we'll be tempted to view the trust in an intention as forward-looking: you trust your later self to remain faithful to your intention. That overlooks how an intra-personal assurance—an invitation to trust—informs an intention. If we view an intention as an intrapersonal trust relation that unfolds through time between distinct selves, earlier and later, which self invites trust and which accepts the invitation? The logic of the "invitation" metaphor gives this answer: the earlier self issues the invitation and the later self, if all goes well, accepts it—trusting the earlier self, not to ϕ (since that's up to the later self), but to have been worthy of trust in forming an intention to ϕ. Though this backward-looking trust relation conflicts with the notion that you "promised yourself you'd ϕ," an intention nonetheless resembles a promise insofar as a trustworthy intention, like a trustworthy promise, serves as a source of planning reasons—of reasons to do things that you would not have reason to do if the intention or promise were not relevantly worthy of your trust.

There are thus two points of resemblance between a promise and an intention. In a promise and an intention alike, one party offers the other an assurance of performance—an invitation to trust that the commitment thereby undertaken will be faithfully executed. And in each, the party who receives an invitation that is indeed worthy of trust thereby also receives reasons to act or plan on the assumption that the commitment will be faithfully executed. The reasons are typically not reasons that support doing these other things in particular but reasons not to avoid doing them given that there are independent reasons to do them, Your promise to help thus gives me reason to plan on moving that heavy couch tomorrow—though the consideration that you would help did not contribute to my decision to move that couch. And my intention to clear my schedule for that hour gives me a reason to persist in my plan to move that couch—though I did not decide to move the couch because I had that gap in my schedule.

We can see the parallel more clearly by reminding ourselves how a promise may simply replace an intention. A would normally manage the picnic himself, let's imagine, but on the present occasion he has other obligations. So B steps in and promises A that she will manage it. Had A managed the picnic, his intention to grill meat would have given him a reason to buy meat—not, of course, a conclusive reason but a pro tanto reason inasmuch as it would make no sense to buy meat that no one will grill—a lacuna filled by his intention to grill. Since A cannot manage the picnic, B's promise to grill the meat fills that gap. And so on for the other intended or promised performances involved in managing the picnic: each gives A planning reasons provided that the commitment in question is worthy of A's trust.

What is it for such a commitment to be worthy of A's trust? Here the parallel deepens: in each case, the commitment crucially serves an understanding shared with A. In the interpersonal case, it is the understanding that A shares with B about the point of the promise: for example, that the promise serves the needs of picnickers that are not served by attempting to picnic in an unexpected thunderstorm. In the intrapersonal case, it is A's ongoing understanding of what he is up to in planning the picnic, which likewise includes the caveat that it makes no sense to persist in the plan in an unexpected thunderstorm. And so we may ask with equal rhetorical force across the two cases: would it constitute a failure to remain faithful to the promise or intention—to "follow through" on it in a way controlled by the understanding that gives the promise or intention its normative content—if the agent in question failed to grill in an unexpected thunderstorm? Obviously not. Obviously, an agent who did grill in an unexpected thunderstorm (under an umbrella to keep the coals hot, but with soggy buns and tastelessly waterlogged meat)—doing what she or he promised or intended rigidly with no acknowledgment that circumstances have changed in ways relevant to the shared understanding at the core of the promise or intention—would show that she or he failed to share that understanding. By grilling in an unexpected thunderstorm, B no more keeps her promise to grill—in the sense that goes with remaining faithful to it—than A simply follows through on his intention to grill.

Imagine now that A holds B to her promise by insisting that, given her promise, she has a promissory obligation simply to grill—whether in a downpour, or in an earthquake, or whatever the circumstances. Contrary to what is sometimes called an "authority view" of promissory obligation,[10] A's refusal to let B off the promissory "hook," in such unexpected circumstances, appears to have no bearing, just as such, on actually keeping B on that hook. What keeps B on the hook are the mutually understood terms of the promissory agreement—which I'm assuming do not include grilling in a thunderstorm, much less in a dangerous natural disaster. The terms of the agreement may include a provision that gives A some authority to interpret how the agreement applies, but even when B thus cedes to A authority to demand performance, A cannot exercise the authority however he wants. There must be some mutually understood point to the promise, defined in terms of how keeping the promise would serve A's interests or needs. The parallel with intention clarifies why the agreement plays this normative role.

This feature of the normative relation is completely obvious for intention: when you form an intention to ϕ at t, you do so with a set of expectations about what the world will be like at t, in respects relevant to your intention, and an implicit understanding of which of these expectations are relevant to your follow through on the intention in this respect: if a relevant expectation is falsified, you should not simply follow through on the intention. In our picnicking example, A expects it not to rain but also expects that no one will show up wearing a bowtie. A has not formulated the latter expectation explicitly in his consciousness, but his betting dispositions, etc., show that he has it, and that it is just as strong as his expectation that it will not rain. If someone does show up in a bowtie, his understanding of the point of intending to grill ensures that the falsification of his expectation tends not at all to show that he ought not to follow through on that intention. Does the difference lie in his consciousness of the expectation? We can easily think of expectations not present to A's consciousness that would nonetheless be relevant to A's follow through on this intention to grill. For example, A expects that a war will not break out among rival armies on the picnic grounds, though he has given the matter no conscious thought. If rival armies do go to war there, he will immediately see that this is relevant to his intention to grill and will not simply follow through on that intention.

These observations clarify how the parallel with promising informs our objection to the authority view. Does B have a promissory obligation to do what she has promised to do unless and until A positively lets B off this "hook"? If B has promised some picnic guest A to grill but war unexpectedly breaks out on the picnic grounds, does A's obstinate insistence that B promised really ensure that B has an obligation to grill—an obligation overridden by other obligations, to be sure, but an obligation nonetheless? By hypothesis, this battlefield scenario formed not even an implicit part of their promissory agreement and in fact runs counter to that agreement, just as—in the intrapersonal parallel—it falsifies relevant expectations informing A's intention. How could B, by virtue of promising with that understanding of the point of the promise, be *on* this hook—imagine, if you need an even more extreme case, a deadly tornado bearing down on them, or warmongering Martians landing on the grounds with a tornado-like descent. If one replies that B ought not to grill merely because her obligation to grill is overridden by an independent obligation not to remain in harm's way, I revert to the simpler case in which grilling is not dangerous but pointless—because it does not serve the mutually understood point of the promissory agreement.[11] B does not need A's permission to manifest her understanding that grilling in such unexpected circumstances would fail to keep her promise to grill for everyone's pleasure on what they all expect will be a Sunday afternoon perfect for grilling, with no forecast of grill-undermining rain or wind, not to mention bellicose Martians.

That parallel between promise and intention yields this formula: a promisor aims to do for the promisee what the promisee would have aimed to do for himself had he formed an intention to do it. The formula does not, of course, mean that promisees are always or even usually in position to intend to do what the promisor has promised to do. What it means is this: just as an intention loses its intrapersonal normative force, requiring redeliberation before rational follow-through, when a relevant expectation informing the intention is falsified, so a promise loses its normative force, no longer requiring performance of the promised act, when a relevant expectation informing the promissory agreement is falsified. What gives promises and intentions their parallel normative structures is the distinctive temporality of their commitments. When you form an intention, you aim to do justice to your ongoing needs in respects relevant to your understanding of the point of the intention. If your needs change because your circumstances unexpectedly change, your rational obligation to do what you intend to do may merely lapse, rather than being outweighed. If your promisee's needs likewise change through changing circumstances, then your obligation to do what you promised may likewise lapse.

We can also frame the parallel in terms of how the commitments give rise to planning reasons. As we've seen, B's promise to φ serves A's planning needs in the way that A's hypothetical intention to φ would serve his own planning needs. The parallel appears to rest on a deeper analogy: between how promissory trust gives planning reasons and how trust in your own intending self makes you rationally coherent.[12] In each case, the rational status appears to derive from vindication of the presumption of trustworthiness informing an invitation to trust. In each case, gaining or retaining the rational status rests, not on responsiveness to positive evidence of trustworthiness—evidence that may be hard to obtain—but on responsiveness to evidence of unworthiness of trust. As the promisee withdraws trust upon receiving significant evidence of the promisor's untrustworthiness, so you redeliberate whether to do what you were intending to do upon receiving significant evidence of your own untrustworthiness in intending. You need not have positive evidence to be guided by evidence. Trust guides you in planning by making available reasons grounded in trustworthiness of which you may lack positive evidence—as long as you also lack evidence that the putative source off the reason is relevantly untrustworthy.[13]

4.5 How Trust, Including Self-Trust, Gives Access to Reasons

At the core of my approach lie the ideas that trust serves as a conduit for giving reasons through assurance, and that this form of reason-giving differs from how a reason is given by evidence of the speaker's reliability. It's a large question how an assurance can give reasons, and how that form of reason-giving is distinctive. I've had my say about it elsewhere in papers on testimony, advice, and promising.[14] For present purposes, we do best to focus on the intrapersonal case, developing the parallel between promises and intentions sketched in the previous section. Continuing that argument, this will help us to see why the condition of concern must inform the condition of fidelity for promises and intentions: it must do so because such concern lies at the core of reason-giving trustworthiness. Though my argument forces us to confront the objections that I'll now consider, my discussion in this section and the next pulls us into issues that run deeper than we can fully investigate here. I return to our core dialectic in Section VII.

Why emphasize intrapersonal reason-giving? And what could such reason-giving have to do with self-trust? Let's begin with some general observations about why we form intentions. Say it is now t_1 and your deliberative question is whether to ϕ at some later time t_2. Why might you resolve the question now, at t_1, by forming an intention to ϕ at t_2, rather than leaving the matter unresolved until t_2? The answer will typically involve your desire to coordinate matters in advance, both because you may now possess better resources, whether better information or increased ability to use it, than you expect to possess at t_2, and because in forming the intention now you give yourself a rational basis for doing other things that you would not do if you could not count on yourself to follow through on that intention. This rational structure emerges especially clearly for sub-plans within an overarching plan—you build the walls of your house today partly because you intend to add a roof tomorrow—but it also emerges when the actions embody separate plans. Say, in election season, you volunteer to campaign for candidate X. Some of your reasons to do so are the reasons to vote for X that informed your decision to vote for X, but one additional reason derives from your intention to vote for X—assuming the intention trustworthy. Your intention to vote for X does not itself provide a sufficient reason to campaign for X, but it does provide one reason, and that reason may even prove necessary: perhaps if you did not intend to vote for X, it would not in context make rational sense for you to campaign for X—given, say, your ineffectiveness in campaigning with an "open mind," your susceptibility to charges of hypocrisy, and the inefficiency of putting off that important decision.

It is thus part of the point of your forming an intention to ϕ that doing so will, you expect, give you reasons to do other things—to do things that you would not regard yourself as having a sufficient reason to do if you did not have this intention to ϕ. I have called these "planning reasons," since they are reasons, grounded in your presumed trustworthiness, that articulate the normative structure of your planning. Note well that I do not claim that forming an intention to ϕ can later give you a reason specifically *to* ϕ. That claim is more controversial than my anodyne observation about the point of intention, since it appears to yield the result that you can illicitly "bootstrap" yourself into possessing reasons by a sheer act of will.[15] When you lack good reason to do what you intend to do, does the fact that you made one error, in forming the intention, mean that you now have a reason to make another error by following through on it? When we examine the role of trust in agency, however, we see that the bootstrapping problem is more specific than merely willing your way into reasons. Say you've formed an intention to ϕ which you treat as giving you a reason to ϕ, and you now worry that this intention may be untrustworthy. If you (re)deliberatively affirm that intention even partly on the basis of that putative reason, you have merely gone round an illicit circle that leaves your worry unaddressed.

Since I'm going to argue that this problem does not arise for reasons to perform actions other than the action that you intend to perform, let's examine how the problem arises. The problem reveals that even if we assume that you are trustworthy in forming an intention to ϕ, we should nonetheless not regard your trustworthiness as giving you a *deliberative* reason to ϕ. Though I eschew the distinction between "objective" and "subjective" reasons, the bootstrapping problem motivates a distinction between "deliberative" and "non-deliberative" reasons. Imagine you forget this intention for a while and then remember it through recognizing your own handwriting in your appointment calendar. You still don't remember the experience of forming the intention, but you treat the handwriting as evidence that you formed it. You now reason as follows: "I'm reliable on the question whether to ϕ. So the fact that I formed an intention to ϕ gives me reason to believe that I ought to ϕ. So I ought to ϕ." And you thereby reaffirm your intention to ϕ. There is nothing inherently wrong with this reasoning, and there need be nothing wrong with reaffirming your intention in this way. The rub for our purposes is merely that this is not a manifestation of normal diachronic agency. You don't govern yourself, looking forward, by leaving a trace of your intention where you expect your future self to discover it, and then offload responsibility to your future self to reason in the way just described. If you expect your future self to redeliberate the question whether to ϕ, now in a way informed by its evidence of your reliability in having formed an intention to ϕ, you aren't inviting that future self simply to follow through on the intention. And if you later find yourself in that predicament looking back, your attempt to cope with the deficit deliberatively marks a contrast with the normal case in which you don't need to redeliberate because—having earlier deliberated—you can remember what you intend and then, trusting your intending self, simply follow through on the intention.

The bootstrapping metaphor thus codifies a puzzle. Part of the point of forming an intention lies in giving your future self reasons to do things that depend on your having this intention. Planning reasons must count as deliberative reasons, since you deliberate—partly but perhaps decisively—from the consideration that you intend to ϕ when you go on to form a further plan whose rationality depends on your assumption that you will ϕ by following through on this intention. But if your intention to ϕ does not give you a deliberative reason to ϕ, we may wonder, how can it give you a deliberative reason to do things that depend on the intention?

We can resolve the puzzle by noting that the bootstrapping problem does not rule out your having a *non*deliberative reason to follow through on that very intention. What would ground that reason is not the sheer fact that you intend to ϕ but your trustworthiness in forming and retaining the intention. No bootstrapping problem infects the idea that your trustworthiness grounds a nondeliberative reason to follow through on an intention, since to say that the reason is "nondeliberative" is to say that you cannot weigh it in deliberation and so cannot go round the illicit circle.[16] If, by contrast, you reaffirm your intention to ϕ by deliberating from your presumed trustworthiness in intending to ϕ, you are illicitly bootstrapping, because that presumption is precisely the question posed by this deliberation. But when you deliberatively weigh a planning reason to do something else, grounded in your presumed trustworthiness in intending to ϕ, you are not illicitly bootstrapping because you are not addressing any question of your trustworthiness in intending to ϕ. The bootstrapping problem arises only when your trustworthiness is specifically in question. If your trustworthiness in intending is not in question, there is no circle in deliberating from the presumption that it gives you planning reasons.

4.6 How Trust, Including Self-Trust, Is Betrayed

What is it for trust, including intrapersonal trust, to be betrayed? Though it may seem like a digression, explaining the possibility of betrayed self-trust lets me reply to a pressing objection to my reliance on the parallel between promising and intending. We have been considering a parallel between reason-giving trustworthiness in promising and reason-giving trustworthiness in intending, a parallel grounded in a deeper parallel between the interpersonal agreement at the core of a promise and the intrapersonal understanding of what you're up to at the core of an intention. It is clear enough how a promisor can be untrustworthy, but what exactly is it to be unworthy of your own trust in intending? If you are then, by my account, you do not get any planning reasons from the intention—so it loses a key part of its point as an intention. How should you respond? We now get what looks like a paradox. Insofar as you do have this intention, it seems you should follow through on it. Insofar as the intention is not worthy of your trust, it seems you should mistrustfully not follow through on it. But there is no paradox; we need merely get clear on what it is to betray your own self-trust. Understanding how self-trust is betrayed will put us on the right track to understand what it is to betray trust more generally and thus how to achieve our ultimate theoretical aim of distinguishing trust from mere reliance.

How could you "mistrust" your own intention? At the core of the present objection lies the observation that when you "mistrust" an intention you make it the case that you no longer have that intention: you reopen your deliberation whether to do the thing in question, which is incompatible with committing yourself to do it in the way of intention.[17] If you cannot simply mistrust your own intention—that is, yourself insofar as you have formed and retain it—how could an intention manifest self-trust? Though you may have worries about an intention that you persist in retaining, just as you may about one of your own beliefs, if you simply "mistrust" your intention, in the way that you might mistrust another's promise, you thereby cease to retain the intention, and for a reason that applies also to belief: both intention and belief manifest trust in your judgment. While there may be special contexts or respects in which you can trust yourself and yet at the same time count as mistrusting that trust, trust in your judgment does not appear to admit that possibility. You cannot trust your practical judgment that you ought to φ in such a way as to count as intending to φ yet at the same time also mistrust that trust in your judgment. But, while you cannot abandon an intention without abandoning the judgment that informs it, it does not follow that the only way to abandon an intention is to abandon the judgment that informs it. You might abandon an intention by mistrusting the judgment that informs it. Our question now is how this works: how might you mistrust a judgment that you nonetheless retain?

What is it to mistrust your own judgment? Let's work within the standard approach that equates your all-things-considered practical judgment that you ought to φ with a doxastic judgment that you have conclusive reason to φ.[18] The view identifies the specifically practical element in a practical judgment with an element in the content of that judgment: the idea that you have a conclusive practical reason. We might ask what it is to judge that you have a *conclusive* practical reason, but I take that notion for granted.[19] I have noted that you cannot mistrust your own belief, apparently for the very reason that you cannot mistrust your own intention: both intention and belief manifest trust in your judgment, and it does not make sense to say that you cannot mistrust this dimension of your own self-trust. As with intention, to mistrust your own belief that p is no longer to believe that *p*: to mistrust the belief is to abandon it. Why not say the same of mistrust in your own judgment? How could you retain your judgment that *p*—say, your judgment that you have conclusive reason to φ—while at the same mistrusting that judgment?

Let me now build up to my proposal. When I speak of "mistrusting" your own judgment, I do not mean mistrusting your faculty of judgment. If "mistrusting your judgment" could only mean mistrusting your faculty of judgment, then when you mistrust your judgment you would be—deliberatively speaking—just stuck. You would have to stop deliberating and merely wait for the bout of self-mistrust to subside. But you are not just stuck when you mistrust your judgment; you can mistrust your judgment in this or that precise respect and resume deliberation by trusting your judgment in other respects. We individuate these "respects" with propositions. Self-mistrust thus typically targets a subject matter, which we individuate with propositions, and a subject matter can be so narrow that it coincides with a single proposition. To say that you mistrust your judgment in the respect individuated by the proposition *p* is to say that you mistrust your judgment on the question whether *p*. Does it follow that you cannot count as judging that *p*? If you were redeliberating whether *p*, then you would not count as judging that *p*. But from the fact that you mistrust your judgment on the question whether *p*, it does not follow that you are redeliberating whether *p*, since you may be deliberating *whether to redeliberate* whether *p*. Reconsidering your judgment that *p* may, in this way, fall short of reconsidering whether *p*.

What is it, then, to consider—again, not idly but with appropriate engagement—whether to reconsider whether *p*? Some ways of considering whether to reconsider whether *p do* amount to abandoning your judgment that *p*. Considering whether to reconsider whether *p* on the basis of a worry about the truth-conducive reliability of the doxastic process whereby you formed your judgment that *p* is the first step, at least, toward abandoning that judgment. Once raised, the worry tends to force open deliberation on the question whether *p*—perhaps not all at once, but unless you simply let go of the worry that's where you will wind up. You cannot settle a non-idle worry about your truth-conducive reliability without reconsidering whether *p*.

But there is another dimension of your reliability that your self-mistrust can target when you mistrust your own judgment: what I'll call your "closure-conducive" reliability. As I use the term, "closure-conducive" reliability is very different from truth-conducive reliability; though we aim at or care about the two species of reliability together, a given subject could at once be closure-conducively reliable without being truth-conducively reliable, and vice versa. The question whether a subject is closure-conducively reliable in believing that *p* is the question whether her doxastic deliberation whether *p* is or was informed by an appropriate implicit conception of when her evidence would epistemically suffice for her to close deliberation with a judgment that *p*. If your worry targets your closure-conducive reliability in judging that *p*, by contrast, you can refrain from reconsidering whether *p*—even while non-idly pressing the worry.

To worry about your closure-conducive reliability in judging that *p* is to worry that the doxastic deliberation informing your judgment was not governed by the appropriate epistemic standard: that your deliberation whether *p* was temporally ill-drawn ("impatient," "impulsive," "too hasty," "rushed") or insufficiently resourced ("complacent," "incurious," "lazy," "parochial"). You know you should not take too long to decide, since life is short, but maybe you are being impatient. You know you should not think too hard about the decision, since these mental resources are finite and also needed elsewhere in your life, but maybe you are just being complacent. This is not yet, in either case, to worry that you made a mistake *within* the deliberation. Your worry targets not how you weighed evidence while deliberating but your implicit conception of what was at stake in the deliberation. You need not worry that you have made an error in your reasoning or are less likely than you had assumed you would be to hit on the truth. What you would learn in learning that you are closure-conducively unreliable is that you are likely to have misassessed what is at stake in your doxastic context. You would learn that you are likely to have misassessed how much or generally what quality of evidence would epistemically suffice for you to close deliberation with a judgment.

When we specify that the doxastic judgment in question has practical content, we can diagnose the predicament you confront in a case of practical self-mistrust: you wonder whether following through on your intention to ϕ will amount to betraying your own trust. In following through, you would manifest trust in your intention, but the betrayal would lie in the judgment that informs your intention, your judgment that you have conclusive reason to ϕ. We could pin the self-betrayal on how this judgment invites your trust—though nothing turns on the metaphor. That's one risk that you run whenever you follow through on an intention: you risk betrayal by your own practical judgment. You can address the risk by being open to self-mistrust. Without yet abandoning your judgment, you can raise the question of your trustworthiness as a worry that you were impatient or complacent in forming it; you thereby worry that your judgment betrays the trust that it invites through representing you as closure-conducively reliable. Combined with relevant truth-conducive reliability, your closure-conducive reliability forms the basis of your worthiness of your own trust as a source of planning reasons. As in the promissory case, responsiveness to betrayal and responsiveness to reasons go hand in hand.

Can we generalize this account beyond betrayed self-trust to betrayed promissory trust? On the account I'm developing, there is room for two explanations of a promisor's, B's, betrayal of your trust: (i) B forgets or rejects her promissory obligation; (ii) B misinterprets that obligation, by misinterpreting how the promissory agreement governs what it demands of her. B might misinterpret the agreement by failing to see that it obligates her to φ. Perhaps she interprets her promise to grill at the picnic as defeated by unexpectedly bowtied attendees or (more realistically) by an unexpected chill in the air, revealing that she misunderstands how relevant others perceive the bearing of weather on picnics. (In her native south, no one would grill in near-freezing temperature, but here in the north people do so regularly.) Or perhaps she fails to interpret her promise as defeated by a thunderstorm, or by a tornado warning. Both type-(ii) violations—both her laxly failing to grill in a chill and her rigidly grilling in a downpour—amount to failures in B's judgment. These failures of judgment betray A's trust as directly as more stereotypical type-(i) violations, wherein B forgets or rejects her promissory obligation.

The parallel with intention thus helps us trace some instances of betrayed trust back to a question of judgment: specifically, how judgment is exercised in interpreting what an understanding of the implicit context and orienting content of a commitment normatively requires of you. Our next step is to see that type-(ii) betrayals of trust reveal most clearly how trust differs from mere reliance. We can treat some type-(i) violations as targeting the condition of fidelity without touching the condition of concern, as when B simply forgets or overlooks or non-culpably ignores her promissory obligation. And we can treat other type-(i) violations as targeting the conditions of fidelity and concern in different respects. If B rejects or spurns or rebels against her promissory obligation, that reveals that she has the wrong attitude toward the promisee, A, thereby violating the condition of concern. But her attitude bears a merely causal relation to her violation of the condition of fidelity: she does not violate both conditions with a single attitude or state of her will. If B rejects the promissory obligation, her failure has these two components: she fails to do what she promised, and the causal explanation of that failure lies in her lack of appropriate concern toward A. The first failure is the same as it would have been if B's failure of performance had manifested mere forgetfulness, and the second failure is the same as it would have been if B had performed but with a contemptuous attitude toward A.

In a type-(ii) violation, by contrast, the two elements do not come apart. Or rather, the only way they come apart is if B does what she has promised to do inadvertently, without any regard to the promise. If we set that sort of case aside, we get the following result. In a type-(i) case, B can violate the condition of fidelity without violating the condition of concern (e.g. B merely forgets to act), and B can violate the condition of concern without violating the condition of fidelity (e.g. B acts with an inappropriate attitude). But in a type-(ii) case, B satisfies the two conditions together: her fidelity is governed by her concern, and a lack of fidelity already manifests a lack of concern. If B fails to perform in a type-(ii) case, that failure manifests the failure of concern inherent in misinterpreting the promissory agreement. And if B fails to show appropriate concern in a type-(ii) case, that failure manifests a failure of fidelity to the promise—unless, again, she just happens to perform the act for unrelated reasons, a possibility that we're setting aside for both types of case. We cannot get a case in which B violates the condition of concern, by misinterpreting what the promise requires of her, yet nonetheless satisfies the condition of fidelity, by doing what she promised to do because she promised to do it, or a case in which B violates the condition of fidelity, by failing to do what she promised to do as an expression of her understanding of the promise, yet nonetheless satisfies the condition of concern, by correctly interpreting what the promise requires of her. In a type-(ii) case, but not in a type-(i), violation of each condition goes with violation of the other, or satisfaction with satisfaction. Type-(ii) violations thus reveal more clearly how trust differs from mere reliance:

they reveal what links the two conditions, violation of which amounts to trust betrayed.

We can draw one further moral from type-(ii) cases. Focusing on such cases lets us see clearly how the Affective and Reactive Attitude Views of trust misconstrue core instances of trust betrayed. The Affective Attitude View can explain type-(i) cases but not type-(ii) cases, for the simple reason that the betrayal of trust that we find in type-(ii) cases need not manifest any ill will toward the promisee. Some type-(ii) cases will prove entirely non-moral—if, for example, B's misinterpretation of the promissory agreement was "innocent" because, as the exculpating catchphrase puts it, "merely a misunderstanding." When B interprets her promissory agreement with A as requiring her to grill only as long as the temperature does not drop close to freezing—thereby misinterpreting what anyone in A's position would have taken for granted about its content, she betrays A's promissory trust, but not in a way that calls for reactive-attitudinal response. At least, we do sometimes encounter cases along these lines: B's misinterpretation is so natural—she's from the South, where it is unthinkable to grill at near-freezing temperatures—that A rightly catches himself before giving in to any impulse toward resentment. There is no ill will, contra the Affective Attitude View. And, contra the Reactive Attitude View, betrayal does not warrant reactive-attitudinal response. But since my Assurance View offers a positive account of betrayed—via the parallel with intrapersonal trust—there is, in the end, no need to treat reactive attitudes as the key to explaining how trust differs from mere reliance: what explains betrayal is what the reactive attitude would, when appropriate, respond to. My alternative three-place analysis, with its emphasis on reason-giving through trust, thus explains both how disappointment need not yield betrayal and how betrayal need not be moral.

4.7 What Then of Trust without Assurance?

The point of the previous section's deep dive into intrapersonal trust was to excavate a structure that explains how it and interpersonal trust univocally risk betrayal. Let's now resume a broader social focus. My approach assigns a role for assurance in mediating trust relations, and that role motivates a novel three-place analysis of trust, on which the fundamental normative structure of a trust relation is not "A trusts B to ϕ" but "A ϕs (or has a reason to ϕ) through trust in B." I have discussed interpersonal cases that appear to vindicate that analysis, but I concede that there are other cases of trust that do not, since they do not contain anything recognizable as an assurance. How does my approach treat such cases? Must I bifurcate my approach and theorize these assurance-free cases on one of the standard models, whether three-place or two-place?

Before I answer, let me provide a brief review. When we focus on assurances such as promises and intentions, in which the conditions of fidelity and concern do not come neatly apart, we see how the risks of trust track the rewards of trust. A promise or intention aims not merely at rigid execution but at fidelity to an understanding, whether the interpersonal understanding of what is at stake for the promisee at the core of a promise or the intrapersonal understanding of what the agent is up to at the core of an intention. This fidelity to understanding informs the trustworthiness grounding the planning reasons that constitute the rewards of trust—reasons for the promisee to plan or act in a way that depends on the promise, or reasons for the agent to plan or act in a way that depends on his own intention.

We have seen how this framework explains how trust can be disappointed yet unbetrayed, since in unexpected circumstances, fidelity to relevant understanding does not require refraining from disappointing the trust (and broader considerations may actually require disappointing the trust—though this is not strictly necessary for trust disappointed yet unbetrayed). The framework also offers a satisfying explanation of how trust can be undisappointed yet betrayed. An affective-attitudinal approach to promissory trust would emphasize the badness of the promisee's attitude in such a case: she does what she promised to do, but in a way that manifests ill will toward the promisee. But if that amounts to a betrayal of trust, it is not a betrayal of specifically promissory trust. Perhaps that explains why Baier, a proponent of that approach, does not regard a promissory assurance as a paradigmatic invitation to trust. On my assurance-theoretic approach, by contrast, the betrayal goes right to the core of the promissory relation. When B rigidly executes her promise to A though it does not serve A's needs in respects relevant to the promissory agreement between them, there is a betrayal of A's trust that may have nothing to do with any ill will that B bears A. B may actually have good will toward A yet nonetheless betray A's trust—A's specifically promissory trust—through confusion over what the interpersonal understanding between them requires of her. Here too we see a parallel with intention. If you act on an intention though relevant expectations—expectations that inform your understanding of what you are up to in intending—go false, you may have betrayed your own trust, by betraying this understanding, without bearing yourself ill will or any other problematic attitude—other than your lack of this intention-specific self-concern.

By "self-concern" here I mean concern to act from this understanding of what you're up to in intending, just as the condition of concern requires that a promisor act from the understanding that she shares with her promisee *qua* parties to the promise. There is an attitude of concern in each case, but it is specific to the normative demands of the promise or the intention. The concern is not an extra element, codifying the role of any further attitude toward the one who offers his trust. And we may say the same of other reason-giving assurances such as testimony and advice. Each brings its own cognate species of concern for the addressee, a species of concern that informs trust by informing the reason-giving relation. Though there is always the possibility that a broader trust relation will be betrayed, betrayal of trust invited by an assurance rests on attitudes that are specific to how that assurance gives reasons.

What then of such broader trust—of trust without assurance? Note first that, like other theorists of trust, I do not aim to explain everything we might call "trust." When you say you "trust" your new toaster (unlike its "untrustworthy" predecessor) not to burn your toast, you mean merely that you rely on the toaster: there is no conceptual space there to distinguish trust from mere reliance. Like other theorists of trust, I aim is to explain that distinction, and so my account is silent about uses of "trust" where the distinction could not apply. The present challenge to my approach is that you can trust someone who has not made an assurance, with trust conceptually distinct from mere reliance on the person. How can an assurance-theoretic approach explain that distinction? How, without an assurance, can trust differ from mere reliance?

We cannot set aside such interpersonal trust, as we might set aside its intrapersonal analogue. How to set aside what at first may look like intrapersonal trust without assurance? Though it is a stretch to appeal to intuitions about self-assurance in intrapersonal practical commitment, there is a kind of case that resembles an intention but without the diachronic complexity that I've argued forms the core of intention. Consider Homer's Odysseus as he confronts the Sirens' song.[20] One reason to distinguish Odysseus's strategy for dealing with expected temptation from an intention is that having his hands tied to the ship's mast prevents more than merely giving in to the Sirens' deadly enticement. If, in an unexpected turn of events, a hurricane blows the Sirens away but also threatens the boat, he'll need to escape those bonds to deal with the emergency. It isn't merely that such pre-commitment carries risks but that the risks are not like the risks of inherent in diachronic agency. When you cope with temptation by forming a resolute intention, inviting your later self's trust, you risk forgetfulness (you may simply not remember your intention), weakness (you may be overcome by the temptation), practical unwisdom (perhaps, as in Huck Finn's resolution to betray his friend Jim, the temptations themselves are backed by stronger reasons), and lack of appropriate self-concern (you may misconstrue the bearing of unexpected circumstances on your intention, in the way that I have argued amounts to betraying your own trust). But you do not typically risk the weirdly mechanical rigidity characteristic of Odysseus's pre-commitment when coping with temptation. Such a strategy may prove helpful in keeping your conduct in line with your reasons, but without an invitation to trust—without what we are conceiving as the intrapersonal analogue of an assurance—it does not involve anything like the self-trust dynamic at the core of an intention.

Though intrapersonal reliance without an assurance falls short of intrapersonal trust, we cannot draw the parallel conclusion for interpersonal reliance and trust. There are several types of interpersonal case to consider, in each of which trust does not respond to an assurance. In a testimonial case, you trust a testifier who has not addressed you, treating her assertion not merely as a reliable guide to the truth but as informed by concern for the context-sensitive epistemic needs of someone in circumstances *like yours*. In an advisorial case, you trust an advisor who has not addressed you, treating her advice not merely as a reliable guide to your reasons but as informed by concern for how someone *like you* would receive it. In a sub-promissory case, your trust in the other party is not informed by an understanding with the diachronic complexity of a promissory agreement: if you merely trust B to φ, with no promise, then you are not relying on B to do justice to your ongoing needs in the specific respect in which you do so when B has promised you to ϕ (unless, of course, φing itself requires such responsiveness).

What do the cases have in common? How might trust without an assurance be betrayed? Without an assurance, B can betray A's trust only under the fiction that B has invited it. In testimonial and advisorial cases, you treat B as concerned with an addressee who resembles you in relevant ways. There are two ways you might do so: you might work from available evidence that this resemblance between you and B's actual addressee does indeed obtain, or (perhaps lacking such evidence) you might treat B's concern as bearing on you more directly. The former option collapses the case into a case of mere reliance, since your normative relation to B now runs through evidence of B's reliability—both in the dimension of truth-seeking and in the dimension of appropriate concern. To trust B in a way that stands opposed to merely relying on B, you would have to take the latter option, treating B's concern as bearing on you directly. But that is to treat B *as if* she had offered you an assurance, as if she had invited your trust. The most interesting sort of case is institutional: you trust institution B to serve as a source of reciprocal planning reasons, as if you stood to it both as promisee (e.g. relying on a school to educate your children) and as promisor (acknowledging its reliance on your support)—even if there is nothing like an actual promise. Though I lack space to give these observations the theoretical development they deserve, I believe that many forms of social trust have this *as-if* structure.

In each such case, treating the trusted as if he, she, or it had invited your trust can give you planning reasons grounded in his, her, or its status as worthy of that trust. Under this fiction, a failure of trustworthiness amounts to a betrayal of your trust. To say that the betrayal unfolds under the fiction captures its two sides: you feel betrayed by the trusted, but the trusted bears no attitude and performs no act specifically addressed *to you*. Is the trusted's worthiness of your trust, in the more favorable case, therefore also fictive? If it is, must we say the same of the reason it grounds? I do not believe that we should answer either question in the affirmative, but to show why would require an inquiry into the nature of reasons—too much for the present occasion. Setting those more difficult general questions aside, we see illustrated again our guiding thesis, that the fundamental normative structure of trust is "A ϕs through trust in B." The point of such a fiction would lie in how it mediates your access to reasons.

Notes

1. For a different account of trust that also emphasizes commitment, see Hawley (2014). In other respects, however, my approach differs substantially from Hawley's. For example, Hawley endorses the traditional three-place analysis, does not distinguish fidelity from "rigid" execution, and does not consider the sort of parallel between the interpersonal and the intrapersonal that informs my approach.
2. See for example, Hardin (2002, Chapter 3); Nickel (2007, Section 6); and Rose (2011, Chapter 9).
3. See for example, Baier (1994, Chapters 6–9); Jones (1996); and McGeer (2008) (on the role of hope in trust).
4. See for example, Holton (1994); Jones (2004); Walker (2006, Chapter 3); Hieronymi (2008); and Helm (2015).
5. Shared by approaches as diverse as Baier (1994), Holton (1994), Hardin (2002), and Hawley (2014).
6. See for example, Lahno (2001); Faulkner (2015); and Domenicucci and Holton (2017).
7. Grice (1957).
8. I discuss cases with this structure more fully in Hinchman (2017).
9. I defend the claims in this sentence and the last in Hinchman (2005a, 2014). In the latter, I argue that testimony resembles promising on the present point, but I do not want to presuppose that argument here.
10. See, for example, Darwall (2006, Chapter 8, 2011); Owens (2006, 2012, Parts II and III); Shiffrin (2008, 2011); and Watson (2009).
11. Again, I'm assuming a stereotypical case in which there is relevant agreement that the thunderstorm undermines the point of the picnic. In a less stereotypical case, we could imagine that a storm has no such consequence, as determined by the less stereotypical agreement defining the case.
12. I explore this deeper analogy in Hinchman (2017) and more fully in "Commitment as Normative Power," in preparation.
13. While we lack space to pursue the parallel further, we might wonder how we develop this capacity for trust: does the development of capacity for diachronic agency internalize proto-promissory relations?
14. See Hinchman (2005a, 2005b, 2014, 2017).
15. Bratman (1987, pp. 23–7, 86–7); Broome (2001). Smith (2016) offers a dissenting perspective.
16. See Hinchman (2003, 2009, 2010) for full argument on this point.
17. For an elaboration of this and related problems, see Kolodny (2005, pp. 528–39). For replies to Kolodny's arguments, see Hinchman (2013, Section III).

18. For an influential version of this approach, see Scanlon (1998, pp. 25–30, 2007).
19. I develop a challenge to this aspect of Scanlon's view of practical judgment in Hinchman (2013, Section VI).
20. For provocative treatments of this case, see Elster (1984, 2000).

References

Austin, J. L. 1975. *How to Do Things with Words* (Cambridge: Harvard University Press).
Baier, Annette. 1994. *Moral Prejudices* (Cambridge: Harvard University Press).
Bratman, Michael. 1987. *Intention, Plans, and Practical Reason* (Cambridge: Harvard University Press).
Broome, John. 2001. "Are Intentions Reasons? And How Should We Cope with Incommensurable Values?," in C. Morris and A. Ripstein (eds.) *Practical Rationality and Preference* (Cambridge: Cambridge University Press), 98–120.
Darwall, Stephen. 2006. *The Second-Person Standpoint* (Cambridge: Harvard University Press).
2011. "Demystifying Promises," in H. Sheinman (ed.) *Promises and Agreements* (Oxford: Oxford University Press), 255–76.
Domenicucci, Jacopo and Richard Holton. 2017. "Trust as a Two-Place Relation," in P. Faulkner and T. Simpson (eds.) *The Philosophy of Trust* (Oxford: Oxford University Press), 149–60.
Elster, Jon. 1984. *Ulysses and the Sirens* (Cambridge: Cambridge University Press).
_______. 2000. *Ulysses Unbound* (Cambridge: Cambridge University Press).
Faulkner, Paul. 2015. "The Attitude of Trust is Basic," *Analysis* 75:3, 424–29.
Grice, Paul. 1957. "Meaning," *The Philosophical Review*, 66:3 (1957), 377–88.
Hardin, Russell. 2002. *Trust and Trustworthiness* (New York: Russell Sage Foundation).
Hawley, Katherine. 2014. "Trust, Distrust, and Commitment," *Noûs* 48:1, 1–20.
Helm, Bennett. 2015. "Trust as a Reactive Attitude," in N. Tognazzini and D. Shoemaker (eds.), *Oxford Studies in Agency and Responsibility*, Volume 2 (Oxford: Oxford University Press), 187–215.
Hieronymi, Pamela. 2008. "The Reasons of Trust," *Australasian Journal of Philosophy* 86:2, 213–36.
Hinchman, Edward. 2003. "Trust and Diachronic Agency," *Noûs* 37:1, 25–51.
_______. 2005a. "Advising as Inviting to Trust," *Canadian Journal of Philosophy* 35, 355–86.
_______. 2005b. "Telling as Inviting to Trust," *Philosophy and Phenomenological Research* 70:3, 562–87.
_______. 2009. "Receptivity and the Will," *Noûs* 43:3, 395–427.
_______. 2010. "Conspiracy, Commitment, and the Self," *Ethics* 120:3, 526–56.
_______. 2013. "Rational Requirements and 'Rational' Akrasia," *Philosophical Studies* 166:3, 529–52.
_______. 2014. "Assurance and Warrant," *Philosophers' Imprint* 14:17, 1–58.
_______. 2017. "On the Risks of Resting Assured: An Assurance Theory of Trust," in P. Faulkner and T. Simpson (eds.), *The Philosophy of Trust* (Oxford: Oxford University Press), 51–69.

Holton, Richard. 1994. "Deciding to Trust, Coming to Believe," *Australasian Journal of Philosophy* 72:1, 63–76.
Hume, David. 1978. *Treatise on Human Nature*, 2nd Edition (Oxford: Oxford University Press).
Jones, Karen. 1996. "Trust as an Affective Attitude," *Ethics* 107:1, 4–25.
_______. 2004. "Trust and Terror," in P. DesAutels and M. Walker (eds.), *Moral Psychology* (Lanham: Rowman & Littlefield), 3–18.
Kolodny, Niko. 2005. "Why Be Rational," *Mind* 114:455, 509–63.
Lahno, Bernd. 2001. "On the Emotional Character of Trust," *Ethical Theory and Moral Practice* 4:2, 171–89.
McGeer, Victoria. 2008. "Trust, Hope, and Empowerment," *Australasian Journal of Philosophy*, 86:2, 237–54.
Nickel, Philip. 2007. "Trust and Obligation-Ascription," *Ethical Theory and Moral Practice* 10:3, 309–19.
Owens, David. 2006. "A Simple Theory of Promising," *Philosophical Review* 115:1, 51–77.
_______. 2012. *Shaping the Normative Landscape* (Oxford: Oxford University Press).
Rose, David. 2011. *The Moral Foundation of Economic Behavior* (Oxford: Oxford University Press).
Scanlon, T. M. 1998. *What We Owe to Each Other* (Cambridge, Mass: Harvard University Press).
_______. 2007. "Structural Irrationality," in G. Brennan, R. Goodin, F. Jackson, and M. Smith (eds.), *Common Minds* (Oxford: Oxford University Press), 84–103.
Shiffrin, Seana. 2008. "Promising, Intimate Relationships, and Conventionalism," *Philosophical Review* 117:4, 481–524.
_______. 2011. "Immoral, Conflicting, and Redundant Promises," in R. J. Wallace, et al. (eds.), *Reasons and Recognition* (Oxford: Oxford University Press), 155–78.
Smith, Matthew. 2016. "One Dogma of Philosophy of Action," *Philosophical Studies* 73:8, 2249–66.
Walker, Margaret Urban. 2006. *Moral Repair* (Cambridge: Cambridge University Press).
Watson, Gary. 2009. "Promises, Reasons, and Normative Powers," in D. Sobel and S. Wall (eds.) *Reasons for Action* (Cambridge: Cambridge University Press), 155–78.

5 Public Trust in Science

Exploring the Idiosyncrasy-Free Ideal

Marion Boulicault and S. Andrew Schroeder[1]

5.1 Introduction

What makes science trustworthy? On what basis should the public trust scientists when they claim that smoking causes cancer, that the earth is divided into tectonic plates, or that bee populations are declining? This chapter examines a compelling answer to that question: the trustworthiness of science is based in part on its freedom from the idiosyncratic values and interests of individual scientists. That is, all else being equal, a trustworthy science will be one in which scientists all converge on the same conclusions, regardless of their personal values and interests.

We analyze this answer—dubbed by Marion Boulicault the "idiosyncrasy-free ideal" (IFI) for science (Boulicault unpublished; cf. Boulicault 2014)—by looking at philosophical debates concerning inductive risk. We examine two recent proposals for handling inductive risk, each of which offers a method of avoiding idiosyncrasy: the High Epistemic Standards proposal as put forward by Stephen John, and the Democratic Values proposal as put forward by Andrew Schroeder.[2] We show how each proposal involves different trade-offs, and draw out the implications of these trade-offs for the question of what makes science trustworthy.

First, a note about what we mean by "trustworthy." The meaning we have in mind is a deflationary one, what many philosophers would call (mere) reliance. When we ask whether the public should trust science, we only mean to ask whether the public should accept scientific claims as true, or as bases for action. This is a much weaker sense of trust than is common in the contemporary philosophical literature, where analyses of trust often include additional conditions. It is common, for example, to hold that warranted trust requires that the trustor have expectations about the trustee's motives, such as that they include good will toward the trustor (cf. Almassi 2012; Baier 1986; Irzik and Kurtulmus *Forthcoming*). We work from a deflationary account because it is our sense that informal, non-philosophical discussions of trust in science often have this account in mind, and also because the two main philosophers with whom we engage employ deflationary accounts (John 2015, 2017; Schroeder *Forthcoming-a*).

5.2 Trusting Science in the Face of Inductive Risk

5.2.1 *The Value-Free Ideal and the Argument from Inductive Risk*

To understand the appeal of the IFI, it helps to look first to a more familiar ground for the trustworthiness of science. According to the value-free ideal (VFI) for science, science is trustworthy because it deals only in facts, and not values. More specifically, the VFI holds that for science to be trustworthy, non-epistemic values—social, political, and other values that do not "promote the attainment of truth" (Steel 2010, 17)—should not influence justificatory reasoning concerning the truth or falsity of scientific claims (Elliott 2011, 304). The thought is that excluding such values secures a kind of objectivity for science, which is a mark of trustworthiness.[3] VFI proponents readily admit that non-epistemic values can and should influence non-justificatory reasoning, for example, reasoning about which research program to pursue, or about what to do with our scientific knowledge once we've discovered it. They are also clear that the VFI is an ideal. Scientists are human, and so it may not be possible to entirely cleanse scientific reasoning of the influence of non-epistemic values. But the idea behind the VFI is that, the closer science can get to eliminating the influence of non-epistemic values in justificatory reasoning, the more trustworthy it will be.

The VFI has been vigorously challenged. Some have argued that it is impossible to draw sufficiently robust boundaries between epistemic and non-epistemic values (Douglas 2000, 560; Rooney 1992, 18). Others, particularly feminist scholars, have questioned the assumption implicit in the VFI that facts and values are in opposition to each other (Anderson 1995), and even the viability of the fact/value distinction itself (Nelson 1990). Here, we focus on a particular challenge to the VFI known as the argument from inductive risk.

First formally articulated by Richard Rudner (1953) and C. West Churchman (1956), the argument from inductive risk starts from the fact (which follows from the nature of inductive reasoning) that evidence never deductively entails the truth of a hypothesis. Because of this, scientists face a trade-off between two types of risk whenever they decide whether to accept or reject a hypothesis: if they require more certainty before accepting a hypothesis, they increase their risk of failing to accept a true hypothesis (known as a "false negative"); if they require less certainty, they increase their risk of accepting a false hypothesis (known as a "false positive").[4] Crucially, the trade-off between these "inductive risks" is extra-evidentiary: empirical evidence cannot tell you how certain you should be before accepting a hypothesis based on a body of evidence. In Wilholt's (2013, 252) words, the decision of how to balance these inductive risks is "underdetermined by the aim of truth" and therefore must be made by appeal to non-evidentiary factors. In particular, inductive risk theorists argue, it should be made by appeal to the relative importance of avoiding false positives versus avoiding false negatives on some issue, which requires a (non-epistemic) value judgment. Thus, even in the ideal, justificatory scientific reasoning by its very nature cannot be value-free, and the VFI must be rejected.

5.2.2 *The Idiosyncrasy-Free Ideal as an Alternative Ground for Trust*

Science's freedom from non-epistemic values has served as a traditional foundation for its trustworthiness. However, if the argument from inductive risk holds, non-epistemic values are essential to scientific reasoning. Does it thus follow that science, even in the ideal, is not trustworthy? Unsurprisingly, this is not the conclusion that most proponents of the argument from inductive risk endorse. Instead, most contend that the argument only shows that value-freedom can't be the right foundation for trust in science. Some inductive risk theorists have proposed alternative foundations for trust. For example, Douglas (2009) endorses a "value-laden ideal" that grounds trust not on the *type* of values (i.e. epistemic vs. non-epistemic values), but on the *kind of role* that values play in science.

In this chapter, we examine a different alternative to the VFI, one that connects trustworthiness not to the influence of *values*, but rather to the influence of *idiosyncrasy*, that is, of factors (values-based or otherwise) that can vary from scientist to scientist. Boulicault (unpublished manuscript) calls this the *idiosyncrasy-free ideal (IFI):*

> **IFI:** In the ideal, justificatory scientific decisions are made in a way free of idiosyncrasy, i.e. free from the influence of particular features of individual scientists.

The IFI can be traced back at least to Isaac Levi (1960). Levi (1960, 356) argued that, even if scientists depend on non-epistemic values in their justificatory reasoning, science remains trustworthy so long as any two scientists, when presented with the same evidence, would make the same decisions, that is, that "two different investigators [given the same evidence] would not be warranted in making different choices among a set of competing hypotheses". For Levi, the key to trust in science is therefore not freedom from values, but freedom from idiosyncrasy. Trust in science "does not depend upon whether minimum probabilities for accepting or rejecting hypotheses are a function of values, but upon whether *the canons of inference require of each scientist that he assign the same minima as every other scientist*" (Levi 1960, 356, emphasis added).

More recently, Torsten Wilholt (2013) has provided one of the more detailed accounts of the IFI in the inductive risk literature. Like Levi, Wilholt argues that when faced with inductive risk, what is important is that all scientists balance those risks in the same way. He suggests that the best way to achieve uniformity is through shared methodological conventions—conventions like "only accept a hypothesis with a p value of at least 0.05." If all scientists adhere to the same methodological conventions, then any scientist faced with the same evidence, regardless of her idiosyncrasies, will make the same decisions and reach the same conclusions. On Wilholt's view, trustworthy science is non-idiosyncratic science.

Why think that the IFI provides a good foundation for trust? Why think that idiosyncrasy-free science is (all else being equal) science worth trusting? One reason is that the IFI helps address a major concern voiced by the public when questioning the trustworthiness of scientific research: the concern that scientists might manipulate their results to justify their preferred conclusions. Medical researchers have been accused of producing results friendly to the pharmaceutical industry (Bhattacharya 2003; Fugh-Berman 2013). Oreskes and Conway (2010) describe how the tobacco and oil industries have mounted a concerted effort to present scientific conclusions in ways that promote their bottom lines. Economists regularly accuse one another of allowing political views to dictate their economic conclusions (Jelveh, Kogut, and Naidu 2018; Thoma 2016). And the heart of the so-called "Climategate" scandal was the claim that climate scientists were manipulating their results in the service of a left-wing agenda ("Closing the Climategate" 2010).

The IFI can't guarantee that social or political views never influence scientists' conclusions. (To let go of the VFI is to acknowledge that values can legitimately play a role in scientific reasoning.) But it can guarantee that (at least in the ideal) particular scientists can't manipulate results in ways that are favorable to their preferred values. The IFI means that scientists on both sides of an issue—those paid by tobacco companies and those aiming to protect public health; those who attend left-wing political rallies and those at home in politically conservative communities—have to play by the same rules.

Wilholt (2013) also offers arguments in favor of the IFI as a ground for trust between scientists. Adherence to the IFI increases the ease and efficiency with which scientists can understand and assess each other's claims, thereby facilitating trust. If each scientist managed inductive risk in her own idiosyncratic way, then scientists would face coordination problems in deciding whether and how to rely on other scientists' conclusions. They would have to engage in arduous examination of other scientists' methodologies to determine how that particular scientist balanced inductive risk. Inductive risk decisions would be "extremely cumbersome to track and take account of by peers. Not only can value judgments vary considerably from individual to individual, it is also usually difficult to guess another person's value judgments on a given subject matter" (Wilholt 2016, 230–1). Although Wilholt's argument focuses on the case of trust between scientists, it could be extended to the case of public trust. While it might be "extremely cumbersome" for a scientist to determine how another scientist balanced inductive risks, that task could be nearly impossible for a lay person (Scheman 2011). The IFI guarantees a uniformity that can assist the public in understanding scientific results, thereby providing a foundation for trust in those results.

Another reason why the IFI might seem an appropriate foundation for trust is the fact that science is an increasingly social and collaborative endeavor. Wilholt (2016) notes, for instance, that an article on one of the particle detectors of the Large Hadron Collider lists 2,926 authors, and that in the United States, the average number of authors per paper in the medical sciences increased from 3.7 to 6.0 between 1990 and 2010.[5] In collaborative research, trust in the group doesn't simply supervene on trust in individuals, and so we need an account of trustworthiness that is group-based. Given that scientific communities are "constituted by shared methodological standards" (Wilholt 2016, 222), it seems plausible that adherence to methodological standards should play an important role in an account of the trustworthiness of science.

5.3 Implementing the IFI

5.3.1 *Wilholt's Framework*

We have suggested, then, that the IFI plausibly provides a foundation for public trust in science, and Wilholt suggests that idiosyncrasy can be avoided through shared conventions for managing inductive risk (i.e. for determining the degree of certainty necessary for accepting a hypothesis). But what, specifically, should those conventions be? Might some conventions for managing inductive risk provide better foundations for trust than others?

At some points Wilholt seems to suggest that the answer to this question is "no." All that matters is that scientists adhere to *some* conventions for managing inductive risk; the content of those conventions is not especially important:

> [W]ith regard to the aim of facilitating reliable assessments of the trustworthiness of other researchers' results, it is crucial that everyone within the community sticks to the same standards and thus the same limitations on DIR [distribution of inductive risks], *but not which particular DIR it is that is set as an ideal*. (Wilholt 2016, 231, emphasis added)

He goes on to suggest, however, that the content of the conventions does matter, saying that they should be grounded in value judgments concerning the relative importance of false positives versus false negatives:

> [The conventions] also represent the research community's collective attempt to find the right balance between power and the two types of reliability. In that sense, they also represent an implicit consensus (or at least an implicit compromise position) of the community with regard to the question of how valuable the benefits of correct results and how grave the negative consequences of mistakes typically are for the kinds of research procedures that are subject to the standards at issue. (Wilholt 2016, 231–2; cf. 2013, 248)

Ultimately, we think the best interpretation of Wilholt's view is as follows: it is important that conventions lie within a certain range of acceptability, but that within that range, the details of the convention aren't especially important. Yet Wilholt doesn't say very much about how to determine that range of acceptability. Two recent articles, however, do offer more detailed proposals for how such conventions could be set: Stephen John's *High Epistemic Standards* approach, and Andrew Schroeder's *Democratic Values* approach. In the remainder of this chapter we will consider each of these proposals, highlighting their implications for the question of public trust in science.

5.3.2 *High Epistemic Standards*

The lesson of the argument from inductive risk is that evidence does not determine how confident a scientist should be in a hypothesis (60%? 95%?) before accepting it. In other words, it does not determine a standard for balancing the inductive risk of accepting a false hypothesis or rejecting a true one. What, then, should the standard be? According to some—for example, Rudner (1953) and Douglas (2009)—we should reject fixed standards and instead adopt "floating standards": different scientists may use different standards for balancing inductive risk based on the perceived importance of false positives versus false negatives.

While this floating standards approach has its appeal, it creates a problem for the public trustworthiness of science. If a scientist uses floating standards, I may have legitimate reasons to distrust her conclusions even if I regard her as more knowledgeable than me about the domain at issue. For example, suppose a scientist reports that a particular insecticide depletes wild bee populations. On the floating standards approach, to know whether I should accept the scientist's claim, I need to know her standards—I need to know how she balances inductive risks. If she is relatively tolerant of false positives (perhaps because she believes the collapse of wild bee populations would be catastrophic), then she might endorse that claim upon being 90 percent convinced it is true. But suppose I am much more worried about false positives (perhaps because I believe that the loss of wild bees would not be so serious, while the lower agricultural yield caused by a failure to use effective insecticides would be devastating). I might think that we should require near-certainty before accepting that an effective insecticide depletes wild bee populations. Thus, it may be rational for me to distrust the scientist's conclusions (even while acknowledging her expertise in the domain).

How might this problem be addressed?[6] John (2015, 2017), echoing Levi and Wilholt, begins by arguing that a critical step to preserving trust in the face of inductive risk is for scientists to reject floating standards in favor of fixed ones, at least when publicly communicating scientific claims. John, therefore, endorses the IFI. His arguments are based primarily on pragmatic considerations concerning communication between scientists and the public. Because there are typically multiple audiences who hold a variety of different epistemic standards and whose identities are *ex ante* unknown to scientists, it is impossible for scientists to tailor their inductive risk decisions so as to keep their value choices in line with all possible users of the scientific knowledge produced (2015, 85). Further, it would take a great deal of time, energy, and expertise for members of the public to dig into the details of scientific reports to determine what particular standards and values the scientists used. Thus, scientific results can be readily interpretable to the public only if they are based on fixed standards (2015, 87–89).

Interpretability, however, is not sufficient for trust. To ground public trust, John argues that those fixed standards must be high—reporting claims only when they are supported by very strong evidence. Only high epistemic standards guarantee (without the need for arduous investigation) that an individual can trust that a particular result meets her own epistemic standards. If I know that scientists demand higher certainty than I would to accept a claim, then whenever scientists report a claim as true, I can safely accept it as well. Thus, fixed, high epistemic standards ground trust by ensuring that scientists' claims are likely to meet most, and ideally all, people's demands for certainty (2015, 88; 2017, 167). On John's proposal, trustworthiness is secured when scientific standards play the role of a very fine sieve, ensuring that only claims that meet nearly everyone's standards are communicated to the public.

5.3.3 *Democratic Values*

Schroeder (*Forthcoming-a*) considers a broader problem than inductive risk: public trust in value-laden science more generally. In addition to managing inductive risk, scientists must make value-laden determinations at other stages of the research process. There doesn't seem to be any value-free way, for example, of creating a comprehensive measure of population health (Murray and Schroeder 2020), or of creating a classification system for instances of violence against women (Merry 2016). For roughly the same pragmatic reasons as John, Schroeder believes that it is important for the trustworthiness of science that the standards used in making these decisions be set in a way that will allow the public to quickly and easily assess their practical relevance. He, like John, argues that this can best be accomplished by taking these decisions out of the hands of individual scientists—as the IFI suggests.

But, also echoing John, Schroeder thinks this isn't enough. Even if all scientists are using the same standards, if the values that lie behind those standards have nothing to do with my values, there is no clear reason for me to trust scientific results based on those standards.

Schroeder's solution to this problem is where he diverges from John. Members of the public often have different values from one another, and so scientists can't choose standards that reflect everyone's values. We are thus faced with a situation where scientists must base their work on values that will reflect the values of some members of the public, while failing to reflect the values of others. In a democracy, when situations arise where important public decisions must be made in a way that reflects some citizens' concerns but not others, we typically (or at least ideally) invoke democratic procedures. Schroeder therefore argues that when scientists must make value-laden decisions in the course of their work, they should typically base their primary conclusions on democratic values—values arrived at through procedures that yield a kind of political legitimacy. Schroeder's hope is that even though democratic procedures may yield values that conflict with my own (I may, essentially, get outvoted in my attitudes toward inductive risk or other value choices), I can nevertheless accept scientific results grounded in those values as a basis for certain kinds of actions, if the appropriate democratic procedures were carried out properly.[7]

Take, for example, John's case of insecticides and bee populations. Imagine that I am personally not very worried about the loss of wild bee populations, and accordingly would prefer acting to reduce insecticide use only if the evidence it harmed bees were near certain. If, however, scientists employ epistemic standards arrived at democratically, I might nevertheless accept their claim that insecticides deplete wild bee populations as a basis for my own decision-making about, for example, whether to protest others' use of insecticides, to support policies that permit or ban insecticides, or perhaps even to use insecticides myself. Even if I don't know the precise standards the scientists employed (because I haven't read or couldn't understand the scientific report), the knowledge that those standards were reached through a fair, politically legitimate process may make it reasonable for me to accept the claims that flow from them as a basis for decision-making.

5.3.4 *High Epistemic Standards, Democratic Values, and the IFI*

John and Schroeder offer different proposals for grounding public trust in the conclusions of value-laden science. Each proposal satisfies the IFI, but in different ways. That is, each proposal takes discretion away from individual scientists by telling them how to handle inductive risk choices (for John's proposal) or value choices more generally (for Schroeder's proposal). Thus, each seeks to prevent the idiosyncrasies of an individual scientist from affecting her results.

John's and Schroeder's proposals diverge, though, when it comes to eliminating other forms of idiosyncrasy. In rejecting "floating standards," John isn't only worried about variation between scientists; he is also worried about variation between cases, topics, or political contexts. John's proposal directs all scientists studying the potentially damaging effects of insecticides on bee populations to use the same (high) standards as scientists studying the potentially damaging effects of herbicides on frog populations, and the same (high) standards as scientists studying bee populations in other countries, or at other times. On Schroeder's proposal, however, epistemic standards could vary between the cases, if democratic procedures show that the public has different attitudes toward protecting bee versus frog populations. And they could also vary from political context to political context, if the members of one political community have different values than the members of another political community. John's view therefore prevents the particular features of individual topics, areas of study, or political contexts from impacting the way scientists handle inductive risk, while Schroeder's doesn't. It is thus possible to interpret the High Epistemic Standards approach as not simply a different *implementation* of the IFI, but as embodying a different and more robust *interpretation* of the IFI: on the Democratic Values approach, the term "idiosyncrasy" refers only to those features that vary between scientists, whereas on the High Epistemic Standards approach, it refers to many additional sources of variation.

This difference, we believe, is useful in framing the strengths and weaknesses of each proposal. As John (2015) acknowledges, the most serious objection to his view is that:

> [L]imiting scientists' public assertions only to claims which meet high epistemic standards may leave them unable (properly) to say very much at all ... [S]cientists may often be in a position where they are the only people aware that certain claims, although not well-enough established to warrant "public" assertion, are well-enough established to warrant action by others in the community. Remaining silent in such cases may seem an unacceptable abrogation of moral duty... (89)

It is uncontroversial that we should sometimes act on the basis of claims about which we are far from certain. Learning that some substance is 70 percent likely to be a serious carcinogen is plenty of reason to avoid it. Learning that some climate policy is 85 percent likely to leave many major cities under water is, for most of us, sufficient reason to reject it. Under the High Epistemic Standards proposal, it would be inappropriate for scientists to publicly report such claims, even if the public overwhelmingly would view the information as decision-relevant. This is obviously problematic.

John thinks that his proposal may be able to get around this problem. He suggests that scientists could report less-than-certain, decision-relevant results in private or "unofficial" settings. In this way, the public would be informed, without compromising the high epistemic standards of publicly or officially communicated science. He admits, however, that creating venues for such unofficial communication is "likely to be both practically and morally complex" (John 2015, 90), in part because policy-makers and the public may be liable to confuse (or be confused by) scientists' "official" and "unofficial" statements, in cases where they diverge. We agree, and so we take this to be a serious concern for John's proposal.[8]

In contrast, Schroeder's proposal doesn't have this problem, since it allows standards to float from case to case or context to context (though not from scientist to scientist). When it comes to dangerous carcinogens and the destruction of cities, the public will presumably want to act on probable but somewhat uncertain claims, and so the Democratic Values proposal will permit scientists to report claims that are far from certain. But on matters of low importance, such as the extent to which drinking green tea stains tooth enamel, or on matters of no obvious immediate practical relevance, such as the discovery of an additional moon orbiting Jupiter, it seems likely that (for reasons similar to those given by John) the public will want scientists to adopt much higher epistemic standards.

At the same time, these differing standards also yield some of the most serious problems for Schroeder's view, as they place significant burdens on both scientists and the public. First, any worked-out version of the Democratic Values view will have to answer broad conceptual questions such as: what is the relevant public whose values ought to be democratically assessed on some particular issue? Given the cross-national and international significance of much scientific research, this is a difficult question to answer. Once an appropriate public has been determined, scientists (or others working on their behalf) must then actually determine the values of this public. Schroeder offers some suggestions for how this might be done, including the use of deliberative polling and citizen science programs. But his suggestions are (as he admits) speculative, and implementing them will be challenging, resource-intensive endeavors.[9]

The public will also face challenges when it seeks to interpret scientific conclusions grounded in democratic values. If scientists report, for example, that an insecticide depletes bee populations, a member of the public can trust that that claim has been established to the level of certainty demanded by the public. But if she wants to know precisely what that level of certainty is—because, perhaps, she herself holds unusually high or low standards—she will have to dig into the details of the study. Wilholt, John, and Schroeder all agree that this is no simple task, and in many cases the complexity of scientific research may make it close to impossible for most non-experts.[10]

5.3.5 *Different Visions of Science*

Which proposal—John's or Schroeder's—provides the better foundation for public trust in science? To answer this question, it helps to see each proposal as motivated by a different vision of science. According to one vision, the goal of science is the accumulation of a store of highly certain facts about the world, that is, a store of truths (or as close as we can get to truths) that we can all rely on with confidence in deciding what to believe and how to act. John's approach is in line with this vision: when scientists employ high epistemic standards, what results is a uniform body of highly certain and thus dependable claims; claims that can be imported and easily applied to different contexts. Schroeder's view doesn't line up so neatly with this vision. His view calls for scientific claims to be tailored to the specific value-laden context in which the claims are produced and communicated. Thus, rather than a uniform body of highly certain claims, Schroeder's approach results in a conglomeration or mixture of claims, each of which is based on context-dependent values.

A second vision of science sees its goal as more to do with action than with fact accumulation. On this view, the goal of science is to improve our lives and to facilitate our interactions with the world around us. Here, the situation is reversed. As we saw earlier, when scientists employing high epistemic standards fail to report a conclusion, it would be inappropriate to conclude that action is not called for. (Knowing that a substance is 70 percent likely to be a serious carcinogen is plenty of reason to avoid it.) If, though, one accepts the legitimacy of democratic processes, then scientific conclusions grounded in democratic values are arguably ones that we as a public ought to act on. The Democratic Values approach could therefore be interpreted as prioritizing an action-oriented view of science.

Each of the proposals seems to align with a different—and appealing—vision of science. Rather than choosing between the Democratic Values and High Epistemic Standards approaches, therefore, in the final section of the paper we show how they might be combined in a way that builds on the strengths of each.

5.4 A Hybrid Approach

5.4.1 *Our Proposal*

We think an attractive implementation of the IFI can be arrived at through a context-dependent trade-off between the more flexible but more resource-intensive Democratic Values approach, and the pragmatically simpler High Epistemic Standards approach. While we don't have the space to work out the details here, we will sketch such a proposal.

First, consider scientific research that has little predictable practical significance. Examples might include the potential discovery of a new moon orbiting Jupiter, or a finding that a particular exercise regimen is marginally more efficient at facilitating weight loss. In such cases, the main drawback of the High Epistemic Standards approach isn't present, since there isn't any serious cost in scientists failing to report a result that is probable but far from certain. Further, in such cases the benefits of the Democratic Values approach aren't especially significant, and so arguably don't justify the resources required to implement it. Overall, then, in cases involving research whose predictable practical significance is relatively small, it seems pragmatically appropriate to omit the intensive public deliberation and input required by the Democratic Values approach in favor of the relative simplicity and transparency of the high epistemic standards approach.

Contrast that with cases where research has clear practical importance—for example, research involving potentially lethal toxins or catastrophic weather events. In such cases less-than-certain information can nevertheless be highly actionable. These are precisely the cases where the High Epistemic Standards approach faces its most serious objections, and where the public input called for by the Democratic Values approach is most critical. For scientists' claims on a matter of great public importance to be trustworthy to the public, it would seem reasonable for the public to insist on having input into the level of certainty the scientists employed. Thus, in such cases, it seems that trustworthiness requires sacrificing the simplicity of the High Epistemic Standards approach for the more complicated but democratically grounded and action-oriented Democratic Values approach, since what the public ultimately cares about in these cases are the consequences of knowledge—for example, protection from toxins or extreme weather events.[11]

We think, then, that in cases where research has little to no practical significance, scientists can best ground public trust through the simplicity, transparency, and uniformity assured by only reporting highly certain claims; while in cases where research has great practical significance, they can best ground public trust by deferring to the public to set the levels of certainty their research must meet. What remain, then, are the cases in the middle: cases where there is either widespread agreement that some research has moderately important consequences (e.g. a finding that drinking coffee modestly increases lifetime cancer risk), or disagreement about the practical significance of research (e.g. findings about the precise stage of development where a human fetus can feel pain, or about the likelihood that a development project will lead to the extinction of an endangered lizard species). These cases, we think, pose problems for both John's and Schroeder's proposals.

To address these middle cases, we tentatively propose using a modified version of Wilholt's conventionalism. Recall that Wilholt argues that it is critical that all scientists manage inductive risk in the same way, but that within a certain range of acceptability, it doesn't especially matter what specific standards they use. We propose that within the middle ground we have identified, it is less important whether scientists employ high epistemic standards or democratic values; it is more important that all scientists approach the research in the same way. Scientists collectively need a relatively clear way of distinguishing research questions that should be governed by high epistemic standards from research questions that should be governed by democratic values. But, as long as that standard calls for research of clear high practical importance to be governed by democratic values and research of clear low practical importance to be governed by high epistemic standards, it is much less important how or where it draws the line between the two types of research.[12]

5.4.2 *Possible Objections*

Though we think our proposed hybrid approach is promising as a foundation for public trust in science, it faces challenges. We will briefly comment on two. The first challenge questions whether our hybrid approach can really claim to combine the best aspects of each view—in particular, whether it can capture the advantages of the High Epistemic Standards approach. John argues that it is important for scientists' standards to be fixed, including across cases. It isn't enough for scientists to *sometimes* use high epistemic standards; in order to ensure that scientific results can be readily interpretable by the public, John thinks it critical that scientists *uniformly* employ high epistemic standards. Our hybrid approach allows for the use of lower standards in certain cases. Doesn't it therefore forfeit core benefits of the High Epistemic Standards approach?

We agree there is a tension here, but think the tension is not as serious as it appears. We presume that John would at least allow epistemic standards to vary by scientific field. High-energy physics, for example, typically uses an incredibly stringent five-sigma standard–accepting a chance of error of less than one in three million—when assessing new discoveries (Staley 2017), and it seems to serve them well. It would be virtually impossible, though, to make any discoveries in behavioral psychology that meet that standard. Rather than telling physicists to employ lower standards or telling psychologists they're out of a job, we presume John would permit standards to vary by discipline, since some hypotheses can be explored (and therefore proven) to a much higher degree of certainty than others. To retain the benefits of his High Epistemic Standards approach, therefore, John will need some way to clearly distinguish and flag research employing the extremely high standards characteristic of high-energy physics from research employing standards more appropriate to behavioral psychology. A hybrid approach like ours could use a similar mechanism to clearly mark off research governed by high epistemic standards from research governed by democratic values. That, we believe, could preserve the benefits of the high epistemic standards approach for research governed by those high standards.

A second challenge to our approach questions the practicality of creating a convention of the sort we propose above, in a way that truly avoids idiosyncrasy. Central to the appeal of IFI-based approaches is that they take value judgments out of the hands of individual scientists, grounding trust by ensuring that the justification of scientific claims is independent of individual idiosyncrasies. Our hybrid approach upholds this ideal regarding decisions about inductive risk, but introduces the need for a new kind of decision: decisions about the practical significance of scientific research. We have argued that research of high practical importance should be governed by democratic values, while research of low practical importance should be governed by high epistemic standards. That means, though, that someone must decide, for any given research question, into which category it falls.

We have already suggested conventionalism as a solution here. But can conventions be established in a way that avoids the sort of idiosyncratic judgment the IFI warns against? Our experience with certain aspects of Institutional Review Boards (IRBs) leads us to believe that this can be done reasonably well. In the United States, IRBs are responsible for ensuring that scientific research meets ethical standards concerning the protection of human research subjects. Most IRBs begin their evaluation process by classifying research into one of three categories: research exempt from review; research subject to expedited review; and research requiring a full review. Although the federal regulations governing this classification are complex, our experience has been that in a large majority of cases there is no disagreement about the proper classification for any particular study.[13] We are therefore hopeful that, in a similar fashion, criteria could be devised that would demarcate research to be governed by high epistemic standards from research to be governed by democratic values. Of course, no criteria of this sort will be perfectly clear. There will be cases in which it is ambiguous which standard should apply to a given research question. But, keeping in mind that the IFI is an ideal rather than a strict requirement, we don't regard that as a serious objection to our proposal. IRB regulations go a long way toward reducing idiosyncrasies in the classification of research as exempt from review, subject to expedited review, or subject to full review. If criteria could be drawn up that did an equally good job of assigning research to high epistemic standards versus to democratic values, we would regard that as a reasonable implementation of the IFI.

5.5 Concluding Thoughts

The driving question of this paper is not a new one. Nor is it specific to science.[14] But questions of trust have a particular character and salience in the context of modern Western science for two reasons. First, science is often portrayed as the ultimate paragon of trustworthiness (Fabiola 2018), to the extent that people who don't trust science are commonly deemed irrational. Second, science is a domain where trust is unavoidable, since the extreme complexity and technical nature of much of modern science means that most non-scientists are unable to directly evaluate scientific evidence (Scheman 2011). No wonder then, that perceived threats to the trustworthiness of science—corporate influences on science (Oreskes and Conway 2010), "p-hacking" controversies, cases of scientific racism (Carroll 2017; Stein 2015), and accusations of liberal biases in science (Inbar and Lammers 2012)—are so unsettling.

With the growing consensus among philosophers of science that the VFI must be rejected, and worries about a "crisis of trust" between scientists and the public (Czerski 2017), there is an urgent need to understand what grounds or could ground public trust in science. In this chapter, we have considered one general solution to this problem—the IFI—which grounds trust in freedom from the idiosyncrasies of individual scientists. Though that general approach has an important history (Boulicault unpublished manuscript) and has been discussed and critiqued (Scheman 2011), we don't think it has received the kind of detailed consideration it deserves, particularly in the inductive risk literature. As the significant differences between John's and Schroeder's proposals show, there is more than one way to implement the IFI. We have proposed and briefly explored a third option, combining John's and Schroeder's proposals. We hope that future work will explore other ways of making science idiosyncrasy-free, with the aim of both shedding further light on the IFI as an ideal for science, and on the question of what makes science trustworthy.

Notes

1. The authors are listed alphabetically and were equal contributors to the paper. We would like to thank the volume editors, Kevin Vallier and Michael Weber, as well as Kevin Elliott, Sally Haslanger, Stephen John, Milo Phillips-Brown, and Kieran Setiya for their insightful comments on earlier drafts of the paper. We would also like to thank Capri D'Souza for her help in preparing the manuscript for final submission.

2. When referring to the co-authors of this chapter individually, we will, awkwardly, use the third person, as we see no better alternative.
3. Though we believe this generally characterizes what a range of scholars have in mind, it is important to note that these concepts are used in a variety of ways in the literature. "Value" is not always clearly or consistently defined, for example, and there are a number of competing conceptions of scientific objectivity (Reiss and Sprenger 2014). See Douglas (2004), Koskinen (2018), Elliott and Resnik (2014), Schroeder (*Forthcoming-a*), Anderson (1995) and Longino (1990) for discussions of the connections between trust, values, and objectivity.
4. Technically, the choice is more complicated, involving at minimum a third option of neither accepting nor rejecting the hypothesis, and thus the choice actually involves a trade-off between three factors: the reliability of positive results, the reliability of negative results, and the method's power (which is the "the rate at which a method or type of inquiry generates definitive results, given a certain amount of effort and resources") (Wilholt 2016, 227). For the purposes of this paper, however, all that matters is that an extra-evidentiary trade-off of some kind must be made, and thus we stick to the more simplified formulation of accept versus reject.
5. Some might take Wilholt's point further and argue that science is necessarily social and collaborative. Consider, for instance, that modern science is partly premised on the notion of replicability, which in principle requires the participation of more than one scientist. As Helen Longino (1994, 143) would put it, a "Robinson Crusoe" scientist simply isn't possible given the nature of the scientific method. Scientific knowledge is, Longino argues, inherently social knowledge.
6. Transparency might appear to provide an easy solution: rather than reporting simply that the insecticide depletes bee populations, scientists could report that *given a particular balance of inductive risks*, they have concluded that the insecticide depletes bee populations. Or, relatedly, they could hedge their assertions, saying only that they are 90 percent confident that the insecticide depletes bee populations. Proposals like these have been discussed extensively in the literature. See Jeffrey (1956) and Betz (2013) for canonical defenses of this sort of approach, and McKaughan and Elliott (2018) for a more moderate proposal. For a variety of reasons, we don't think transparency solves the problem of public trust in value-laden science, and the main authors we will discuss agree (John 2018; Schroeder *Forthcoming-a*). Accordingly, we will for the remainder of the paper assume that transparency isn't, by itself, an adequate solution to challenges posed by inductive risk.
7. The precise form of these procedures is a complicated matter, requiring careful work in political philosophy. As Schroeder (*Forthcoming-a*, *Forthcoming-b*) notes, however, there is no reason to think these procedures will always or even usually be simple majoritarian ones.
8. We believe a second concern with John's proposal, which he does not discuss, is that it can't easily be applied to many other cases in which science is arguably value-laden. Unlike attitudes toward inductive risk, there is no clear way to order many other decision factors on a scale from more to less epistemically conservative. If, as Schroeder and many others have argued, the value choices that need to be made by scientists go beyond inductive risk, and if these value choices also raise issues connected to public trust, then John's proposal will need to be supplemented by another account to handle those choices. Schroeder's proposal, on the other hand, can be extended to all value choices. We set aside this concern in the paper, though, and accordingly will focus only on cases of inductive risk.

9. For some of the challenges involved in bringing public deliberation into scientific research, see OpenUpSci (2019) and Sample et al. (2019). It is worth noting, though, that the many of the challenges facing the Democratic Values view are no more (and no less) serious than those facing any democratic approach to public decision-making. Thus, in a sense, the success of the Democratic Values proposal hinges on the success of democracy-based approaches to decision-making more generally. Putting this point in the language of trust, the Democratic Values view underwrites trust only to the extent that democratic processes more generally underwrite trust.
10. One way of putting a key difference between John's and Schroeder's views is that they make different kinds of information accessible to the public. On the High Epistemic Standards approach, the public can quickly ascertain the specific standard used, but it would be very hard for them to know how that standard compares to the public's values. On the Democratic Values approach, the public can quickly ascertain the relationship between the standard employed and the public's values, but it would be much harder for them to know the specific standard used.
11. It also seems likely that in many such cases, some of the more serious objections to the Democratic Values approach lose some of their force. There is presumably less need, for example, to conduct a resource-intensive focus group to determine whether the public wants to know about substances 70 percent likely to be lethal toxins, and it is more probable that different publics are likely to reach similar conclusions on such issues.
12. In saying that it is much less important where the line is drawn, we don't mean to suggest that all ways of drawing the line are valid. Distinctions could easily be made, for example, in a sexist or racist way—a real concern, given the long history of sexist and racist research practices—which would obviously be unacceptable. This points to the importance of thinking carefully how such a convention is created. For example, a convention created with the input of a wide range of voices, including voices traditionally marginalized within science, is far more likely to be a just one (see e.g. Longino 1990).
13. For the regulations, see 45 CFR 46 (2016). Many IRBs produce clearer and somewhat simplified versions to facilitate their own work—for example, see University of Southern California (n.d.). To be clear, we are not endorsing all aspects of the IRB process. We focus solely on the initial determination concerning the appropriate level of review, and the extent to which existing guidelines ensure that the decision is made in a non-idiosyncratic way.
14. Questions of trust can be posed in any instance of epistemic dependence, that is, any circumstance in which there is knowledge exchange between individuals or groups. For instance, one might wonder what makes the court system worthy of public trust, or why we should trust the claims of journalists.

References

45 CFR 46 of October 1, 2016, Protection of Human Subjects." Code of Federal Regulations, annual edition (2016): 128–48. https://www.govinfo.gov/content/pkg/CFR-2016-title45-vol1/pdf/CFR-2016-title45-vol1-part46.pdf.

Almassi, Ben. 2012. "Climate Change, Epistemic Trust, and Expert Trustworthiness." *Ethics and the Environment* 17: 29–49.

Anderson, Elizabeth. 1995. "Knowledge, Human Interests, and Objectivity in Feminist Epistemology." *Philosophical Topics* 23 (2): 27–58.

Baier, Annette. 1986. "Trust and Antitrust." *Ethics* 96 (2): 231–60.

Betz, Gregor. 2013. "In defence of the value-free ideal." *European Journal for Philosophy of Science* 3: 207–20.

Bhattacharya, Shaoni. 2003. "Research Funded by Drug Companies Is 'Biased.'" New Scientist. May 30, 2003. https://www.newscientist.com/article/dn3781-research-funded-by-drug-companies-is-biased/.

Boulicault, Marion. Unpublished manuscript. "A Tale of Two Ideals: Values and Idiosyncrasy in Science."

———. 2014. "Science, Values and the Argument from Inductive Risk: In Favour of a Social Alternative to the Value-Free Ideal." M.Phil. Dissertation. Cambridge, UK: University of Cambridge.

Carroll, Aaron E. 2017. "Did Infamous Tuskegee Study Cause Lasting Mistrust of Doctors Among Blacks?" *The New York Times*, December 21, 2017, sec. The Upshot. https://www.nytimes.com/2016/06/18/upshot/long-term-mistrust-from-tuskegee-experiment-a-study-seems-to-overstate-the-case.html.

Churchman, C. West. 1956. "Science and Decision Making." *Philosophy of Science* 23 (3): 247–49.

"Closing the Climategate." 2010. *Nature*, 468 (7322): 345–345. https://doi.org/10.1038/468345a.

Czerski, Helen. 2017. "A Crisis of Trust Is Looming between Scientists and Society—It's Time to Talk." *The Guardian, January* 27, 2017, sec. Science. https://www.theguardian.com/science/blog/2017/jan/27/a-crisis-of-trust-is-looming-between-scientists-and-society-its-time-to-talk.

Douglas, Heather. 2000. "Inductive Risk and Values in Science." *Philosophy of Science* 67 (4): 559–79.

———. 2004. "The Irreducible Complexity of Objectivity." *Synthese* 138 (3): 453–73.

———. 2009. *Science, Policy, and the Value-Free Ideal.* Pittsburgh, PA: University of Pittsburgh Press.

Elliott, Kevin. 2011. "Direct and Indirect Roles for Values in Science." *Philosophy of Science* 78 (2): 303–24.

Elliott, Kevin and David Resnik. 2014. "Science, Policy, and the Transparency of Values." *Environmental Health Perspectives* 122: 647–50.

Fabiola, Gianotti. 2018. "Science Is Universal and Unifying." World Economic Forum. January 18, 2018. https://www.weforum.org/agenda/2018/01/science-is-universal-and-unifying/.

Fugh-Berman, Adriane. 2013. "How Basic Scientists Help the Pharmaceutical Industry Market Drugs." *PLOS Biology* 11 (11): e1001716. https://doi.org/10.1371/journal.pbio.1001716.

Inbar, Yoel and Joris Lammers. 2012. "Political Diversity in Social and Personality Psychology." SSRN Scholarly Paper ID 2002636. Rochester, NY: Social Science Research Network. https://papers.ssrn.com/abstract=2002636.

Irzik, Gürol and Faik Kurtulmus. *Forthcoming*. "What is Epistemic Public Trust in Science?" *British Journal for Philosophy of Science*, https://doi-org.ccl.idm.oclc.org/10.1093/bjps/axy007.

Jeffrey, Richard. 1956. "Valuation and Acceptance of Scientific Hypotheses." *Philosophy of Science* 23 (3): 237–46.

Jelveh, Zubin, Bruce Kogut, and Suresh Naidu. 2018. "Political Language in Economics." SSRN Scholarly Paper ID 2535453. Rochester, NY: Social Science Research Network. https://papers.ssrn.com/abstract=2535453.

John, Stephen. 2015. "Inductive Risk and the Contexts of Communication." *Synthese* 192 (1): 79–96. https://doi-org.libproxy.mit.edu/10.1007/s11229-014-0554-7

———. 2017. "From Social Values to P-Values: The Social Epistemology of the Intergovernmental Panel on Climate Change." *Journal of Applied Philosophy* 34 (2): 157–71. https://doi.org/10.1111/japp.12178.

———. 2018. "Epistemic Trust and the Ethics of Science Communication: Against Transparency, Openness, Sincerity and Honesty." *Social Epistemology* 32 (2): 75–87.

Koskinen, I. 2018. "Defending a Risk Account of Scientific Objectivity." *The British Journal for the Philosophy of Science*. 71 (4):1187–1207. https://doi.org/10.1093/bjps/axy053.

Levi, Isaac. 1960. "Must the Scientist Make Value Judgments?" *The Journal of Philosophy* 57 (11): 345–57.

Longino, Helen E. 1990. *Science as Social Knowledge : Values and Objectivity in Scientific Inquiry*. Princeton, New Jersey: Princeton University Press.

Longino, Helen E. 1994. "The Fate of Knowledge in Social Theories of Science." In *Socializing Epistemology : The Social Dimensions of Knowledge*, edited by Frederick F. Schmitt, 135–57. Studies in Epistemology and Cognitive Theory. Lanham, MD: Rowman & Littlefield Publishers.

McKaughan, Daniel and Kevin Elliott. 2018. "Just the Facts or Expert Opinion? The Backtracking Approach to Socially Responsible Science Communication." In *Ethics and Practice in Science Communication*, edited by Susanna Priest, Jean Goodwin, and Michael Dahlstrom, 197–213. Chicago: University of Chicago Press.

Merry, S. E. 2016. *The Seductions of Quantification: Measuring Human Rights, Gender Violence, and Sex Trafficking*. Chicago: University of Chicago Press.

Murray, Christopher and S. Andrew Schroeder. 2020. "Ethical Dimensions of the Global Burden of Disease." In *Measuring the Global Burden of Disease: Philosophical Dimensions*, edited by Nir Eyal, Samia A. Hurst, Christopher J. L. Murray, S. Andrew Schroeder, and Daniel Wikler. Oxford: Oxford University Press.

Nelson, Lynn Hankinson. 1990. *Who Knows: From Quine to a Feminist Empiricism*. Philadelphia : Temple University Press.

OpenUpSci. 2019. "Opening up Science for All!" *Ten Challenges and Barriers to Public Engagement and Citizen Science* (blog). January 16, 2019. https://research.reading.ac.uk/openupsci/2019/01/16/challenges-and-barriers-to-public-engagement-and-citizen-science/.

Oreskes, Naomi and Erik M. Conway. 2010. *Merchants of Doubt: How a Handful of Scientists Obscured the Truth on Issues from Tobacco Smoke to Global Warming*. Reprint edition. New York, NY: Bloomsbury Press.

Reiss, Julian and Jan Sprenger. 2014. "Scientific Objectivity." In *The Stanford Encyclopedia of Philosophy*, edited by Edward N. Zalta. Stanford, CA: The Metaphysics Research Lab, Center for the Study of Language and Information, Stanford University. https://plato.stanford.edu/archives/win2017/entries/scientific-objectivity/.

Rooney, Phyllis. 1992. "On Values in Science: Is the Epistemic/Non-Epistemic Distinction Useful?" *PSA: Proceedings of the Biennial Meeting of the Philosophy of Science Association* 1992 (January): 13–22.

Rudner, Richard. 1953. "The Scientist Qua Scientist Makes Value Judgments." *Philosophy of Science* 20 (1): 1–6.

Sample, Matthew, Marion Boulicault, Caley Allen, Rashid Bashir, Insoo Hyun, Megan Levis, Caroline Lowenthal, et al. 2019. 11(4): 043001. "Multi-Cellular Engineered Living Systems: Building a Community around Responsible Research on Emergence." *Biofabrication*, June. https://doi.org/10.1088/1758-5090/ab268c.

Scheman, Naomi. 2011. *Shifting Ground: Knowledge and Reality, Transgression and Trustworthiness*. New York: Oxford University Press. 207–233. http://site.ebrary.com/id/10483505.

Schroeder, S. Andrew. *Forthcoming-a*. "Democratic Values: A Better Foundation for Public Trust in Science." *British Journal for Philosophy of Science*. https://doi.org/10.1093/bjps/axz023.

———. *Forthcoming-b*. "Thinking about Values in Science: Ethical versus Political Approaches." *Canadian Journal of Philosophy*. https://doi.org/10.1017/can.2020.41

Staley, Kent. 2017. "Decisions, Decisions: Inductive Risk and the Higgs Boson." In *Exploring Inductive Risk: Case Studies of Values in Science*, edited by Keven Elliott and Ted Richards. Oxford: Oxford University Press.

Steel, Daniel. 2010. "Epistemic Values and the Argument from Inductive Risk." *Philosophy of Science* 77 (1): 14–34.

Stein, Melissa N. 2015. *Measuring Manhood: Race and the Science of Masculinity, 1830–1934*, 3rd edition. Minneapolis: University of Minnesota Press.

Thoma, Mark. 2016. "There's a Conservative Bias in Economics." *The Week*, June 25, 2016. https://theweek.com/articles/631010/theres-conservative-bias-economics.

University of Southern California. n.d. "Levels of IRB Review | Office for the Protection of Research Subjects | USC." Accessed August 11, 2020. https://oprs.usc.edu/irb-review/types-of-irb-review/.

Wilholt, Torsten. 2013. "Epistemic Trust in Science." *The British Journal for the Philosophy of Science*, 64: 233–53.

———. 2016. "Collaborative Research, Scientific Communities, and the Social Diffusion of Trustworthiness." In *The Epistemic Life of Groups: Essays in the Epistemology of Collectives*, edited by Michael S. Brady and Miranda Fricker. New York, NY: Oxford University Press.

6 Justified Social Distrust

Lacey J. Davidson and Mark Satta

6.1 Introduction

Human social life requires frequent interaction between strangers. Such interaction typically works best when there is widespread trust that other people normally contribute to the collective success of others by upholding certain standards of behavior. Such widespread trust is a remarkable achievement, especially given how little information we have about most of the people with whom we interact. This general trusting attitude toward relevant others allows people to engage in a wide variety of large-scale pro-social and cooperative behaviors that would otherwise be impossible. This includes the creation of sustained culture and normative rules, which can provide great personal and collective benefits.[1]

Many scholars have theorized that these cooperative trusting behaviors gave rise to and are now supported by a norm system of some kind (see Kelly and Davis 2018 for an overview). Among these scholars, some (Bicchieri 2006; Vallier 2019) argue that *social trust* plays an essential stabilizing role in cooperative systems. A public demonstrates social trust when most members believe that others in the same public are contributing to the goals and projects of one another by complying with shared social norms. Kevin Vallier (2019) has argued that people have moral reasons to act in ways that sustain the system of social trust; they have moral reasons to be trustworthy and act as if others are trustworthy with respect to upholding social norms. However, these moral reasons to act as if others are trustworthy obtain only when such trust is epistemically justified, that is, when individuals have good reasons to believe that others will comply with norms (Vallier 2019, 52–57). Beliefs that constitute trust and stabilize norms must be at least truth approximate.

Vallier's approach to the social trust literature operates under the assumptions that (1) individuals are generally epistemically justified in believing that others will comply with norms,[2] and (2) existent social norms benefit a public's members. Our purpose here is to examine cases when either (1) some members of a public lack epistemic justification for the belief that others will comply with particular norms (because they have evidence that others in fact do not) or (2) the upholding of some social norms is harmful to some people in the community. In these cases, social trust is undermined either by norm-violating actions or by the upholding of harmful norms. When individuals or groups consistently flout certain standards for behavior or uphold harmful norms, other (and sometimes even the same) individuals and groups may question the extent to which their community is trustworthy. When such barriers for social trust are present, individuals are unable to fully obtain the collective benefits supported by systems of social trust. Under such circumstances, not only do some members of a public lack justification for social trust, but they also have justification for social *dis*trust. It is crucial to note that this kind of social distrust is the downstream effect of social conditions that are not worthy of social trust. Thus, creating social trust should be first and foremost a task of creating social conditions that merit social trust.

In this paper we describe the concept of justified social distrust and put forward empirical evidence that there are some groups of people who are justified in their social distrust even when within a majority trusting society. The central example we will focus on is the anti-Black racism woven into many of the United States' social norms and practices and the justified social distrust developed by many Black people living in the United States in response. When social distrust is present, we lose out on the important benefits of social trust like the stability of social institutions.[3] Although social trust can be both valuable and a moral good (Vallier 2019), social trust cannot and should not be maintained when a community's social norms systematically benefit some while harming others. Our social norms must benefit people of all racial identities within the public in order to secure social trust and the valuable things social trust brings to a society.

In the weeks following the murder of George Floyd, the call to build trust between police and communities reverberated on many news programs. Such narratives often suggest the problem is that Black people don't trust the police. These narratives imply that Black people need to be more trusting and that Black people's lack of trust is a root cause of police violence. In this paper we counter this narrative by arguing that (re)establishing social trust first requires becoming *trustworthy* so that members of a community may be justified in *trusting*.[4]

We'll proceed in the following way. In section 6.2, we provide empirical data about the systemically racist social and material conditions in the United States. In section 6.3, we develop our account of justified social distrust against the backdrop of Vallier's (2019) conception of social trust. Drawing on the information provided in section 6.2, we argue that for many Black people living in the United States the necessary conditions for social trust (Vallier 2019, 48) have not been met. We also argue that there are many practices and actions that actively work against the meeting of the conditions for social trust such that many Black people are also justified in their social *dis*trust. In section 6.4, we explore pathways for building trust. Because social trust ought to be epistemically justified, building social trust requires changing the world before changing people's minds. That is to say, the first step in building social trust is to become more trustworthy so that social trust is epistemically justified.

Before proceeding, we offer two points about our methodology. First, the accounts of social trust that we focus on in this paper are largely cognitivist accounts of social trust that place emphasis on the beliefs of individuals. We think this framework is useful for parsing out our account of social distrust, especially since we focus on the epistemic justification of social distrust. That said, we also think there is good evidence supporting the view that there are important non-cognitivist features of social norms such as *feelings* about what one ought to do and *behavioral inclinations* to comply with norms (Richerson and Boyd 2005; Henrich 2015; Kelly and Davis 2018; Sripada and Stich 2007). If the function of the norm system relies on much more than beliefs, then changing beliefs won't necessarily be enough to change norms or to regain trust.[5] Further, there may be cases in which norms shift without changes in beliefs (Paluck 2009; Paluck, Shepherd, and Aronow 2016). So, while we focus on the doxastic features of social distrust, we are not committed to a view in which beliefs are the only mechanism for supporting or shifting social norms or social trust.

Second, this chapter is primarily an exercise in non-ideal theory. What we mean here is that we wish to start with the material conditions and lived experiences of real people living in the United States and to theorize with these experiences at the center. We take our approach to be guided and inspired by feminist and critical race theory (for specific examples see: Moraga and Azaldúa 1981; Harris 2020; hooks 1984; Mills 2005). From this robust literature, there are three primary methodological principles we aim to center in this chapter. First, we aim to focus on the experiences of those most oppressed given current power structures, lest we be tempted to treat those who suffer the most as outliers in an otherwise just system. Second, we embrace the claim that we cannot conceive of the proper goals or ideals to build social trust in our society without assessing the current social structures and the material conditions supported by these structures. Theorizing from this approach does not lend itself to over simplification, and we see this as a strength rather than a weakness. Finally, we come to this work and write this chapter as white embodied people and non-ideal theory allows us to acknowledge the ways this shapes our experiences and can limit our perspectives.

6.2 Material Conditions and Lived Experiences

In this section of the chapter, we will review some of the unjust material conditions experienced by Black people in the United States, focusing on mass incarceration, policing and police brutality, housing, barriers to generating wealth, and healthcare. We take these conditions to be produced and maintained by systemic racism, which shows up in our interpersonal interactions, our social norms, procedures and policies, and institutions. We take a descriptive approach in this section that is informed by Harris' (2018) approach in "Necro-Being: An Actuarial Account of Racism." He argues that racism is a "polymorphous agent of death" that shows up in many ways and modes, and we move forward from this framework in giving a descriptive account here that does not require a neat, complete, or unified account of the causes or explanations for these material conditions.

The Movement for Black Lives (2020) specifically highlights the war on Black communities in mass incarceration and policing. They write, "Policing, criminalization, and surveillance have increasingly become the primary and default responses to every conflict, harm, and need, including those flowing from systematic displacement and divestment from infrastructure and programs aimed at meeting basic needs in working class and low-income communities." This war on Black communities impacts the lived experiences of Black people in their everyday lives as they go to work and school, spend time with their families and friends, and sleep in their homes at night.

According to the NAACP (2020), "African Americans[6] are incarcerated at more than five times the rate of whites," making up 34 percent of the correctional population while representing only 13 percent of the population of the United States. The lifetime likelihood of imprisonment for Black men born in 2001 is 1 in 3 while it is 1 in 9 for white men, and the lifetime likelihood of imprisonment for Black women is 1 in 18 in comparison to 1 in 111 for white women (The Sentencing Project 2020).

Incarceration rates are influenced by arrest rates and sentencing. The ACLU found that "a Black person is 3.73 times more likely to be arrested for marijuana possession than a white person, even though Blacks and whites use marijuana at similar rates." Starr and Rehavi (2013) found that prosecutors were nearly twice as likely to charge Black defendants with crimes that have mandatory minimum sentences, increasing incarceration time. As argued by Alexander (2010) in *The New Jim Crow* and DuVernay in the documentary *13th* (2016) mass incarceration is an updated mechanism of control that replaced enslavement and Jim Crow laws.

As should be expected, mass incarceration has effects beyond the experience of the person who is incarcerated. A key finding of the Economic Policy Institute's "Mass Incarceration and Children's Outcomes" found that an "African American child is six times as likely as a white child to have or have had an incarcerated parent" (Morsy and Rothstein 2016). In addition, many of those who are incarcerated were previously the family's primary income provider, which has longstanding effects on financial stability (Western and Pettit 2010). There are also many barriers to re-entry, such as legal discrimination in housing, work, and financial assistance, which increases the "collateral consequences" of incarceration such as unemployment, housing insecurity, poverty, and recidivism (Pinard 2013).

Alongside mass incarceration is policing and police brutality. The data on police brutality is difficult to track because only certain data is required to be collected and it is collected and reported by police departments themselves (Goldberg 2020), but the testimony of Black people and the available data shows robust anti-Black police brutality. A Human Rights Watch (2019) study of policing in Tulsa, Oklahoma from 2012–17 found that "Black people in Tulsa are 2.7 times more likely to be subjected to physical force by police officers than white people on a per capita basis" (6) and "2.3 times more likely than white people to be arrested" (7). In an analysis of New York City's Stop and Frisk program, Fryer (2018) found that "on non-lethal uses of force—putting hands on civilians (which includes slapping or grabbing) or pushing individuals into a wall or onto the ground, there are large racial differences. In the raw data, blacks and Hispanics are more than fifty percent more likely to have an interaction with police which involves any use of force" (3–4). Using 911 call data from two unnamed cities, Hoekstra and Sloan (2020) found that, "while white and black officers use gun force at similar rates in white and racially mixed neighborhoods, white officers are five times as likely to use gun force in predominantly black neighborhoods."

According to the organization Mapping Police Violence, in 2017, "Black people were more likely to be killed by police, more likely to be unarmed and less likely to be threatening someone when killed." Specifically, 27 percent of those killed by the police in 2017 were Black, which is a stark over representation in comparison to the population. Here are just some of the names of Black people killed by the police in the last five years: George Floyd, Breonna Taylor, Atatiana Jefferson, Aura Rosser, Stephon Clark, Botham Jean, Philando Castille, Alton Sterling, Michelle Cusseaux, and Freddie Gray (for more information, see Chughtai 2020). Breonna Taylor was *sleeping in her bed* when she was shot eight times and killed by police who entered her home using a "no-knock warrant" and after the suspect had already been apprehended by other members of the police department. For Black people, police violence is a part of what it means to be policed.

In addition to the violence endured by institutions meant to "protect and serve," Black people have been denied equal access to good housing and to opportunities to generate wealth throughout the entirety of US history. These barriers to housing and wealth-accumulation have in turn denied Black people equal access to education and educational resources, sufficient nutrition, employment, and reliable transportation between home and work.

The specific structure of the barriers to housing and wealth has changed many times since the end of the antebellum enslavement of Black people. The cruelties of unjust labor practices in the South, such as share cropping, led many Black people to move from the rural South into Northern US cities during World War I and in the five decades that followed (Wilkerson 2010). But through the combined and often coordinated efforts of private and public actors, on both state and federal levels, Black people were barred from obtaining the most desirable housing reserved for white people (Rothstein 2017).

In the private sphere, these barriers were created by racially restrictive covenants whereby entire white neighborhoods agreed via contract not to sell homes to Black people (Rothstein 2017, Ch. 5), by the refusal of many financial institutions to give mortgages to prospective Black homeowners (Stocker-Edwards 1988), and by the nationally coordinated commitment of real estate agents to uphold racial segregation in housing (Szto 2013). Both the Supreme Court and numerous state courts upheld racially restrictive covenants as constitutional in the early decades of the twentieth century (Rothstein 2017, Ch. 5). It wasn't until 1948 that the Supreme Court finally acknowledged that enforcement of racially restrictive covenants was unconstitutional (*Shelley v. Kraemer*).

Public and private housing discrimination against Black people persisted well beyond the era of racially restrictive covenants. Until the passing of the Fair Housing Act of 1968, it was legal in the United States to deny important housing services to particular communities, most notably Black communities. In a process now known as redlining, financial and other important institutions continued to systematically withhold services from neighborhoods based on the ethnic or racial make-up of the neighborhood. These institutions also used the racial and ethnic makeup of neighborhoods to determine the value of homes, with the highest value being given to homes in exclusively white neighborhoods. In turn, the Federal Housing Administration used these racist determinations of home values as a cornerstone of its housing policy for much of the early twentieth century up through 1968. As a result, many white people and white suburban neighborhoods received substantial government subsidies that were denied to Black people and other People of Color. This led to the underdevelopment of Black neighborhoods that were deemed by financial institutions, realtors, and state and federal governments to be "undesirable" or "insecure." This *de jure* segregation continues to affect segregation and community resources today (Rothstein 2017).

These racist housing policies have had long lasting consequences on the material circumstances of Black people in the United States. For many living in the United States, home ownership is the chief means of accumulating wealth (Oliver and Shapiro 1995; Szto 2013). Historian Richard Rothstein provides a vivid example:

> [M]ost African Americans have suffered under this *de jure* system [of unconstitutional housing discrimination] ... For example, many African American World War II veterans did not apply for govern-guaranteed mortgages for suburban purchases because they knew that the Veterans Administration would reject them on account of their race, so applications were pointless. Those veterans then did not gain wealth from home equity appreciation as did white veterans, and their descendants then could not inherit that wealth as did white veterans' descendants. With less inherited wealth, African Americans today are generally less able than their white peers to afford to attend good colleges. (Rothstein 2017, xi)

These downstream effects of past systemic racial discrimination in housing are not the only ways in which systemic racism still makes it difficult for Black people to own homes and accumulate wealth. Historian Keeanga-Yamahtta Taylor outlines in her book *Race for Profit* that in the over 50 years since the passage of the 1968 Fair Housing Act, actors in the private sector, such as financial institutions, have continued to exploit Black people for profit. Taylor refers to these racist practices as "predatory inclusion," which she describes as follows:

> Predatory inclusion describes how African American homebuyers were granted access to conventional real estate practices and mortgage financing, but on more expensive and comparatively unequal terms. These terms were justified because of the disproportionate conditions of poverty and dilapidation in a scarred urban geography that had been produced by years of public and private institutional neglect. When redlining ended, these conditions of poverty and distress became excuses for granting entry into the conventional market on different and more expensive terms, in comparison with the terms offered to suburban residents. (Taylor 2019, 5)

Taylor also recounts how real estate and mortgage bankers have sought out low income home buyers in order to profit off the possibility that they will "fail to keep up with their home payments and slip into foreclosure" (Taylor 2019, 5). Such practices began shortly after the passage of the Fair Housing Act and continued right through "the acceleration of subprime lending in the atmosphere of deregulation in the late 1990s and the early 2000s" which "resulted in unprecedented home losses for African Americans" (Taylor 2019, 262).

Black people living in the United States also have inferior health outcomes. For example, the infant mortality rate for Black women's babies born in the United States is about twice as high as it is for babies born to white, Asian, or Hispanic women (Galvin 2019). Black people in the United States have also often been subject to unjust forms of medical experimentation. Journalist Harriet Washington summarizes the situation as follows.

> The experimental exploitation of African Americans is not an issue of the last decade or even the past few decades. Dangerous, involuntary, and nontherapeutic experimentation upon African Americans has been practice widely and documented extensively at least since the eighteenth century. (Washington 2006, 7)

In her book *Medical Apartheid*, Washington outlines not only historical abuses of Black people by the hands of medical practitioners in the United States, but also a litany of abuses that have occurred in more recent decades such as radiation experiments conducted on Black Americans, research on Black prisoners, and US military bioterrorism targeted against Black people living in the United States (2006). She offers far more information about such abuses than can be summarized in this chapter, so we will focus on one example of medical abuse against Black people in the United States discussed by Washington and others: the compulsory sterilization of Black women and other Women of Color.[7]

Compulsory sterilization in the United States began within eugenics programs aimed at ending things like "hereditary insanity" and primarily targeted institutionalized individuals. From the origin of the practice, forced sterilizations were considered to be a justified public health strategy. When the Supreme Court heard *Buck v. Bell* (1927), they ruled the practice constitutional "for the protection and health of the state." Though these practices began inside of mental health institutions, the precedent set by *Buck v. Bell* allowed states to begin sterilizing individuals that had not been institutionalized, often through coercion and deceit.

In the first half of the twentieth century, California far outpaced other states in terms of the number of compulsory sterilizations performed. Eventually states like Virginia and North Carolina performed more compulsory sterilizations within particular years, but the over 20,000 sanctioned compulsory sterilizations in California between 1909 and 1979 remains unmatched (Stern 2005, 1128–9). Historian Alexandra Minna Stern, in seeking to offer a partial explanation for the longevity of the practice in California, writes that "from the outset, California defined sterilization not as a punishment but as a prophylactic measure that could simultaneously defend the public health, preserve precious fiscal resources, and mitigate the menace of the 'unfit' and 'feebleminded'" (Stern 2005, 1130). Alongside other groups, such as Mexican women, African Americans were among those that were disproportionately targeted for compulsory sterilization in California (Stern 2005, 1131).

The 1950s and 1960s saw increased compulsory sterilization of women in southern states like North Carolina and Virginia (Sebring 2012; Stern 2005, 1132). Rationales for sterilization during these periods included concerns about bad parenting and population burdens, along with punitive rationales (Paul 1968; Stern 2005, 1132). During this period Black women (along with other socially vulnerable populations) continued to be disproportionately affected (Stern 2005, 1132). Perhaps the most well-known case in this era is the compulsory sterilization of two African American sisters, Minnie Lee and Mary Alice Relf. Minnie Lee and Mary Alice received tubal ligations when their mother—who was known by staff to be illiterate—signed an "X" to consent for what she thought were routine birth control injections. These procedures were done at a Health, Education, and Welfare (now the Department of Health and Human Services) clinic in Montgomery, Alabama. When the Southern Poverty Law Center (SPLC) filed a lawsuit, *Relf v. Weinberger* (1973), a "district court found an estimated 100,000 to 150,000 poor people [often People of Color] were sterilized annually under federally-funded programs."

Though many of the state laws sanctioning compulsory sterilization have been repealed, and informed consent laws have replaced them, the threat of compulsory sterilization is still alive for many Black women due to non-compliance with the current laws by healthcare providers. For example, between 2006 and 2010, in two California state prisons over 150 female prisoners were sterilized shortly after giving birth in a manner that failed to comply with state law (Ohlheiser 2013). This included the testimony of one inmate who stated that "she was pressured to agree to a tubal ligation while strapped down and sedated in preparation for a C-section" (Ohlheiser 2013).

This is just one example of how disparate treatment of Black people in comparison to white people in the United States medical system has disproportionately harmed Black people living in the United States. The lived experiences of Black people in the United States are a part of an oppressive system that has resulted in Black people being over-policed and disproportionately incarcerated while being denied equal opportunities to housing, wealth, education, and employment. Part of this experience is being part of a broader white-dominant culture in which many white people fail to understand or acknowledge the nature of Black people's oppression. Throughout this section, we have emphasized the ways in which these practices have been considered normal practices throughout US history and these conditions are often produced by the very institutions meant to increase quality of life (at least in theory), such as policing, housing institutions, and healthcare. We review these conditions to ground our theorizing of justified social distrust.

6.3 Justified Social Distrust

As discussed in the introduction, social trust can be socially valuable. It supports our moving through the world with each other by stabilizing widespread pro-social and cooperative behaviors and associated social institutions (Vallier 2018). Thus, individuals have good reasons to trust those they interact with so that social trust arises on the group level. However, as emphasized in the introduction, social trust cannot arise under conditions in which individuals and groups are untrustworthy, because social trust must be epistemically justified to function. Under conditions of widespread social oppression, social trust cannot be created or maintained. Working from Vallier's (2019) definition and conditions for social trust, we explore the conditions for social distrust, focusing on the ways distrust can be epistemically justified. We do this through both conceptual analysis and through the case of anti-Black racism in the United States.[8] To move toward outlining distrust, we'll proceed as follows. First, we'll highlight two important features of trust from the interpersonal trust literature[9] that will be relevant to social trust and distrust: the distinction between reliance and trust and accounts of justification for trust. Second, we'll give an overview of the concept of social trust grounded in the social norms literature and as developed by Vallier (2019). Third, moving from the material conditions caused and maintained by systemic anti-Black racism and white supremacy, we'll give an account of social distrust. Working through the literature in this way demonstrates that social distrust is conceptually coherent with philosophical accounts of trust.

6.3.1 What is Trust? How Is It Justified?

Annette Baier (1986) distinguishes between trusting someone and *merely* relying on someone or something (further theorized by Holton 1994; Townley and Garfield 2013). When we *rely* on someone, we expect someone to do something. For example, we rely on the owner of the corner deli to sell food that has been stored at the proper temperatures to prevent the growth of listeria. In short, we rely on them to prevent food poisoning because food poisoned customers are bad for business. If she fails to do so, we are prepared to be disappointed, perhaps dismayed that we have to find a new place for lunch, a new place with more reliable corned beef. However, when we *trust* individuals, rather than merely rely on them, we are prepared to react to them in a different kind of way, in many cases because we depended on their *goodwill* toward us.[10] According to Holton (1994), "In cases where we trust and are let down, we do not just feel disappointed ... We feel betrayed" (66). Say I've developed a relationship with the deli owner, and I come to believe that they care for my well-being and health. Now, I no longer merely rely on them for my daily lunch, I've come to trust them. Thus, if the deli owner serves me meat they know to be at a high risk for contamination, no longer have they just let me down. They've betrayed me. In short, when we trust, we bring in the possibility of responding to others with the uniquely human relational "reactive attitudes" (Strawson 1974) like those of resentment, gratitude, betrayal, and forgiveness. This is important because trust, lack of trust, and distrust are tied to emotional responses, not just doxastic states.

Alongside this distinction, we can also distinguish between two different accounts of the justification for interpersonal trust. There are two basic kinds of accounts of the justification of trust: evidence-directed and end-directed. On the first account, trust is justified when it is fitting, and trust is fitting when we have good reasons to believe that others have good will toward us. Put another way, it is appropriate to have the attitude of trust toward individuals only when the persons have qualities or tendencies that make them trustworthy. The second type of account is end-directed. Here, trust is justified when it is instrumentally valuable for things like cooperation (Gambetta 1988; Hardin 2002). On these accounts, one could be justified in trusting another even if one lacked good evidential reasons to do so but had good practical reasons to do so. Though trust may be epistemically unwarranted, we are justified in trusting when it leads to desirable outcomes. In this paper, we will work from the evidence-directed account of trust. Although we certainly think that trust is valuable for practical reasons, including the positive or valuable systems supported by trust, we will not use an end-directed conception of justification for trust that relies on these values. We will assume that trust that is justified in the evidence-directed sense will also generally be instrumentally valuable and lead to social goods in many cases. We will maintain the distinctions between reliance and trust, on the one hand, and between evidence-directed and end-directed justification for trust, on the other, as we move to our discussion of the group-level concepts of social trust and distrust.

6.3.2 Social Trust

As described by Vallier (2019), social trust is a group-level state of affairs dependent on the beliefs of members of a public about other members of their public.[11] For clarity, we will begin with Vallier's definition of social trust:

> *ST:* A public exhibits social trust to the extent that its participant members generally believe that other participants are necessary or helpful for achieving one another's goals and that (most or all) members are generally willing and able to do their part to achieve those goals, knowingly or unknowingly, by following moral rules where moral reasons are sufficient to motivate compliance. (37)

Here, Vallier identifies what he takes to be the necessary conditions for a public to exhibit social trust. The first condition, the belief that others are helpful for achieving one's goals, comes from Cristiano Castelfranchi and Rino Falcone's (2010) view that "a truster only trusts when she has a goal that the trustee is required to facilitate" (Vallier 2019, 25). Vallier labels this the *reliance* condition. Remember, though, that trust requires something over and above reliance. The second condition, identified with "willing and able" in Vallier's definition, is the *competence* condition of trust. Third, we come to the reason why individuals comply with moral rules (a type of social norm), which for Vallier must be moral reasons. These moral reasons motivate due to some internal moral, rather than prudential, commitment to upholding the norm.[12] On Vallier's (2019) account of moral rules, which is embedded in a much larger argument about peaceful political life, individuals have a moral obligation to be trustworthy and to treat others as trustworthy to support a system of social trust. Thus, unless individuals are given sufficient epistemic justification to believe that others are not trustworthy, the belief in the trustworthiness of others should be the default.

We've said a little bit about norms and the norm system in the introduction, but since social trust is grounded in social norms, it will be helpful to say a bit more about norms. There is no widespread agreement here. But, because the social trust literature has largely focused on Bicchieri-style norms, we'll start here, remembering that ultimately we endorse a more non-cognitivist view of norms in which reportable or accessible beliefs[13] need not always be necessary for behavior change. For Cristina Bicchieri (2006, 2017), social norms are group-level behavioral regularities that are stabilized through a preference to conform to a standard of behavior on the condition that individuals within a reference network have beliefs about what others will do (empirical expectations) and beliefs about what others think should be done with respect to a particular behavior (normative expectations). Social norms are conditional preferences, which is what makes them different from moral norms for Bicchieri (2017). Individuals do not prefer to conform to social norms outside of their empirical and normative exceptions about others in their reference network. In addition to conditional preferences, norms are stabilized through punishment and sanction. When a norm is important within a reference network, individuals are consistently positively sanctioned for norm-adherence and negatively sanctioned for norm-violations.[14] Because social norms are independent from personal preferences and do not necessarily meet needs, "[w]ithout these systems of sanctions, the norm could easily fall apart" (Bicchieri 2017, 39). Norms play an essential role in the regulation of behavior within particular reference networks.

Building off this explanation of group-level behavioral regularities, Vallier (2019) utilizes Gerald Gaus' (2011) notion of moral rules to begin his analysis. Bicchieri-type norms are explicitly non-moral in nature, that is, individuals only comply with norms conditionally, not based on a personal moral conviction to follow the norm independently from what others do and think. On Gaus' picture, however, moral rules are based on reciprocal obligation in which we mutually expect one another to follow the moral rules (117). This can be interpreted as a conditional preference, and therefore "count" as a social norm using Bicchieri's conception, because the moral rule would not persist independently of reciprocal obligation. Vallier's (2019) account moves from these conceptions of social norms such that his view of trust cannot be separated from them.

Now that we've unpacked Vallier's definition of social trust, we can move forward in building our conception of social distrust that is the primary aim of this paper. Our purpose here is not to challenge Vallier's definition for social trust, but rather to offer a new conceptual tool for understanding the actual material and epistemic conditions in which find ourselves. In other words, we think an understanding of social trust is incomplete without acknowledging the many reasons social distrust is justified.

On Vallier's account of social trust, we make sense of the "public" in a fairly straightforward manner as a conceptual tool for talking about different groups of people, the norms with which they comply, and the behavior regularities within a group. However, we'll see that when we begin to talk of social distrust, this notion quickly becomes more complicated. For example, the United States is not just one public. Rather it is made up of many smaller communities that make up various publics with different sets of social norms. What counts as norm compliance in one public can constitute a norm violation within another. Publics do not fall exclusively along socially constructed social group kinds, and there are no monolithic publics that adequately represent essential qualities of one or another social or cultural group. Still, publics are often made up of individuals who share similar social identities.[15] Because these social identities are inextricably tied to social power and privilege, it is not surprising that certain publics have imposed, collected, and maintained power throughout the comparatively short history of the United States. These differences in power matter because they can change the ways in which individuals and communities (can and should) react to norm violations. Though made of many publics, we can also speak of a US public because of the large-scale social cooperation, particularly with respect to public institutions and government services; however, we must always recognize that this public is not a monolith and that the different publics within the US matter greatly to our theorizing. Due to the ways in which publics are loosely correlated with social identities that lead to differences in social power, coupled with these large-scale coordination needs, we are often unable to discuss what this heterogeneous public believes or has experienced as a whole. When we talk about the larger public that is the United States, we must include the ways in which individuals and groups have been oppressed and marginalized through unjust systems. Moving from this understanding of multiple, differently situated publics, we can begin to analyze the concept of social distrust in the context of the United States and the publics that comprise it.

6.3.3 Social Distrust

According to Vallier's definition, social trust requires that individuals within a public generally believe that others are relevant and useful for achieving each other's goals and that they are generally willing to contribute to the achievement of those goals through complying with moral rules. In addition, the compliance with moral rules is motivated by moral reasons, that is, because one believes that the norm in question is normatively binding or expected.[16] In order for this trust to be stable, the individual's beliefs must be epistemically justified. This requirement means that members of a public must actually be trustworthy to comply with moral rules. We are interested here in cases where many members of a public have good epistemic reasons to actively distrust other members of the public with respect to moral rules. This active distrust is not the same as merely not trusting (D'Cruz 2020; Krishnamurthy 2015). For example, if a person formed the belief that everyone is irrelevant for achieving one another's goals, that is, they hold a metaphysical view in which every person is an individual actor who acts completely independently from their community, that person would no longer have personal social trust. These are not the cases we're interested in. Rather, we'd like to illuminate cases in which individuals within a public are justified in distrusting others in a public and in fact do distrust.

As with trust, we'll begin with the reliance condition. In order for trust to get off the ground, A has to believe that B is necessary or relevant to contributing to A achieving some goal. Thus, for distrust, A must believe that B is either irrelevant or harmful to A in achieving some goal. On the account of distrust we'll build, *irrelevance* gets at the base of the reliance condition (without it we can't have trust) and *harmful* points to the kind of behaviors within a public that will most effectively justify social distrust. Let's go back to the redlining example from section 6.2. The history of systematically denying Black people the material resources required to invest in their communities, as well as persisting material conditions caused by this history, justifies Black individuals in believing that others are harmful to achieving their goals of living in economically flourishing and resource rich communities, owning a home, or starting their own business. Though this example is specific to one area of life, it is perhaps one of the most important areas that serves as the foundation for other goals and life projects. The practice of redlining provides a strong example to clarify the absence of reliance within social distrust.

Failure to meet the reliance condition for trust is sufficient for establishing non-trust. However, our goal here is to flesh out an active social distrust. So, we will explore the competence condition of social trust. For a public to be socially trusting, members must believe that other members are willing and able to follow moral rules that contribute to their goals. The literature on social trust seems to assume a tight relationship between moral rule compliance and contributing to one another's goals. However, in the development of the concept of social distrust, we will pull apart these two concepts and argue that compliance with some moral rules of a public are helpful in contributing to one another's goals while other moral rules are only helpful to some members of a public's goals due to social location.[17] We can see this distinction with two examples. Let's begin with an example that is consistent with the social trust literature, that is, a situation in which others following a norm *would* be helpful to achieving one's goal. Jack works at a company that uses anonymous review of résumés in the first round of application review. Jack's company instituted this policy after noticing that the candidates selected for the second round of review were often all or mostly white and, after a few months, most employees have internalized motivation to comply with the policy. Sherri is a Black woman applying for a job where Jack works. Jack's friend Nathan is also applying for the job. Jack would like to work with Nathan, so instead of following the company policy, Jack looks at the names on the résumés to make sure he puts Nathan into the next round. In doing so, he also sacrifices the anonymity of the rest of the candidates. In this case, Jack's non-compliance with the moral rule does not contribute to Sherri's goal of moving onto the next round of review, where his compliance would have (compliance ensures that reviewers' explicit or implicit biases do not influence their decisions). We can understand this case straightforwardly with social distrust: Jack violated a social norm, and if everyone did this, then social trust would be undermined. Now let's look at an example where *compliance* with norms undermines trust.

We can go back to the redlining example here. Howard is a Black man with the goal of obtaining a business loan to open a hardware store in his neighborhood. Howard relies on Brian the banker to approve them for the business loan. Brian denies Howard's loan based on a moral rule supported by law. Brian invests the money he would've loaned to Howard in another neighborhood. Here, the following of the moral rule supports Brian's goals but not Howard's goals. Thus, in this case, Howard believes that Brian will follow the norm (Brian does) but Howard does not believe that Brian's following the norm will help Howard achieve his goal in any way. In this case, compliance with the social norm actually harms Howard. It would have been more helpful to Howard if Brian would have questioned the moral rule and acted in a different way. But Howard does not believe that Brian will do so because Howard knows that there are consequences for violating social norms. Though redlining is just one example, there are many other cases where social norm compliance does not contribute to oppressed people's goals. For example, it is often a norm violation in the larger public of the United States to interrupt a racist joke, question your company's hiring practices, call out someone's behavior, suggest or make changes to your department's climate to make it more inclusive, or criticize the police. There are many times when upholding social norms harms individuals who are already oppressed within current social conditions.[18]

With this analysis of the reliance condition and the competence condition, we have come to a basic definition of social distrust. To reflect the two situations explored above, the competence condition has been split into two conditions: one, where upholding social norms would be helpful to the achievement of goals, and two, where challenging a norm would be helpful to the achievement of goals.

> *SD:* A public exhibits **social distrust** to the extent that its participants generally believe that some or most other participants undermine one another's goals because participants are either unwilling or unable to facilitate one another's goals due to their (i) disobeying helpful or just social norms or (ii) obeying harmful or unjust social norms.

Notice that social distrust may be exhibited by a public situated within a larger public that exhibits social trust. This may be the case due to meta-norms about the scope of social norms. An individual may disobey a helpful or just social norm because they consider the person to be outside of their moral community. In other words, the norm is not a limitation on their behavior with respect to certain relevant others. This is governed by a sort of meta-norm that sets the conditions for when and how certain standards of behavior are required by norms. In this case, the meta-norm is unjust while the norm may be just or helpful (in the presence of a just meta-norm). This can allow for the maintenance of social distrust in the public at large and distrust within certain sub-publics.

Social distrust is justified when members of a public have good reasons for believing that some or most of the members of their public will violate helpful or just norms or uphold clearly harmful norms. This justification stems from the experience of living in a society where social power distributes the means for survival and flourishing in unjust and oppressive ways. The social and material conditions faced by Black people in the United States reviewed in section 6.2 provide compelling reasons for believing that others are not trustworthy. In this chapter we wish to emphasize that we have a collective responsibility to become more trustworthy instead of focusing on changing the minds of those who exhibit justified social distrust.

6.4 Building Trust

Social trust does not relate to only one set of norm-governed behaviors or one group in particular, but rather involves beliefs about norm compliance in general. This means that social trust can still be justified to some degree when members of a public are justified in distrusting a particular group to break or uphold norms. However, when a particular case of untrustworthiness is embedded within a system of untrustworthy groups and individuals, that is, when people are justified in socially distrusting, it is especially difficult to build trust between individuals and between individuals and groups or public entities. In the larger public of the United States, it is essential that the larger society work to create social conditions that are worthy of Black people's trust. Such changes would benefit Black people by reordering society in a way that better respects their dignity and meets their needs. Such changes would also benefit all members of the United States by contributing to the creation of a public that can support epistemically justified social trust. In this final section, we explore potential pathways for building trust within a public that has been and continues to behave in untrustworthy ways toward those who are oppressed by individual, cultural, and material structures within that public.

The first potential pathway is a central part of the motivation for this paper. When conditions are such that social distrust is justified, it is essential that the public acknowledge these conditions with honesty and transparency. In other words, when social distrust within a public is justified and members of that public behave in ways that reflects their distrust, we should acknowledge that such a distrusting response is justified. Being honest about past mistakes can provide evidence that one is becoming more trustworthy, and a commitment to transparency can help prevent backsliding into untrustworthy or other harmful practices. Harriet Washington showcases the importance of acknowledging wrongdoing with transparency and honesty in her discussion of former US Secretary of Energy Hazel O'Leary's response to a history of clandestine radiation research conducted on Americans—mostly People of Color—without their consent. Washington (2006, 240–1) writes as follows:

> In 1993, DOE secretary Hazel O' Leary, the first African American to hold that position, displayed refreshing candor as she reacted to graphic press allegations of the government's experimentation on its own citizens. She admitted the agency's guilt and ordered the selective declassification of vital nuclear information. In December 1993, she ordered the opening of all DOE records of the 435 human radiation experiments conducted between 1944 and the 1990s. O'Leary's investigation ushered in a new atmosphere of openness to replace decades of Machiavellian Cold War secretiveness. As she explained "We've learned that openness helps to bring a corrective to government, and quickly."

In the short-run, such revelations may instill greater distrust in those who had not previously suspected such wrongdoing. In the long-run, however, transparency and honesty alongside reform are essential components to building trust.

A second potential pathway for building trust is for members of a public to listen to those who exhibit distrust, with an expectation that such people have perspective and experiences worth learning about. If one embodies a dominant identity within a public and, as a result, does not have epistemic justification for social distrust, it may be easy or tempting to claim that those exhibiting distrust are being irrational or too sensitive.[19] Such dismissive reactions to epistemically justified distrust further degrade trust because they provide additional justification for the distruster's distrust by providing additional evidence that the reliance and competence conditions for social trust are not met. When those with dominant identities reject what individuals who have been oppressed say about that very oppression, they show themselves to be untrustworthy members of a public. The better course of action is to take the time to listen to those who have been oppressed and to be prepared to learn things that challenge one's current perceptions of society.

Though this may sound fairly straightforward, it is very difficult in practice. Because of social positioning and the differing epistemic resources available to those in various social positions, it can be difficult to understand and believe others speaking from different social positions (Dotson 2011). In addition, as Charles Mills (1997) argues, the epistemic resources available to those in dominant social positions are meant to obscure conditions of oppression. Thus, socially dominant ways of thinking and knowing do not lend themselves to this practice.

Moving from these general approaches for building trust, we will now present a theoretical and practical difficulty for building trust, along with two specific strategies that distrusted entities might engage in to build trust. When the conditions for social distrust have been met, individuals who respond rationally to reasons will exhibit behaviors that are consistent with such distrust. Thus, for example, if they distrust medical professionals, they will rationally avoid the doctor or at the very least be hesitant. Remember, however, that social distrust functions at the group level. This means that communities with members who are justified in socially distrusting will exhibit these distrust-consistent behaviors. These distrust-consistent behaviors will be enacted toward the distrusted community as a whole (individual members of the distrusted community need not have individually behaved in untrustworthy ways). Because these behaviors are supported by shared justified beliefs, the behaviors may persist over time. Thus, the distrust-consistent behavior may become a social norm itself that is in some ways independent from the epistemic justification of the distrust. For example, we can imagine a social norm of *Avoid Doctors* supported by the following conditional preference:

> *Avoid Doctors*: The *Avoid Doctors* norm is a rule of behavior that individuals prefer to conform to on the condition that they have the factual beliefs that (1) most people in their reference network will avoid doctors when possible and (2) most people in their reference network have a belief that they ought to avoid doctors when possible.

Notice that the norm itself, at least when articulated within the Bicchieri (2017) framework, does not include the epistemic justification for the behavior of avoiding doctors. This does not mean that the epistemic justification does not play a role; in fact, the personal normative beliefs supporting (2) likely involve epistemic justification for distrust of doctors. However, this means that the group-level regulation of behavior is something over and above specific cases of justified distrust. Thus, building trust requires not only providing first-order evidence to people that they can trust their doctors; it also requires providing higher-order evidence that social perceptions are changing in an epistemically justified way toward greater trust in doctors. These tasks must be rooted in changing social conditions, and not merely changing social messaging. That is to say, it is not enough just to argue that doctors are trustworthy.

With this in mind, we can identify some more specific strategies public health entities can adopt for building trust. As we emphasized earlier, these strategies will not include ignoring or dismissing the epistemic justification for distrust. Rather, it requires acknowledging the distrust and moving from this location. In her discussion of potential roads for norm change, Bicchieri notes that a public commitment to change can be useful. In the case of a hospital or other public health entity, a costly signal of this type might look like a public acknowledgement of historical involvement with morally bad practices and a commitment to avoiding such practices in the future. Bicchieri (2017) writes, "Nothing will convince others about the depth of our commitment like a costly signal" (191). Though she is discussing norm change within communities that already trust one another to comply with social norms, this idea can be extended to communities that do not trust one another when the threat to the promiser's reputation is high enough. In other words, something must be at stake on the part of the promiser if they do not fulfill their promise to the promisee. If, on the other hand, there will be no damage to reputation if the promiser does not uphold her promise, the public commitment will not be very effective. Thus, the health entity's public commitment must include some strategies for accountability.

Though this public commitment may improve things a bit, it does not undo the epistemic justification for distrust. Not only must the health entity follow through on their commitment, they may have to engage in other actions that begin to unravel the distrust and the behavioral norms that come with it (Tam 2021). One strategy might be to begin to train and hire medical professionals that are members of the public who have been previously harmed by the bad past actions of medical establishments. Here we mean a long-term commitment that includes identifying young people from oppressed communities who are interested in health-related careers, supporting them through schooling and training, and guiding them through the hiring process. Though this is a long process, if the doctors in question are individuals from the community with this norm, eventually the beliefs supporting *Avoid Doctors*, for example, will begin to be undermined. This improves trust of medical entities by changing the social positions of those who are working and providing services within this entity.

In summary, building trust in societies that exhibit justified social distrust is difficult because of the distrust already present, but it is not impossible. Potential pathways for building trust include transparency and honesty, acknowledging that many individuals are justified in distrusting entities, listening with an open-mind to the reasons people offer for their distrust, being willing to take costly actions in order to earn trust, and making long-term investments in those who are part of communities that have been oppressed.

6.5 Conclusion

In this paper we have developed the concept of social distrust and provided empirical evidence that the conditions for justified social distrust are met for Black people living in the United States who continue to be oppressed due to numerous social and material conditions set up and maintained by individuals and institutions holding the most power in the United States. Our goal in delineating such a concept is to provide the conceptual tools for those embodying dominant social identities to take responsibility for and work toward building social trust. Perhaps the most important point here is that individuals in dominant social positions need to first work on themselves, toward becoming a people worthy of trust, before focusing on changing the beliefs or behaviors of others. All too often in US history the emphasis has been on compelling those who have already been oppressed to change. The argument we've given in this paper shifts the responsibility to those that have proved themselves untrustworthy and provides potential pathways for building a society that everyone can trust.

Notes

1. See Henrich (2015) for a more detailed argument about how culture drives human evolution and increases evolutionary adaptivity.
2. Depending on the theory of norms one is using, this point may be somewhat trivial. For example, on Bicchieri's (2006, 2017) account, norms are behavioral regularities that are sustained by certain psychological states (beliefs about what others will do and what others think people should do). Thus, if individuals have epistemic access to these behavioral regularities, and they have no reason to believe that change is on the horizon, they are epistemically justified in their belief that others will continue to follow the norm and that others believe individuals ought to follow the norm. However, behavior regularities only capture what most people in a society do. We hope to complicate this picture throughout the paper.
3. There may be times when instability of a social institution is a good thing. For example, instability can cause harmful institutions to lose their effectivity. As we develop the concept of justified social distrust, we'll explore this possibility further.
4. Some institutions, such as the police, may be incapable of becoming more trustworthy. In such cases, the path to building trust is to re-imagine our institutions.
5. Vallier (2018) makes clear that his account of Social Trust is a cognitivist account that identifies beliefs as necessary for Social Trust (46–47). We neither endorse nor reject this view.
6. Throughout the paper, we will use the language for racial and ethnic categories used within a study or report when discussing the findings of that study or report. For example, if the study or report uses "African Americans," we will use that term when discussing the findings of the study or report.
7. We use the term "compulsory sterilization" as an umbrella term that covers both instances in which an outside party puts undue pressure on someone else to give up their ability to reproduce (coerced sterilization) and instances in which an outside party sterilizes someone without gaining permission from the person sterilized (forced sterilization).
8. Social oppression persists for many additional communities (for one example, see Davidson and Satta 2021), but focusing in on anti-Black racism in the United States is useful because of the paradigmatic ways in which both social and epistemic injustice have been a consistent part of the nation's history and persists into the present.
9. We begin with interpersonal trust because it is the foundation of the philosophical literature on trust.

10. This dependence relation can be cashed out using different concepts. Vallier (2018), for example, argues that we depend on another's acting out of moral reasons in upholding trust. The conceptual framework we lay out here is agnostic on this point. See note 14 for further explication.
11. Bicchieri (2017) uses the concept of reference network rather than publics.
12. Vallier does not require that these moral reasons solely motivate every time the trustee acts. Rather, the truster must believe that these moral reasons are psychological accessible and would motivate the trustee to act. The important thing is that the trustee does not comply for morally bad reasons. For more details on the internalization of norms and normative motivation for compliance, see Kelly (2020).
13. This gets particularly philosophically sticky depending on what one thinks a belief is. If, for example, beliefs are attributed based on what one does (Hunter 2011), then behavior change is belief change. On this view, a self-report of a belief may be incorrect. It may also depend on the cognitive structure of belief. For example, does a change in an association or non-propositional attitude constitute a belief change? These questions will all matter when thinking about whether an account is cognitivist or non-cognitivist. Bicchieri (2006) limits her discussion of belief to empirical and normative expectations and does not give an account of belief in general (13–15). From here we can glean that she thinks beliefs are based on evidence (what other people do or the consequences of what they do) and they are causal (they cause preferences to comply with norms). See Kelly and Davis (2018) for a glimpse into why we might think something different is going on in Bicchieri's (2006, 2017) accounts than in more clearly non-cognitive accounts.
14. Both positive and negative sanctions vary in severity depending on the norm. Some positive sanctions are liking, appreciating, respect, etc. Some negative sanctions are disliking, social ostracism, and physical violence. According to Bicchieri (2017), norms that are perceived to be onerous are accompanied with stronger negative or positive social sanctions to maintain their stability in light of disagreement (38–39).
15. The philosophical, scientific, sociological, and anthropological research in this area is rich and is outside the limitations of this paper. For a good philosophical overview, see Mallon (2016).
16. This replaces the goodwill-type conditions (Jones 1996) in the definitions of interpersonal trust discussed earlier in the section. A condition like this is added because of the intuition that A does not trust B to ϕ if B only ϕs out of fear of being sanctioned or to improve only her own life.
17. Of course, there are interesting and non-interesting cases were people's goals are not supported. Say A's goal is to kill every person wearing a green shirt. It is clear that other's compliance with the moral rules will not help A achieve her goal. Thus, there are all kinds of goals that are not supported by moral rules. These are not the interesting cases. Here, our aim is to explore cases where every day goals having to do with basic human functioning are not supported by the current social norms and this non-support is along racial or other social category lines.
18. For an argument that following the racialized social contract enforces white racial dominance, see Mills (1997).
19. This is a common reaction of dominant groups to the testimony of people who have been and continue to be oppressed. This is a form of gaslighting (for more on gaslighting, see Abramson 2014; Berenstain 2020; Cherry 2018; Cooper 2015; Ruíz 2020).

References

Abramson, Kate. "Turning Up the Lights on Gaslighting." *Philosophical Perspectives* 28, no. 1 (2014): 1–30.

Alexander, Michelle. *The New Jim Crow: Mass Incarceration in the Age of Colorblindness*. New York, NY: The New Press, 2010.

Baier, Annette C. "Trust and Antitrust." *Ethics* 96 (1986): 231–60.

Berenstain, Nora. "White Feminist Gaslighting." *Hypatia* 35, no. 4 (2020): 733–758.

Bicchieri, Cristina. *The Grammar of Society: The Nature and Dynamics of Social Norms*. Cambridge, UK: Cambridge University Press, 2006.

Bicchieri, Cristina. *Norms in the Wild: How to Diagnose, Measure, and Change Social Norms*. New York, NY: Oxford University Press, 2017.

Castelfranchi, Cristiano and Falcone, Rino. *Trust Theory: A Socio-Cognitive and Computational Model*. West Sussex, UK: Wiley, 2010.

Cherry, Myisha. "The Errors and Limitations of Our 'Anger-Evaluating' Ways." *In The Moral Psychology of Anger*, edited by Myisha Cherry and Owen Flanagan, 49–65. London: Rowman & Littlefield, 2018.

Chughtai, Alia. "Know their Names: Black People Killed by the Police in the U.S." Al Jazeera, Webpage. 2020. Accessed July 31, 2020. https://interactive.aljazeera.com/aje/2020/know-their-names/index.html.

Cooper, Brittney. (2015). "Black America's 'Gaslight' Nightmare: Psychological Warfare Being Waged Against Black Lives Matter." *Salon*. Retrieved from <https://www.salon.com/2015/09/02/black_americas_gaslight_nightmare_the_psychological_warfare_being_waged_against_black_lives_matter/>.

Davidson, Lacey J. and Mark Satta. "Epistemology of HIV Transmission: Privilege and Marginalization in the Dissemination of Knowledge." In *Making the Case: Feminist and Critical Race Theorists Investigate Case Studies*, edited by Heidi Grasswick and Nancy Arden McHugh. Albany, NY: State University of New York Press, 2021: 241–268.

D'Cruz, Jason. "Trust and Distrust." In *Routledge Handbook of Trust and Philosophy*, edited by Judith Simon. New York, NY: Routledge, 2020.

Dotson, Kristie. "Tracking Epistemic Violence, Tracking Practices of Silencing." *Hypatia* 26, no. 2 (2011): 236–57.

DuVernay, Ava. *13th*. New York, NY: Netflix, 2016.

Fryer, Roland G. "An Empirical Analysis of Racial Differences in Police Use of Force." Working Paper 22399. *National Bureau of Economic Research*. Webpage, (2018). Accessed July 31, 2020. https://www.nber.org/papers/w22399.pdf.

Galvin, Gaby. "Black Babies Face Double the Risk of Dying Before Their First Birthday." *U.S. News & World Report*. (2019) Accessed on August 10, 2020: https://www.usnews.com/news/healthiest-communities/articles/2019-08-01/black-babies-at-highest-risk-of-infant-mortality.

Gambetta, Diego (editor). *Trust: Making and Breaking Cooperative Relations*. New York, NY: Basil Blackwell, 1988.

Gaus, Gerald. *The Order of Public Reason: A Theory of Freedom and Morality in a Diverse and Bounded World*. New York, NY: Cambridge University Press, 2011.

Goldberg, Nicholas. "We Need a Lot More Data on Police Abuse. Here's Why." *Los Angeles Times* (June 17, 2020) https://www.latimes.com/opinion/story/2020-06-17/police-shootings-data.

Hardin, Russell. *Trust and Trustworthiness.* New York, NY: Russell Sage Foundation, 2002.

Harris, Leonard. *A Philosophy of Struggle: The Leonard Harris Reader.* Bloomsbury Academic, 2020.

Harris, Leonard. "Necro-Being: An Actuarial Account of Racism." *Res Philosophica* 95, no. 2 (2018): 273–302.

Henrich, Joseph. *The Secret of Our Success: How Culture Is Driving Human Evolution, Domesticating Our Species, and Making Us Smarter.* Princeton, NJ: Princeton University Press, 2015.

Hoekstra, Mark and Carly Will Sloan. (2020). "Does Race Matter for Police Use of Force? Evidence from 911 Calls." National Bureau of Economic Research Working Paper 26774 (2020). https://www.nber.org/papers/w26774.

Holton, Richard. "Deciding to Trust, Coming to Believe." *Australasian Journal of Philosophy* 72, no. 1 (1994): 63–76.

hooks, bell. *Feminist Theory: From Margin to Center.* Cambridge, MA: South End Press, 1984.

Human Rights Watch. "'Get on the Ground!': Policing, Poverty, and Racial Inequality in Tulsa, Oklahoma: A Case Study of US Law Enforcement." Webpage. (2019) Accessed July 31, 2020. https://www.hrw.org/sites/default/files/report_pdf/us0919_tulsa_web.pdf.

Hunter, David. "Alienated Belief." *Dialectica*, 65, no. 2 (2011): 221–40.

Jones, Karen. "Trust as an Affective Attitude." *Ethics* 107 (1996): 4–25.

Kelly, Daniel. *Emotion Researcher*, (June, 2020): 36–45. http://emotionresearcher.com/internalized-norms-and-intrinsic-motivations-are-normative-motivations-psychologically-primitive/.

Kelly, Daniel and Taylor Davis. "Social Norms and Human Normative Psychology." *Social Policy and Philosophy*, 35, no. 1 (2018): 54–76. http://doi:10.1017/S0265052518000122.

Krishnamurthy, Meena. "(White) Tyranny and the Democratic Value of Distrust." *The Monist*, 98 (2015): 391–406.

Mallon, Ron. *The Construction of Human Kinds.* New York, NY: Oxford University Press, 2016.

Mills, Charles. *The Racial Contract.* Ithaca, NY: Cornell University Press, 1997.

Mills, Charles. "'Ideal Theory' as Ideology." *Hypatia* 20, no. 3 (2005): 165–84.

Moraga, Cherríe and Gloria E. Anzaldúa (editors). *This Bridge Called My Back: Writings by Radical Women of Color.* Watertown, Massachusetts: Persephone Press, 1981.

Morsy, Leila and Rothstein, Richard. "Mass Incarceration and Children's Outcomes: Criminal Justice Policy is Education Policy." Economic Policy Institute. (2016) Accessed July 31, 2020. http://epi.org/118615.

Movement for Black Lives. "End the War on Black Communities." Webpage. (2020) Accessed July 31, 2020. https://m4bl.org/policy-platforms/end-the-war-on-black-communities/.

NAACP. Criminal justice fact sheet. Webpage. 2020. Accessed July 31, 2020. https://www.naacp.org/criminal-justice-fact-sheet/.

Ohlheiser, Abby. "California Prisons Were Illegally Sterilizing Female Inmates." *The Atlantic*, July 7, 2013. Retrieved from https://www.theatlantic.com/national/archive/2013/07/california-prisons-were-illegally-sterilizing-female-inmates/313591/.

Oliver, Melvin L. and Thomas M. Shapiro. *Black Wealth/White Wealth: A New Perspective on Racial Inequality*. London: Routledge, 1995.

Paluck, Elizabeth Levy. "Reducing Intergroup Prejudice and Conflict Using the Media: A Field Experiment in Rwanda. *Journal of Personality and Social Psychology* 96, no. 3 (2009): 574–87.

Paluck, Elizabeth Levy, Hana Shepherd, and Peter M. Aronow. "Changing Climates of Conflict: A Social Network Experiment in 56 Schools." *Proceedings of the National Academy of Sciences* 113, no 3. (2016): 566–71.

Paul, Julius. "The Return of Punitive Sterilization Proposals." *Law & Society Review* 3, no. 1 (1968): 77–106.

Pinard, Michael. "Criminal Records, Race and Redemption." *New York University Journal of Legislation & Public Policy* 16 (2013): 963–97.

Richerson, Peter J. and Robert Boyd. *The Origin and Evolution of Cultures*. New York, NY: Oxford University Press, 2005.

Rothstein, Richard. *The Color of Law: A Forgotten History of How Our Government Segregated America*. New York, NY: Liveright Publishing, 2017.

Ruíz, Elena. "Cultural Gaslighting." *Hypatia* 35, no. 4 (2020): 687–713.

Sebring, Serena. "Reproductive citizenship: Women of Color and coercive sterilization in North Carolina." Dissertation, Duke University, Department of Sociology (2012).

Sripada, Chandra and Stephen Stich. "A Framework for the Psychology of Norms." In *The Innate Mind: Culture and Cognition*, edited by Peter Carruthers, Stephen Laurence, and Stephen Stich, 280–301. New York, NY: Oxford University Press, 2007.

Stern, Alexandra Minna. "Sterilized in the Name of Public Health Race, Immigration, and Reproductive Control in Modern California." *American Journal of Public Health*, 95, 7 (2005): 1128–38.

Stocker-Edwards, Stanley, P. "Black Housing 1860-1980: The Development, Perpetuation, and Attempts to Eradicate the Dual Housing Market in America." *Harvard BlackLetter Law Journal* 5 (1988): 55–88.

Starr, Sonja B. and M. Marit Rehavi. "Mandatory Sentencing and Racial Disparity: Assessing the Role of Prosecutors and the Effects of *Booker*." *The Yale Law Journal* 123, no. 2 (2013): 2–80.

Strawson, P. F. *Freedom and Resentment and Other Essays*. New York, NY: Routledge, 1974.

Szto, Mary. "Real Estate Agents as Agents of Social Change: Redlining, Reverse Redlining, and Greenlining." *Seattle Journal for Social Justice* 12, no. 1 (2013): 1–59.

Tam, Agnes. "A Case for Political Epistemic Trust." In *Social Trust*, edited by Kevin Vallier and Michael Weber. Routledge, 2021.

Taylor, Keeanga-Yamahtta. *Race for Profit: How Banks and the Real Estate Industry Undermined Black Homeownership*. North Carolina: University of North Carolina Press, 2019.

The Sentencing Project. "Criminal Justice Facts." Webpage. (2020). Accessed July 31, 2020. https://www.sentencingproject.org/criminal-justice-facts/.

Townley, Cynthia and Jay L. Garfield. "Public Trust." In *Trust: Analytic and Applied Perspectives*, edited by Pekka Mäkelä and Cynthia Townley, 95–108. Amsterdam, the Netherlands: Rodopi Press, 2013.

Vallier, Kevin. "Social and Political Trust: Concepts, Causes, and Consequences." Knight Foundation, (2018). http://kf.org/vallier.

Vallier, Kevin. *Must Politics Be War? Restoring Our Trust in the Open Society*. New York, NY: Oxford University Press, 2019.

Washington, Harriet A. *Medical Apartheid: The Dark History of Medical Experimentation on Black Americans from Colonial Times to the Present*. New York, NY: Anchor Books, 2006.

Western, Bruce and Becky Pettit. "Collateral Costs: Incarceration's Effect on Economic Mobility." Washington, D.C.: The Pew Charitable Trusts, 19, Figure 10 (2010).

Wilkerson, Isabel. *The Warmth of Other Suns: The Epic Story of America's Great Migration*. New York, NY: Random House, 2010.

Part III

The Ethics and Politics of Social Trust

7 "I Feared For My Life"

Police Killings, Epistemic Injustice, and Social Distrust

Alida Liberman

7.1 Introduction

Police officers who shoot unarmed or unthreatening civilians often attempt to defend themselves by claiming that they feared for their lives. Call this *the fear excuse.* In many cases, this fear is greatly out of proportion to the officer's evidence about the actual risk of harm, and the degree of fear felt by the officer is not epistemically justified. While it is important to recognize that people of all races and genders are killed by police, many of the most high-profile cases in which the fear excuse was invoked involve the deaths of Black men.[1] Here are just a few examples—and there are many more[2]—in which an officer killed an unarmed or unthreatening Black man or boy and an unjustified fear excuse was accepted by the US legal system:

1. In Dallas, Texas in 2014, Jason Harrison's mother called the police for assistance with her son, who she said had schizophrenia and bipolar disorder and was off his medication. Jason was holding a screwdriver; officers John Rogers and Andrew Hutchins shouted at him to drop it. They shot him five times within five seconds when he did not immediately comply. The officers claimed to fear for their lives, and were not indicted.[3]
2. In 2014, 12-year-old Tamir Rice was playing with a toy gun in a park in Cleveland, Ohio, which is an open-carry state; he was shot by officer Timothy Loehmann within two seconds of the officers' arrival in a patrol car. Loehmann appealed to fear and was not indicted.[4]
3. In North Charleston, South Carolina in 2015, officer Michael Slager shot Walter Scott in the back while he was running away. The first trial led to a hung jury. (Although Slager later pled guilty to federal charges and was sentenced to 20 years in prison, at least some members of the first jury accepted his fear excuse.)[5]
4. In Minneapolis, Minnesota in 2016, Philando Castile proactively announced that he was carrying a licensed firearm and told officer

Jeronimo Yanez that he was reaching for his wallet; Yanez shot and killed him in front of his girlfriend and her 4-year-old daughter. Yanez appealed to fear and was acquitted.[6]

5 In Indianapolis, Indiana in 2017, Aaron Bailey had just crashed his car so forcefully that the airbag deployed before he was shot from behind and killed by officers Carlton Howard and Michael Dinnsen. Based on a fear excuse, the officers were not indicted. The IMPD police chief called for the officers to be fired, but a civilian police merit review board accepted their fear excuse and declined to fire them in a 5-2 verdict.[7]

If an officer accurately perceives that a suspect is armed and is actively attempting (or is about to attempt to) fatally attack the officer or an innocent third party, and there is no way to disarm the suspect or avoid the threat apart from fatally shooting them first, it is natural and appropriate for the officer to feel fear. In such cases, shooting in self-defense (or defense of others) is merited. However, in this paper I argue that serious problems arise with the way in which the fear excuse is deployed in practice. Claims to have felt genuine fear, regardless of whether the fear was justified, are routinely accepted by the legal system (including district attorneys, grand juries, judges, and trial juries). These legal decisions then lead to widespread and unreflective acceptance of the fear excuse by the general public. Both types of acceptance are problematic in a variety of ways.

The most obvious and important wrong that results from inappropriate acceptance of the fear excuse is that victims of police shootings do not receive justice. Officers in these cases quite literally get away with murder, and the victim's family and community receive no closure or formal acknowledgment of the fact that they have been seriously wronged. This culture of impunity might also lead to enormous additional harms in the future, since officers may be more likely to shoot first and ask questions later if they feel confident that they will almost certainly be protected from prosecution or punishment.

Less obvious are the pervasive epistemic harms that stem from acceptance of the fear excuse. Epistemic injustice refers to harm to epistemic agents as knowers, or to the ways in which one's capacity to comprehend information and contribute to discourse can be inappropriately hampered or damaged for reasons having to do with one's (usually marginalized or oppressed) social identity.[8] In this paper, I explore how the fear excuse leads to epistemic injustices of multiple sorts, and investigate the negative impact these epistemic harms are likely to have on levels of trust between Black people and the police and between Black people and the White majority. I aim to explain how acceptance of the fear excuse creates or contributes to epistemic injustice in a way that hinders social trust, and to use this discussion to draw general lessons for the ways in which epistemic injustice can contribute to social distrust.

I focus primarily on the impact of police shootings in the United States. This is in part because there are many cases to grapple with—as police killings are much more frequent in the United States than in other developed countries,[9] and the fear excuse is deeply entrenched in the American popular imagination and legal system—and in part because these killings have been highly publicized (and politicized) in recent years in ways that are likely to impact broader social trust levels. However, since widespread acceptance of the fear excuse for police killings will presumably lead to epistemic injustice anywhere it occurs, my particular arguments may apply *mutatis mutandis* in other contexts. Furthermore, my general claims about the connection between epistemic injustice and distrust are broadly applicable in a wide range of settings.

In Section 2, I frame the problem by reviewing empirical data about the number of people killed by police, the low likelihood of indictment or conviction when an officer kills an unarmed person, and low rates of trust between police officers and the Black community. I argue in Section 3 that the fear excuse is frequently epistemically unjustified. I explore how acceptance of the fear excuse can subject victims and witnesses of police shootings to testimonial and other forms of epistemic injustice in Section 4. In Section 5, I illustrate how widespread acceptance of the fear excuse enables and encourages the dominant group to maintain false beliefs, which harms them as knowers by making it harder for them to learn the truth, and often leads them to commit further harms against the marginalized. I argue that this is an instance of a particular kind of epistemic injustice against dominant groups that I call *ignorance bolstering*. Finally, in Section 6 I review multiple ways in which testimonial injustice and ignorance bolstering can undermine social trust, both when it comes to police shootings and more broadly.

7.2 Empirical Data

American law enforcement agencies are not required to comprehensively report data about police use of force. Because the data that the FBI and CDC compile about fatal shootings by police is incomplete, journalists must do their best to fill in the gaps. In raw numbers, more White people are killed by police than are people of color. According to data compiled by the *Washington Post,* in 2019 approximately 40.5 percent of victims were White, 25 percent were Black, 16.5 percent were Hispanic, 4 percent were members of other races, and race was unknown or unreported for the remaining 14 percent.[10] However, these numbers do not tell the whole story, given the racial demographics of the United States and the percentage of victims of different races who are unarmed. While different analyses of the data yield different results, it is clear that the likelihood of being shot and killed by a police officer is significantly higher for Black Americans than it is for White Americans.[11]

For example, a *ProPublica* analysis found that "the 1,217 deadly police shootings from 2010 to 2012 captured in the federal data [which is incomplete] show that blacks, age 15 to 19, were killed at a rate of 31.17 per million, while just 1.47 per million white [non-Hispanic] males in that age range died at the hands of police," making the risk of death for young Black males 21 times greater than for young White males (Gabrielson et al. 2014). James Buehler surveyed death certificates between 2010 and 2014 to find that "although non-Hispanic White males accounted for the largest number of deaths [by law enforcement], the number of deaths per million population among non-Hispanic Black and Hispanic males were 2.8 and 1.7 times higher, respectively, than among White males" (2017 295). The *Washington Post's* analysis of its own data found that White Americans are killed by police at rate of 13 per million while Black Americans are killed by police at a rate of 32 per million. And in a statistical analysis using the *Washington Post's* data for 2015, Justin Nix et al. found that "although roughly twice as many White civilians died by police gunfire as Black civilians (495 vs. 258), more unarmed Black civilians (38) were shot and killed than unarmed White civilians (32)" (2017: 324). They also found that in the cases surveyed, "Black civilians who died by police gunfire were more than twice as likely as Whites to have been unarmed, holding all else constant" (325). Drawing on data compiled by *The Guardian* for 2015, Franklin Zimring (2017) found that "the death rate for Blacks/African Americans per population is 2.3 times the White non-Hispanic rate and 2.13 times the *Guardian*-based Hispanic/Latino rate" (46).

Police officers who kill civilians are very rarely criminally prosecuted or convicted. Between 2005 and May of 2017, around 1,000 people per year were killed by police in the United States, but only 82 officers total were charged with murder or manslaughter after an on-duty shooting, and only 29 were convicted, with just one officer convicted of intentional murder.[12] Given the disproportionate rates of police violence against Black people and the low level of accountability, it is not surprising that levels of trust in the police are low among Black Americans. Gallup polling from 2015 to 2017 found that 61 percent of Whites but only 45 percent of Hispanics and 30 percent of Blacks reported having a "great deal" or "quite a lot" of confidence in the police.[13] Pew Research Center polling from 2016 found that "only about a third of blacks but roughly three-quarters of whites say police in their communities do an excellent or good job in using the appropriate force on suspects, treating all racial and ethnic minorities equally and holding officers accountable when misconduct occurs," and that only 14 percent of Black respondents report having a lot of confidence in their local police (compared to 42 percent of White respondents and 31 percent of Hispanic respondents of any race).[14] These trends are robust; a meta-analysis of over 100 articles about attitudes toward the police found that "the majority of research indicates that blacks view the police less favorably than whites" in both the United States and the United Kingdom (Brown and Reed Benedict 2002: 547). While this data does not establish that police killings of people of color that go unpunished directly contribute low trust rates, it would be very surprising if there was no effect.[15]

7.3 Problems with the Fear Excuse

Since 1989, determinations of whether a police officer used excessive force have been governed by the Supreme Court decision *Graham v. Connor,* which mandates that the use of force be "objectively reasonable" (in contrast with earlier standards that required assessing an individual officer's motives).[16] Specifically, the court decreed that "the 'reasonableness' of a particular use of force must be judged from the perspective of a reasonable officer on the scene, rather than with the 20/20 vision of hindsight," taking into account the fact that split-second decisions must be made (*Graham v. Connor* 1989). To determine whether a shooting was objectively reasonable, courts must assess what any reasonable police officer on the scene would perceive in the moment force was applied and how they would react in response. *Graham v. Connor* opens the door to very broad acceptance of the fear excuse, for it is extremely deferential to officers' subjective perceptions, including their factually mistaken judgments. In practice, officers' appeals to fear are routinely accepted as exculpatory by judges and juries, even in cases in which the victim in fact posed no threat and the evidence that the victim appeared genuinely threatening is thin at best. As Devon W. Carbado notes, "an officer's testimony that he/she feared for his/her life, that he/she was in a high-crime area, that it was late at night, and that he/she thought the suspect had a gun, will often be enough to support the conclusion that the officer acted reasonably" (2016: 1518).

There are at least three ways in which the fear excuse is frequently epistemically unreliable. First, in an environment in which racial bias is commonplace, appealing to how a "reasonable officer" is likely to feel will not always be an accurate guide to whether defensive shooting was actually justified. Because the United States has a long and deep history of strong narrative connections between blackness and criminality, we should expect that even an otherwise "reasonable" officer might (perhaps only implicitly) assume that Black men are more dangerous than White men, and accordingly be likely to feel disproportionate levels of fear when interacting with Black men.[17] As Rebecca Wanzo (2015) puts it, "people consistently associate black men, in particular, with crime .... Because it is always 'reasonable' to fear blackness in US culture, the affective response of the police can itself function as evidence, constructing the criminality they seek to enforce" (230).[18] Mayo Moran (2003) offers a similar critique of the reasonable person standard in the law more generally, noting that what is "reasonable" is often conflated with what is "normal" or "ordinary," and that when this happens,

> we can expect many problems with these conceptions to "seep" into determinations under the objective standard. ... Conceptions of what is normal or ordinary have also exhibited serious and systematic defects ... For many groups, including women, those disadvantaged on racial, religious, or ethnic grounds, the poor, and those with mental or physical disabilities, conceptions of what is normal or natural have been and continue to be used to justify discriminatory treatment (125).

A standard of objective reasonableness need not be racially biased in these ways in principle; it would be possible to adhere to a conception of a "reasonable" officer that was not conflated with ordinariness or typicality, and did not the let the implicit or explicit biases of actual officers seep in. However, in practice it is easy for bias to creep in, and we must be on guard against this in applying *Graham* and assessing individual instances of the fear excuse.

Second, police officers are frequently subject to training that teaches them to be overly fearful in encounters with civilians, which makes it difficult for them to accurately assess the actual risk of harm. This means that an officer's feeling of fear might stem not from genuinely fearsome circumstances, but from the fact that they have been trained to see danger in every encounter, and to accordingly vastly overestimate the risk that they will be harmed or killed on the job and therefore have inappropriately high levels of fear during all interactions with suspects. This fact has been highlighted by commentators on opposite ends of the political spectrum. For example, writing in *The National Review,* David French points out that police officers

> are often taught from the very beginning that their (admittedly dangerous) job is more dangerous than it is. They're shown video after video—and told story after story—about routine calls that immediately escalate into fatal encounters, where unsuspecting cops are killed or maimed. This truth, however, sometimes leads to a deception, to a mindset that enhances the sense of risk way out of proportion to the actual threat. I consistently see videos and reports of police opening fire in circumstances that are more reminiscent of the conduct of troops on patrol, or—even more disturbingly—less restrained than troops on patrol. (2018)

Law professor (and former police officer) Seth Stoughton makes a similar point in *The Atlantic*:

> Police training starts in the academy, where the concept of officer safety is so heavily emphasized that it takes on almost religious significance. ... They learn that every encounter, every individual is a potential threat. They always have to be on their guard because, as cops often say, "complacency kills." Officers aren't just told about the risks they face. They are shown painfully vivid, heart-wrenching dash-cam footage of officers being beaten, disarmed, or gunned down after a moment of inattention or hesitation. They are told that the primary culprit isn't the felon on the video, it is the officer's lack of vigilance. ... More pointed lessons come in the form of hands-on exercises. ... There are countless variations, but the lessons are the same: Hesitation can be fatal. So officers are trained to shoot before a threat is fully realized, to not wait until the last minute because the last minute may be too late. (2014)

Stoughton goes on to point out that this fear is usually unmerited, noting that between 2003 and 2013, "in percentage terms, officers were assaulted in about 0.09 percent of all interactions, were injured in some way in 0.02 percent of interactions, and were feloniously killed in 0.00008 percent of interactions."[19]

Daniel Mears et al. point out that prior encounters can lead to availability biases, noting that if officers have recently interacted with hostile, dangerous, or non-compliant citizens, they "may be more likely to view a citizen during a subsequent encounter as uncooperative. The citizen might be acting cooperatively, but availability error leads the officer to interpret the citizen's actions in a manner that accords with, or has been colored by, selecting information that was most readily available to him or her prior to the encounter" (2017: 16). The same is presumably true of police training that disproportionately highlights the dangers officers are likely to encounter. Such training makes the real—although very small—risk of harm officers face in each interaction extremely salient, and encourages an availability bias that leads to inappropriately high levels of fear. To accept a fear excuse when an officer's fear stems, at least in part, from the way risk is overemphasized in their training is to accept an epistemically unjustified response as justification for defensive shooting.

Finally, judges and juries who routinely accept the fear excuse tend to presume that a feeling of fear for one's life justifies shooting to kill in any situation in which that fear is sincerely felt. But this is not always so. While a feeling of fear is often a reliable guide to what reasons you have (e.g. feeling afraid when a car is swerving toward you in a crosswalk and jumping out of the way to avoid it), fear does not always and automatically provide a good reason for action (e.g. feeling afraid of a spider on the wall, or fearing that the plane you are about to board will crash). Sometimes an officer's fear is merited, and defensive action is justified in response. At other times, an officer's fear is not merited—perhaps it stems from racial stereotyping, or from the availability bias—and defensive action is not justified.

Accepting that sincerely felt fear for one's life always licenses defensive shooting presumes a necessary connection between fear and action where there is none. Because of the biases just addressed, officers may genuinely fear for their lives even when interacting with an individual who is not in fact fearsome. Accepting this as a justification for lethal force presumes that shooting to kill is always the best (or, at least, an appropriate) response to a feeling of fear. However, this is not always the case. We are capable of taking a step back from our emotions and deciding what to do rather than instantly reacting in a less-than-fully conscious way. As philosopher Louis Columbo notes in an essay criticizing the fear excuse:

> As the tradition of virtue ethics stretching back at least to Aristotle argues, we can exert control over our responses to such fear. I'm sure we can all find examples, even in our own lives, where we have chosen not to let fear prevent us from embarking on some chosen course of action. Habituating ourselves to respond appropriately to fear is the mark of a virtuous, and we should say, free human being. … [A]s representatives of the state, armed representatives at that, entrusted with the power to use force against a civilian population, police officers should be held to higher standard [sic] of behavior, and citizens should have a right to expect that the officer they are engaging with will not respond simply from fear, even in tense encounters. (2017)

Similarly, Christine Tappolet (2010) argues against the thesis of motivational modularity applied to fear, according to which emotional motivations are behavioral dispositions that are innate, are triggered by narrow stimuli, and automatically lead to particular behaviors (such as fight, flight, or freeze) without requiring real thought or decision on behalf of the agent. Instead, she proposes that fear "facilitates but does not necessitate certain actions" (335). If this is so, then a police officer who feels a strong surge of fear when confronting, say, a Black male reaching into his pocket during a traffic stop could refrain from immediately shooting without hesitation, and could instead assess whether the man is reaching for his wallet, attempt to de-escalate the situation, or use a non-lethal method of force.

It is natural to expect—particularly in light of the training they receive—that officers will feel fear when confronting an unknown person, especially if that person is potentially armed or is suspected of having committed a crime. But such fear need not drive officers' behavior in a mechanical or inexorable way. And given that the objective risks of harm are quite low in most cases, that the police have a special responsibility to protect citizens, and that the costs of a false positive are extremely high, there are good reasons for officers to avoid letting fear drive them to overhasty responses that involve deadly force. This is not to claim that defensive shooting is never necessary; sometimes, officers encounter genuine threats and must protect themselves. But the mere presence of fear does not always entail that there is a genuine threat, and it is epistemically unjustified to presume that it does.

7.4 Police Shootings and Epistemic Injustice Against Victims

I have argued that the fear excuse is problematic because it is epistemically unreliable. Widespread acceptance of the fear excuse in the legal system and among the public also leads to serious epistemic harms against a wide range of people. The most obvious harms are to witnesses of police shootings who are subject to *testimonial injustice* in Fricker's sense of receiving an inappropriate credibility deficit that stems from an identity-related prejudice. For example, upper- or middle-class White judges or jury members might discount the credible testimony of working-class non-White witnesses who they perceive to be unreliable due to prejudiced assumptions about race, class, or linguistic style.[20] Widespread popular endorsement of the fear excuse—by courts, police organizations and their supporters, and the general public—can also lead to unjust credibility deficits against surviving victims and witnesses in a broader way. Victims and witnesses are in an excellent epistemic position to know whether the victim's behavior was indeed threatening. But their credible testimony that the victim's behavior was in fact *not* fearsome is often inappropriately doubted or discredited by both courts and members of the public, which harms them as knowers. If an officer's subjective and *unmerited* feeling of fear is taken to be the primary or sole determining factor of whether a shooting was justified, the testimony of victims and witnesses fails to serve as countervailing evidence to the officer's narrative of what happened. And if a self-reported feeling of fear is broadly presumed to be nearly unassailable proof that the victim was indeed threatening, the contrary testimony of those who know better is prevented from making its proper contribution.

Sometimes, this happens for identity-prejudicial reasons. For example, some White Americans are overly quick to ignore or downplay the testimony of Black witnesses and activists because they dismissively presume that they always and automatically favor of members of their own racial group. But unjust credibility deficits stemming from acceptance of the fear excuse need not be directly rooted in prejudice. Someone might dismiss the testimony of victims and witnesses not because they are racially prejudiced, but because they are strongly inclined to trust in the court system, or to automatically defer to the judgments of police officers.

Regardless of the motivation for it, such dismissals are seriously epistemically harmful. In extreme cases, credibility deficits of this sort can lead to *testimonial quieting* in Kristie Dotson's sense, in which a speaker's testimony is so systematically undervalued and cast aside that "an audience fails to identify a speaker as a knower" in the first place (2011: 242). Repeated testimonial injustices can also lead to what Dotson calls *testimonial smothering*, or "the truncating of one's own testimony in order to insure [sic] that the testimony contains only content for which one's audience demonstrates testimonial competence" (249), which occurs "because the speaker perceives one's immediate audience as unwilling or unable to gain the appropriate uptake of proffered testimony" as a result of pernicious ignorance (244). And all of these epistemic harms can lead to further material harms: if racial discrimination is not taken seriously by the majority of the population, it is unlikely to be directly grappled with or rectified.

The most serious epistemic injustices that acceptance of the fear excuse leads to are against victims, witnesses, and their supporters. However, there are also epistemic harms that befall the White majority, who are sustained in their ignorance. This both harms the dominant group as knowers—albeit in a comparatively minor way—and frequently leads them to go on to harm marginalized others as knowers. I call this type of harm *ignorance bolstering,* and I explore it in the next section.

7.5 Police Shootings and Epistemic Injustice Against the Dominant Group

The narratives that are promulgated by governmental or other sources of authority and by arbiters of popular culture (such as courts, schools and universities, the media, the entertainment industry, and corporate advertisers) about a topic deeply influence what people believe about that topic. Sometimes, these institutions actively encourage people to form certain beliefs (e.g. through advertisements, proclamations, or public service announcements). They also frequently discourage people from exploring contrary beliefs by presenting an easy and robust narrative that inhibits people's desires to dig deeper or learn more. For example, American politicians, pundits, preachers, and teachers routinely portray the United States as a fundamentally meritocratic system in which hard work guarantees success, and in which failure is evidence of laziness or bad choices.[21] In light of these portrayals, privileged Americans tend to accept this narrative and believe that their country is a genuine meritocracy, while many oppressed Americans know otherwise through experience. Or consider how the tobacco industry worked strategically for years to downplay the risks of tobacco use by (among other tactics) emphasizing personal responsibility for health in their advertising and political lobbying and funding research studies meant to sow doubt and undermine scientific consensus about the harms of smoking; similar tactics are employed by the fossil fuel industry to create doubt about the reality of climate change (Oreskes and Conway 2010). Such framing makes it much harder than it otherwise would be for consumers to comprehend the true risks of smoking and global warming.

When the narratives that are endorsed and disseminated are false or are grounded in flawed epistemic standards, they influence what people believe in a pernicious way by shoring up their ignorance. This phenomenon of *ignorance bolstering* makes it much harder—although not impossible—for people to know the truth (or to have well-justified beliefs).[22] While this can happen in a wide range of scenarios, it is especially likely when this truth is in some way psychologically difficult for the majority of believers to accept—perhaps because it challenges a cherished self-conception (e.g. that I deserve my success because I've worked hard for it, while those who are unsuccessful deserve their failures), or because it doesn't easily square with other beliefs that one holds dear (e.g. that a robust social safety net or redistribution of resources is unnecessary because all had an equal chance to acquire wealth).

To illustrate with a relatively subtle example, consider the "Happy Cows" campaign sponsored by the California Milk Advisory Board starting in the early 2000s. These television advertisements portrayed anthropomorphized dairy cows in a sunny green field engaged in playful activities such as posing for pictures with tourists, complaining about the weather when a single cloud appears, and enjoying a "foot massage" when an earthquake happens. Other ads feature cows from different geographic areas "auditioning" to become a happy California cow in the style of a reality television program. Each spot ends with the tagline "Great milk comes from happy cows. Happy cows come from California. Make sure it's made with real California milk."[23] The ads strongly imply that most California dairy cows are well-treated and live in open-air pastures, when in fact the majority of them live miserable lives on industrial farms.[24] Accordingly, viewers are likely to unreflectingly and falsely presume that California dairy cows are happy.

This is not to say that believers cannot overcome their ignorance, or are not ultimately responsible for failures to do so. The truth is out there to be discovered by anyone with access to the internet or a library. Plenty of privileged Americans are able to ask tough questions and listen to the testimony of their disadvantaged fellow citizens to discover that society is not as meritocratic as it may first appear, and many people are able to think critically and see through the machinations of Big Tobacco and fossil fuel lobbyists. Consumers can learn about the grim realities of California dairy farms, especially since animal rights organizations promote counter-narratives.[25] But these believers are not as responsible as they would have been had their ignorance not been bolstered. And the institutions doing the bolstering are also responsible to some degree for enabling this ignorance.

How to apportion this responsibility is a challenging task that must be tackled on a case-by-case basis, although we can speculate about some general trends. For example, it seems likely that those whose ignorance is bolstered will be more responsible if their false beliefs are likely to harm others, or if counter-narratives about the truth are widespread and readily available, or if the ignorance bolstering stems from a single source and is not pervasive across multiple authoritative institutions. It also seems likely that the institutions that bolster ignorance will be more responsible when the stakes are high and when the flawed epistemic standards are being promoted in a deliberate way.

Ignorance bolstering harms people as knowers by making it harder for them than it needs to be to learn the truth about important and relevant topics. This is an epistemic harm that is wrong for institutions to inflict. This is because it is in general wrong to make it significantly and unnecessarily harder for someone to acquire important true beliefs or shed pernicious false beliefs. We should not make it more challenging than it needs to be to acquire valuable forms of knowledge, including self-knowledge.

Should ignorance bolstering be considered a form of epistemic injustice? On some accounts, the targets of epistemic injustice must be subject to prejudice based on an oppressed or marginalized social identity. For example, on Fricker's (2007) account "the central case of testimonial injustice is *identity-prejudicial credibility deficit*" (28), while hermeneutical injustice results from "having some significant area of one's social experience obscured from collective understanding owing to a structural identity prejudice in the collective hermeneutical sense" (155). Ignorance bolstering does not generally involve identity prejudice. Nor is it restricted to those who are members of marginalized or oppressed groups.[26] I wish to remain neutral about whether epistemic injustice requires prejudice or marginalization, and readers who want to restrict epistemic *injustice* to cases involving prejudice and/or oppression are free to think of ignorance bolstering as an epistemic harm of a different sort.

Widespread acceptance of the fear excuse—both by the legal system and subsequently by members of the public—when police officers kill unarmed or unthreatening civilians greatly bolsters the White majority's ignorance. It makes it harder for White Americans to know the truth about police violence, and to truly understand the wrongs that have befallen their fellow citizens who are unjustly killed by the police.[27] Accepting fear that is in fact unreasonable as a legitimate justification for "reasonable" defensive shooting authorizes a flawed standard of reasonableness, according to which conduct that is not in fact fearsome is unquestioningly treated as such. This enables many to entrench themselves in comforting but false beliefs. Police officers can continue to believe that their fellow officers' actions are virtually always unproblematic, while the White majority can continue to believe that anyone who is harmed by police must deserve it: if it was reasonable for an officer to feel fear, the victim must not have been harmless after all.

This entrenchment is especially risky since it concerns comforting or convenient beliefs that are challenging to grapple with even when ignorance is not bolstered.[28] Acceptance of the fear excuse fosters ignorance of hard truths that are emotionally difficult or stressful for the White majority to accept: it is easier to think that the system is fundamentally just and that police officers treat citizens of all races fairly than it is to recognize that your fellow citizens are sometimes unjustly harmed or killed with impunity by those who are supposed to be their protectors. Especially as movements like Black Lives Matter raise public awareness, and protests against police brutality and violence increase in visibility, reliable information about the extent of police violence against minority communities is readily available, and plenty of White folks are able to see through the flimsiness of the fear excuse in many cases. Those who do not see through it remain culpable, to varying degrees, for their ongoing ignorance. But our legal and political institutions share some of this culpability for creating a system in which it is harder for the White majority to learn the truth.

Ignorance bolstering differs from willful hermeneutical ignorance—in which dominant knowers remain ignorant because they deliberately refuse to acknowledge or accept the interpretive or hermeneutical tools offered by marginalized knowers—in that it focuses not on the way those who remain ignorant epistemically harm the marginalized, but on how those who enable ignorance epistemically harm those who remain ignorant.[29] In many cases, ignorance bolstering encourages people to persist in their willful hermeneutical ignorance, and can serve to rationalize this ignorance or insulate it from critical reflection. This illustrates one way in which ignorance bolstering makes it more likely that the majority—including both those who are perniciously resistant to accepting painful truths and those who are sincere and well-meaning in their effort to understand racial injustice—will commit further direct epistemic wrongs against people of color by inappropriately discrediting their testimony and resisting their interpretive tools. These dominant knowers are still ultimately culpable for perpetrating these harms. But because their ignorance has been bolstered and rationalized, it is deeper and harder to overcome, and the institutions that maintain these standards are culpable to some degree as well.

7.6 Epistemic Injustice and Epistemic Distrust

The epistemic injustices that stem from the fear excuse—that is, testimonial injustices against victims and witnesses of police shootings and ignorance bolstering against the dominant group—are also harmful in a non-epistemic way, for they can lead to decreased levels of social trust, including decreased trust in the legal system.[30] Acceptance of the fear excuse is likely to undermine trust between people of color and police officers in ways that do not depend on epistemic injustice: because people of color know that police officers frequently get away with killing members of their group with impunity, they may presume that officers are unlikely to treat them well or report truthfully on their interactions. (While this is not true of all officers, this presumption will sometimes be accurate.)[31] Conversely, officers who know that people of color are unlikely to trust them might be less willing to extend trust in return. Once we bring epistemic injustice into the picture, though, we can see that trust is undermined in even more ways than this.

We can distinguish between *practical trust*, or trusting in people as actors, and *epistemic trust*, or trusting in them as bearers of information. As Katherine Hawley (2017) notes, the distinction between epistemic trust and practical trust is blurrier than it may first appear: conveying information is itself a way of acting. We also frequently ground our trust in people's actions in the information that they convey to us about what they plan to do, and the trust we place in the information others give us can have concrete practical consequences. Epistemic injustice primarily impacts epistemic trust, as it raises challenges for properly contributing information to and accurately receiving information from social discourse. But given Hawley's observations, it is likely that a decrease in epistemic trust has an impact on practical trust as well.

In the rest of this section, I explore how the epistemic injustices that result from acceptance of the fear excuse can undermine or inhibit social trust. For purposes of this discussion, dominant knowers include many (although not all) White Americans who resist acknowledging the reality of police violence, along with any people of color who are similarly resistant. Marginalized knowers include victims and witnesses of police shootings, their supporters, and members of groups who are disproportionately likely to be victims of police violence more generally.[32] The institutions that perpetrate testimonial injustices against marginalized knowers and bolster the ignorance of dominant knowers include the legal system that broadly accepts the fear excuse, police unions and advocacy groups that unquestioningly endorse it, and media outlets that report uncritically on it. Actual causes and rates of trust or distrust among members of these groups are empirical claims that I will not attempt to offer or assess here. Rather, my aim is to investigate the impact that epistemic injustices stemming from the fear excuse have on a number of conditions that must be present as a conceptual matter for rational trust to be possible. These conditions apply to a range of substantive accounts, and I will not presuppose any particular account of the nature of trust or of when trusting is warranted. (Readers whose preferred account includes different conditions are invited to reflect on whether and how epistemic injustice undermines them).

7.6.1 *Presumption of Good Will*

It is widely agreed that trust is a normatively robust notion that includes but goes beyond mere reliance.[33] The trustor must presume good intentions on the part of the trustee in a way that makes the trustor susceptible to betrayal. As Annette Baier puts it, "the trusting can be betrayed, or at least let down, and not just disappointed. … When I trust another, I depend on her good will toward me. … Where one depends on another's good will, one is necessarily vulnerable to the limits of that good will. One leaves others an opportunity to harm one when one trusts, and also shows one's confidence that they will not take it" (1986: 235). We can think about this in terms of sincerity: the trustor must presume that the trustee is genuine in her desire to act as she claims she will or to convey true information. It is this presumption of good will that makes broken trust result in resentment rather than mere disappointment; we take violations of trust personally. Presumptions of good will are necessary for epistemic trust as well as for practical trust; it does not make sense to depend on someone as an actor or as a conveyer of information unless you believe that they will not betray you. And both sorts of trust induce more than mere reliance.

Epistemic injustice undermines the presumption of good will between marginalized knowers and the institutions that contribute to ignorance bolstering, as well as between marginalized knowers and dominant knowers. This can contribute to marginalized knowers' distrust of both these institutions and dominant knowers. First, because the legal system, police unions, and the media reporting on these issues repeatedly commit testimonial injustices against Black victims of police violence and their communities, Black folks might reasonably (and in many cases rightly) presume that these institutions are unlikely to treat them well in the future or to report truthfully on their interactions more generally. They may wonder: if courts are so deferential to police officers' claims of fear that they do not even indict (let alone convict) officers who shoot Black people out of unreasonable fear, why expect courts to provide Black citizens with justice in any area? Second, widespread ignorance bolstering might lead Black victims of police violence to deny the presumption of good will among non-sympathetic White folks. If many members of the White majority are resistant to learning the truth about police violence—whether because of pre-existing racial prejudice, because their ignorance has been bolstered, or for both reasons—the Black minority may reasonably (and, again, in many cases rightly) perceive that the White majority lacks good will toward them. Why would you make yourself vulnerable to betrayal by someone who persists in believing falsehoods about you?

7.6.2 *Presumption of Competence*

In addition to presuming that the trustee is sincere, it is widely agreed that a rational trustor must presume that the trustee is competent.[34] I should not trust you to prepare a meal for me if I do not believe you to be a decent cook who can follow food safety guidelines; it does not make sense to trust you to explain how cricket works unless I believe that you understand the game. The fear excuse can undermine this presumption of competence in multiple ways. First, the testimonial injustices that participants in the legal system commit against victims of police violence is evidence that they are not competent knowers in this area. Judges and juries who inappropriately dismiss reliable witnesses for prejudiced reasons are not good at their jobs: their aim is to uncover the truth, and their testimonial injustices prevent them from successfully doing so. It follows that Black folks will recognize that judges and juries who inappropriately accept the fear excuse are incompetent, and will accordingly decrease levels of epistemic trust in them. Second, ignorance bolstering can damage members of the dominant group's competence as knowers, and the (accurate) perception of this incompetence is likely to decrease marginalized knower's trust in them. That is, those whose ignorance is bolstered are less able to accurately judge whether an instance of police violence or apparent racial bias was reasonable, and marginalized knowers who recognize this incompetence will have less reason to place epistemic trust in them.

Finally, ignorance bolstering may also lessen White people's trust of Black people, insofar as it decreases White people's confidence that Black people are competent knowers about police shootings in particular and about racial oppression more generally. White folks who have not experienced racial discrimination personally and have had their ignorance bolstered might reason along roughly these lines: "Our generally trustworthy legal system concluded that the officer's fear for his life was reasonable. So it must be the supporters of the victim who are being unreasonable in claiming racial bias where none exists. And if they are being unreasonable about this, it is likely that they are being unreasonable about other accusations of racial bias or discrimination." Such reasoning might make members of the White majority less likely to accept Black people's testimony about their own oppression in the future, and to accordingly commit additional epistemic injustices against them, such as presuming that Black people who share their experiences of racial discrimination are overreacting, "playing the race card," or being deceptive.[35]

7.6.3 *Epistemic Vigilance*

Gloria Origgi points out that the amount of epistemic trust we place in people depends not just on presumptions of sincerity and competence but on "a complex of judgements, heuristics, biased social perceptions and previous commitments we rarely take the time to unpack when we face the decision to accept or reject a piece of information" (2012: 223). She points out that epistemic trust involves both "a *default trust*, which is the minimal trust we need to allocate to our interlocutors in order for any act of communication to succeed; and a *vigilant trust,* which is the complex of cognitive mechanisms, emotional dispositions, inherited norms, reputational cues we put at work while filtering the information we receive" (224). We must interpret the information others present to us in deciding whether and to what extent to trust them, and many social factors affect this process of interpretation. The cognitive devices and social cues that affect these interpretations are greatly influenced by our broader culture and the ideology of our society. Narratives that stem from ignorance bolstering are part of this culture and ideology; they impact our default interpretations in ways that we might not even be aware of. This makes it easier and more likely for people to circumvent the due diligence that is ordinarily needed to assess high-stakes beliefs: falling back on the fear excuse prevents one from carefully investigating each instance of police violence for what it is.

Origgi (2012) lays out a number of factors that influence vigilant trust and affect our interpretations. Among them are "internalized social norms of complying to authority" and "socially distributed reputational cues," along with our "emotional reactions" and "moral commitments" (227). Ignorance bolstering that flows from the narratives of those in positions of authority who enjoy strong positive reputations is especially likely to have a large impact on vigilant trust, as are narratives that connect to our emotions and moral commitments. To illustrate how vigilant trust works, consider again the Happy Cows campaign. When viewing these ads, we don't decide whether to believe their claims by carefully judging the accuracy of the information they convey in isolation. After all, the ads present images that are clearly false; cows don't send in audition tapes. But the ads link up with a broader social context in which most Americans have no personal experience with and little knowledge of modern farming, yet are continuously presented with narratives of idyllic small farm life throughout their lives—first in picture books and children's TV programs, and later in grocery stores and food advertisements. The ads also connect to viewers' predispositions to trust television advertisements in general, and to trust public-service announcements in particular. In light of this, many who view the ads will more-or-less automatically slot them into their existing conception of a tranquil farm filled with happy animals, and will accordingly believe without much reflection that California cows are happy.

Acceptance of the fear excuse functions in a similar way. When dominant knowers hear about a police shooting or witness people protesting one, they generally don't decide what to believe and whether to trust protestors by carefully judging the accuracy of the information conveyed in isolation. Rather, they draw on the narratives they have encountered throughout their lives, narratives that include a connection between blackness and criminality, the presumption that racial minorities in America are not subject to serious discrimination and "play the victim" to receive special privileges, acceptance of the fear excuse, and more. These narratives are then interpreted in light of dominant knowers' predispositions to trust or distrust legal institutions, along with whatever existing moral or emotional commitments (e.g. to racial justice, or to racial solidarity with their fellow White Americans) are relevant. In light of this, many White people who hear about police shootings will more-or-less automatically slot this into their existing conceptual framework, and will accordingly believe that the officers did no wrong. This leads resistant White folks to distrust Black people (and their non-Black allies) who testify about and protest against police violence, because these narratives go against the background presumptions that constitute resistant White people's vigilant trust.

7.6.4 *Willingness to Revise Beliefs*

The final condition I will address is not a constraint on when trust is possible in general, but rather a constraint on when it is possible to trust in challenging contexts. In some cases, trust requires more than just vulnerability to betrayal. When an action or belief is especially challenging, trusting someone to perform that action or convey that belief can require a deeper form of vulnerability that risks a more serious kind of harm than betrayal, and which accordingly requires a deeper degree of courage and commitment to engage in. Consider someone who has been repeatedly cheated on by every romantic partner they have had in the past, believes for this reason that monogamous relationships inevitably end in heartbreak, and is considering entering into a new monogamous romantic partnership. Trusting the new partner to be faithful requires an openness to revising one's conception of the world; the would-be trustor must be prepared to change their basic conception about what a romantic partnership can be like if trust is to occur. The same is true of epistemic trust. Believing someone about a topic that challenges one of your core beliefs requires a similar form of vulnerable openness to revision; accepting that your society is not fundamentally meritocratic when you thought it was requires not only reassessing your beliefs about success and merit, but also being willing to reassess your beliefs about your own deservingness.

When people's ignorance is bolstered, it is very easy for them to ignore hard truths, especially truths that implicate them in wrongdoing. Ignorance bolstering encourages resistance to belief revision as the path of least resistance for dominant knowers. Amia Srinivasan (2016) criticizes Jason Stanley's claim that elites sustain bad ideology because they engage in "identity protective legitimation" in which they fend off counter-evidence to their false ideologies that threatens their conceptions of themselves, claiming instead that

> No doubt psychological phenomena like confirmation bias, wishful thinking and motivated reasoning have some explanatory role to play. But isn't the simpler, more structural explanation of why elites hold onto their elite ideology simply that their experience of the world, rather than resist their cherished self-conception, everywhere confirms it? (376)

Ignorance bolstering helps to confirm the self-conceptions of dominant groups: it prevents people from being vulnerable to radical revision by strongly affirming the comforting stories that (they think) they know about themselves and their society.

An unwillingness to revise one's beliefs contributes to dominant knowers' distrust of marginalized knowers in a straightforward way. Those in the White majority who are resistant to epistemically trusting the victims of police violence about whether fear was reasonable and whether force was justified lack the vulnerability that is required to update their conceptions of themselves and their societies. Police officers are frequently in an even more resistant position, because they are more deeply invested in the belief that officer shootings are generally justified. If officers are to epistemically trust victims, they must be willing to engage in a difficult, sometimes courage-requiring process of belief revision. Widespread acceptance of the fear excuse by the legal system, popular press, and general public makes it harder for this to occur.

7.7 Conclusion

Acceptance of the fear excuse is seriously harmful: it denies justice to victims and their families, and frequently leads to the perpetration of testimonial and other forms of epistemic injustice against victims and eyewitnesses. It also bolsters the ignorance of the White majority, making it harder for them to learn difficult truths about their own society. All of these injustices inhibit the necessary preconditions on social trust in a variety of ways, and arguably are likely to lead to the additional harm of decreased rates of trust among the White majority, the Black minority, and the institutions that maintain the excuse.

However, this analysis has more general lessons for the impact of epistemic injustice on social trust. Testimonial injustice can undermine presumptions of good will and competence in many ways. For example, those who are financially privileged often hold classist attitudes that lead them to doubt the testimony of the financially disadvantaged about whether the system is meritocratic. This can in turn lead the financially disadvantaged to refrain from trusting the financially privileged, because they (rightly) believe that they lack good will toward those whom they falsely perceive as undeserving or lazy.

Ignorance bolstering likewise decreases presumptions of good will and competence, impacts epistemic vigilance, and inhibits the willingness to revise challenging beliefs in multiple ways. For example, the ignorance bolstering of the financially privileged stemming from acceptance of the myth of meritocracy in our school systems, political discourse, and popular culture can lead the privileged to refrain from trusting the financially disadvantaged. When this happens, the privileged (wrongly) believe that the disadvantaged are incompetent judgers of whether results are meritocratic (e.g. that they are unable to recognize their own responsibility for their misfortune) or are lacking in good will (e.g. that they are seeking "handouts"). The myth of meritocracy is also entrenched in our popular culture in ways that greatly affect the default presumptions we make. And the financially privileged are likely to be very resistant to revising their self-conceptions, in part because their ignorance has been bolstered so much that these conceptions seem obviously true to them. Similar patterns are likely to apply (including in overlapping and intersectional ways) to a wide range of other areas in which epistemic injustice contributes to a breakdown in social trust.[36]

Notes

1. I focus primarily on police killings of Black men because my target in this paper is the fear excuse, which has been most prominently invoked in these cases. In adopting this narrow focus, it is especially important not to overlook the Black women (including disproportionate numbers of Black trans women) who have been killed by police and whose stories often do not get as much attention; see http://aapf.org/sayhernamereport.

2. Other prominent cases in which police officers who killed unarmed or unthreatening Black men and successfully avoided criminal prosecution or conviction by claiming to have feared for their lives include the deaths of John Crawford III, Samuel DuBose, Jonathan Ferrell, and Stephon Clark. This list is not exhaustive, and includes only high-profile cases that received extensive media coverage and in which there is no doubt about whether the victim was behaving in a threatening manner. It also does not include cases in which the fear excuse was invoked by police officers who killed unarmed or unthreatening Black women or people of other races, in which there is conflicting testimony about whether the victim was behaving in a threatening manner, or in which the aggressor was not a police officer (e.g. when civilian "neighborhood watch" coordinator George Zimmerman was acquitted for killing 17-year-old unarmed Trayvon Martin on the basis of a fear excuse).
3. https://www.dallasobserver.com/news/grand-jury-declines-to-charge-dallas-cops-who-shot-mentally-ill-man-holding-a-screwdriver-7182223.
4. https://www.nytimes.com/2015/12/29/us/tamir-rice-police-shootiing-cleveland.html.
5. https://www.nytimes.com/2016/12/05/us/walter-scott-michael-slager-north-charleston.html.
6. https://www.cnn.com/2017/06/16/us/philando-castile-trial-verdict/index.html.
7. https://www.indystar.com/story/news/201741/10/31/special-prosecutors-decision-aaron-bailey-shooting-what-we-know/819199001/ and https://www.theindychannel.com/news/local-news/crime/civilian-merit-board-clears-impd-officers-in-aaron-bailey-shooting-in-5-2-vote.
8. The concept of epistemic injustice was brought into the mainstream analytic philosophy literature by Fricker (2007). See McKinnon (2016) for an overview of the concept, including references (438, note 7) to earlier (and often overlooked) work on the same themes from Black feminists and other feminists of color.
9. See Zimring (2017, Ch. 4) for a detailed comparison of both rates of police killings and rates of attacks on police in the United States compared to other developed countries. Rates in the United States are significantly higher; using data from 2012, Zimring found that "the U.S. rate of police killings is 4.6 times that of Canada, twenty-two times that of Australia, forty times higher than Germany's, and more than 140 times the rate of police shootings deaths of England and Wales" (77).
10. The *Washington Post* has the most comprehensive data set available; see https://www.washingtonpost.com/graphics/investigations/police-shootings-database/ for data from 2015 to 2020. Most police killings involved armed suspects: of the 999 people killed by police in 2019, 894 were armed with a gun (598), knife (172), vehicle (64), or other weapon (60). The remainder were armed with a toy weapon (30), were unarmed (55), or were of unknown armed status (20). This database does not state whether armed suspects were actively threatening officers at the times of their deaths, whether unarmed suspects were nevertheless dangerous (e.g. attempting to seize an officer's weapon), or what the severity of the threat was (e.g. whether it could have been averted with non-lethal force).
11. These results do not explain what causes the racial discrepancy in the number of unarmed people killed by police. As Shane et al. note in an analysis of the *Post* data, "The results presented here do reveal higher rates for Blacks in fatal encounters, but these findings are aggregated incidents that fail to account for characteristics of the encounter. Whether these

differences are attributed to bias or something else, such as disproportionate involvement in crime remains unanswered" (2017: 106). However, Kahn et al. used different data to find that "using real-world police suspect use-of-force data and controlling for relevant suspect and case variables ... Black and Latino suspects received higher levels of police force earlier in interactions, whereas White suspects escalated in force at a greater rate after the initial force levels compared with racial minorities," which suggests "that racial stereotypes may, at least in part, play a role during these initial actions" (2017: 122).

12. See Stinson (2017); see also Kindy and Kelly (2015) for detailed analysis of the rates of charges and convictions of officers between 2005 and 2015. Exceptions to this trend do occur. For example, in August 2018, Officer Roy Oliver was convicted of murder for the shooting of unarmed 15-year-old Jordan Edwards; Oliver fired into the car Edwards was in as it was driving away. See https://www.nbcdfw.com/news/local/Sentencing-Underway-for-Ex-Balch-Springs-Officer-Convicted-of-Murder-491972191.html.
13. https://news.gallup.com/poll/213869/confidence-police-back-historical-average.aspx.
14. http://www.pewsocialtrends.org/2016/09/29/the-racial-confidence-gap-in-police-performance/#fn-22079-2.
15. See Bradford, Jackson, and Hough (2017) for an overview of empirical data about levels of trust in the police among members of different racial and ethnic groups. Other factors that are strongly correlated with low levels of trust are perceptions of procedural unfairness in actions by officers and residency in deprived neighborhoods with high levels of aggressive policing aimed at maintaining order.
16. I offer a more thorough assessment of the moral and epistemic flaws in the standard application of *Graham* in (Liberman, unpublished manuscript). See Ross (2002) for an account of how *Graham* differs from previous standards and an analysis of how it was applied between 1990 and 2000. See also the RadioLab: More Perfect podcast episode "Mr. Graham and the Reasonable Man" (https://www.wnycstudios.org/story/mr-graham-and-reasonable-man) for an accessible overview of the case and its impact.
17. See Mears et al. (2017) for an overview of how police officers and citizens rely on cognitive biases and decision-making heuristics in their interactions with each other, and how these cognitive shortcuts can lead to racially biased application of force by police.
18. Jamelle Bouie (2017) echoes this idea in an opinion piece for *Slate*: "Jeronimo Yanez's fear, like Timothy Loehmann's fear and Randall Kerrick's fear reflects a tradition of fear, a custom of fear, a praxis of fear. If, in America, fear of black people is prima-facie reasonable, then the police who kill them will always find a sympathetic ear, a juror or jurors who agree that a 'reasonable officer' would have been afraid."
19. For the FBI database of police officers assaulted and killed while in the line of duty (for each year between 1996 and 2018), see https://ucr.fbi.gov/leoka/.
20. This happened to Rachel Jeantel, who testified for the prosecution during George Zimmerman's trial for the murder of Trayvon Martin. Linguist John Rickford points out that during Jeantel's nearly six hours of testimony, most of which was in fully grammatical AAVE, "people castigated her 'slurred speech,' bad grammar and Ebonics usage, or complained that, 'Nobody can understand what she's saying'" (2013). Rickford worries that "whether they understood her literally or not, Jeantel's vernacular, her eye rolls, stares and palpable 'attitude' may make it difficult for the

jury [consisting of five White women and one Latina woman] to relate to and be convinced by her" (*ibid.*). One of the jurors in the case admitted as much in an interview on CNN with Anderson Cooper (https://www.youtube.com/watch?v=AMWybF6nUQ0).

Juror B37: I didn't think it [Jeantel's testimony] was very credible, but I felt very sorry for her ... I think she felt inadequate toward everyone because of her education and her communication skills. ...

Anderson Cooper: Did you find it hard at times to understand what she was saying?

Juror B37: A lot of the times. Because a lot of the times she was using phrases I have never heard before, and what they meant.

Anderson Cooper: So you didn't find her credible as a witness?

Juror B37: No.

21. For a detailed account of how the wealthy tend to underestimate the role of luck in their success and how the myth of meritocracy is broadly harmful, see Frank (2016).
22. See Eagleton (2007) for an introduction to the concept of ideology; one way to understand ignorance bolstering is as an exploration of the way in which ideology can lead to a particular kind of epistemic harm to the dominant group.
23. See https://www.youtube.com/playlist?list=PLvNmB3tPlwYVpGqH-qidCNUNBvtHjXbAu for a playlist of the ads.
24. See the US Humane Society's report on the welfare of dairy cows here: http://www.humanesociety.org/assets/pdfs/farm/hsus-the-welfare-of-cows-in-the-dairy-industry.pdf.
25. PETA sued the California Milk Advisory Board for false advertising in 2002. In 2003, a judge threw out the suit—not because the advertising wasn't false, but because the laws prohibiting false advertisement that apply to individuals do not apply to the government: http://articles.latimes.com/2003/mar/27/business/fi-cows27.
26. Tessman (2005) argues that oppression is both (materially and morally) harmful to the oppressed as well as morally harmful to the oppressors, who are prevented from fully exercising virtue and thereby prevented from fully flourishing. Her argument is structurally similar to mine: while the harms to marginalized groups are the most serious, the same circumstances that harm the marginalized also lead to harms to the dominant group.
27. See Pipkins (2019) for a textual analysis of how "law enforcement officers involved in shootings of unarmed people of color have a tendency to portray themselves as vulnerable and in fear of losing their lives" and how these narratives enable them to "gain empathy from the public and potential jurors ... to avoid blame for their actions" and to "reinforce the racist ideology that people of color, especially Black individuals, are naturally dangerous" (193).
28. See Wieland (2017) for an account of willful ignorance cashed out in terms of convenience.
29. See Pohlhaus Jr. (2012) for an articulation of willful hermeneutical ignorance; see also themes developed in Collins (2000), Mills (2007), and Medina (2013) on the epistemology of ignorance.
30. Kevin Vallier articulates a notion of legal trust that "involves trust in legal officials and not just trust in other citizens" (2019: 142). This can come apart from social trust, since "it is possible to trust your fellow citizens to abide by moral and even legal rules while thinking that the judicial system and the police are corrupt and unjust" (*ibid.*). The epistemic injustices stemming from the illegitimate application of the fear excuse to police shootings seem liable to undermine both social trust and legal trust.

31. For a discussion of epistemically justified social distrust (of both sensible and pernicious sorts), see Davidson and Satta (this volume, Chapter 6).
32. Other groups that are disproportionately likely to be victims of police shootings include people with mental illness, people with disabilities, homeless people, Latinx people, and Native Americans.
33. See McLeod (2015) for an overview, as well as McCraw (2015).
34. See McLeod (2015) for more on the competence conditions on trust.
35. For example, in an interview with Donald Trump in 2017, Sean Hannity mentioned the deaths of Trayvon Martin, Freddie Gray, and the civil unrest in Ferguson after the death of Michael Brown before dismissively saying "every two to four years the Democrats will play the race card." It is plausible to interpret Hannity as subjecting those who protested against these deaths (imprecisely referred to here as "Democrats") to unjust credibility deficits, perhaps stemming from racist prejudice. For a transcript, see https://factba.se/transcript/donald-trump-interview-sean-hannity-october-11-2017.
36. Thanks to Josh Crabill, Andy Cullison, Asia Ferrin, A. K. Flowerree, Camil Golub, Claudia Mills, Peter Murphy, Julia Staffel, Alberto Urquidez, Kevin Vallier, and audiences at Bowling Green State University (2018), the Rocky Mountain Ethics Congress (2018), Radical Philosophy Association (2018), and the Prindle Institute's Young Philosophers Lecture Series (2018) for helpful discussion of this paper.

References

Baier, Annette. 1986. "Trust and Antitrust." *Ethics* 96: 231–60.

Bouie, Jamelle. 23 June 2017. "The Cloak of 'Fear'." *Slate*. URL: http://www.slate.com/articles/news_and_politics/politics/2017/06/why_fear_was_a_viable_defense_for_killing_philando_castile.html

Bradford, Ben, Jonathan Jackson, and Mike Hough. 2015. "Trust in Justice." *The Oxford Handbook of Social and Political Trust*. Oxford University Press.

Brown, Ben and Wm. Reed Benedict. 2002. "Perceptions of the Police: Past Findings, Methodological Issues, Conceptual Issues and Policy Implications." *Policing* 25(3): 543–80.

Buehler, James W. 2017. "Racial/Ethnic Disparities in the Use of Lethal Force by US Police, 2010–2014."*American Journal of Public Health* 107(2): 295–7.

Carbado, Devon W. 2016. "Blue-on-Black Violence: A Provisional Model of Some of the Causes." *Georgetown Law Journal* 104: 1479–529.

Collins, Patricia Hill. 2000. *Black Feminist Thought: Knowledge, Consciousness, and the Politics of Empowerment*. Routledge.

Columbo, Louis. 26 July 2017. "Use of Force: Law Enforcement in the United States." *Public Seminar*. URL: http://www.publicseminar.org/2017/07/use-of-force/

Dotson, Kristie. 2011. "Tracking Epistemic Violence, Tracking Patterns of Silencing." *Hypatia* 26(2): 236–57.

Eagleton, Terry. 2007. *Ideology: An Introduction*. Verso.

Frank, Robert H. 2016. *Success and Luck: Good Fortune and the Myth of Meritocracy*. Princeton University Press.

French, David. 29 March 2018. "The Police Shooting of Stephon Clark is Deeply Problematic." *The National Review*. URL: https://www.nationalreview.com/2018/03/the-police-shooting-of-stephon-clark-is-deeply-problematic/

Fricker, Miranda. 2007. *Epistemic Injustice: Power and the Ethics of Knowing*. Oxford University Press.

Gabrielson, Ryan, Eric Sagara, and Ryann Grochowski Jones. 10 October 2014. "Deadly Force in Black and White." *ProPublica*. URL: https://www.propublica.org/article/deadly-force-in-black-and-white

Hawley, Katherine. 2017. "Trust, Distrust, and Epistemic Injustice." In *The Routledge Handbook of Epistemic Injustice* ed. Ian James Kidd, José Medina, and Gaile Pohlhaus Jr. Milton: Routledge.

Kahn, Kimberly Barsamian, Joel S. Steele, Jean M. McMahon, and Greg Stewart. 2017. "How Suspect Race Affects Police Use of Force in an Interaction Over Time." *Law and Human Behavior* 41(2): 117–26.

Kindy, Kimberly and Kelly, Kimrbiell. 11 April 2015. "Thousands Dead, Few Prosecuted." *The Washington Post*. URL: https://www.washingtonpost.com/sf/investigative/2015/04/11/thousands-dead-few-prosecuted/

Liberman, Alida. Unpublished manuscript. "Reasonableness and Police Use of Force: Why *Graham vs. Connor* is Flawed."

McCraw, Benjamin. 2015. "The Nature of Epistemic Trust." *Social Epistemology* 29(4): 413–30.

McKinnon, Rachel. 2016. "Epistemic Injustice." *Philosophy Compass* 11(8): 437–46.

McLeod, Carolyn. Fall 2015. "Trust." In *The Stanford Encyclopedia of Philosophy* ed. Edward N. Zalta. https://plato.stanford.edu/archives/fall2015/entries/trust/

Mears, Daniel P., Craig O. Miltonette, Eric A. Stewart, and Patricia Y. Warren. 2017. "Thinking Fast, Not Slow: How Cognitive Biases May Contribute to Racial Disparities in the Use of Force in Police-Citizen Encounters." *Journal of Criminal Justice* 53: 12–24.

Medina, José. 2013. *The Epistemology of Ignorance: Gender and Racial Oppression, Epistemic Injustice, and Resistant Imaginations*. Oxford University Press.

Mills, Charles. 2007. "White Ignorance." In *Race and Epistemologies of Ignorance* ed. Shannon Sullivan and Nancy Tuana: 11–38. SUNY Press.

Moran, Mayo. 2003. *Rethinking the Reasonable Person: An Egalitarian Reconstruction of the Objective Standard*. Oxford University Press.

Nix, Justin, Bradley A. Campbell, Edward H. Byers, and Geoffrey P. Alpert. 2017. "A Bird's Eye View of Civilians Killed by Police in 2015." *Criminology and Public Policy* 16(1): 309–40.

Oreskes, Naomi, and Erik M. Conway. 2010. *Merchants of Doubt : How a Handful of Scientists Obscured the Truth on Issues from Tobacco Smoke to Global Warming*. New York: Bloomsbury Press.

Origgi, Gloria. 2012. "Epistemic Injustice and Epistemic Trust." *Social Epistemology* 26(2): 221–35.

Pipkins, Martel A. 2019. "'I Feared for My Life": Law Enforcement's Appeal to Murderous Empathy." *Race and Justice* 9(2): 180–96.

Pohlhaus, Gaile Jr. 2012. "Relational Knowing and Epistemic Injustice: Toward a Theory of *Willful Hermeneutical Ignorance*." *Hypatia* 27(4): 715–35.

Rickford, John. 10 July 2013. "Rachel Jeantel's Language in the Zimmerman Trial." *Language Log*. URL: http://languagelog.ldc.upenn.edu/nll/?p=5161

Ross, Darrell L. 2002. "An Assessment of *Graham v. Connor*, Ten Years Later." *Policing: An International Journal of Police Strategies and Management*. 25(2): 294–318.

Shane, Jon M., Brian Lawton, and Zoë Swenson. 2017. "The Prevalence of Fatal Police Shootings by U.S. Police, 2015–2016: Patterns and Answers from a New Data Set." *Journal of Criminal Justice* 52: 101–11.

Srinivasan, Amia. 2016. "Philosophy and Ideology." *Theoria: Revista de Teoría, Historia y Fundamentos de la Ciencia* 31(3): 371–80.

Stinson, Phillip. 20 April 2017. "Police Shootings Data: What We Know and We Don't Know (PowerPoint Slides)." *2017 Urban Elected Prosecutors Summit.* Available at https://scholarworks.bgsu.edu/crim_just_pub/78

Stoughton, Seth. 12 December 2014. "How Police Training Contributes to Avoidable Deaths." *The Atlantic.* URL: https://www.theatlantic.com/national/archive/2014/12/police-gun-shooting-training-ferguson/383681/

Supreme Court of the United States. 1989. *Graham v. Connor*, 490 U.S. 386.

Tappolet, Christine. 2010. "Emotion, Motivation and Action: The Case of Fear." In *Oxford Handbook of Philosophy of Emotion* ed. Peter Goldie: 325–45. Oxford University Press.

Tessman, Lisa. 2005. *Burdened Virtues: Virtue Ethics for Liberatory Struggles.* Oxford University Press.

Vallier, Kevin. 2019. *Must Politics Be War? Restoring Our Trust in the Open Society.* Oxford University Press.

Wanzo, Rebecca. 2015. "The Deadly Fight Over Feelings." *Feminist Studies* 41(1): 226–31.

Wieland, Jan Willem. 2017. "Willful Ignorance." *Ethical Theory and Moral Practice* 20: 105–119.

Zimring, Franklin E. 2017. *When Police Kill.* Harvard University Press.

8 Convention, Social Trust, and Legal Interpretation

*Ira K. Lindsay**

Governance by law is a conventional practice. By this I mean that following the law, as opposed to acting on one's best non-legal reasons, is a convention. Government officials, including judges, civil servants, government lawyers, and legislators are charged with interpreting and applying the law in a great range of situations in which they have some discretion as to how to act. Rule by law (rather than by personal command, decree or whim), requires that they attach a great deal of importance to what the law tells them. Conscientious officials should prefer to follow the law, even at some cost to their other aims. But they are unlikely to do so unless they believe that other actors who might have differing moral or political views will also follow the law. In part this is because if one's political rivals do not follow the law, it is hard not to feel unfairly disadvantaged if one follows the law at some cost to one's own normative principles or material interests. In part this is because law cannot perform its coordinating function if legal officials ignore the law when they find it convenient to do so. There is little point to being a lone law-abiding official.

If this analysis is correct, we should expect social trust to play a large causal role in creating and maintaining rule by law. In a high trust environment, officials might go to great lengths to faithfully interpret and apply the law even when doing so does not result in their preferred outcome. In a low trust environment, officials might pay lip service to the law but largely ignore it to the extent that they can do so without being sanctioned. Frequent, serious violations of law by officials undermine trust and encourage others to ignore the law. Since any political system has a limited ability to monitor and sanction its officials, legal systems with low trust between officials will tend to degenerate. Similarly, disagreements between legal officials about the content or proper application of the law will tend to undermine the trust between officials that enables the system to function effectively.

The importance of trust between legal actors provides strong reasons to prefer legal methods that increase agreement about the content and proper application of the law *independently* of any epistemic considerations. This insight has significant import for both legal interpretation and institutional design. Methodologies for legal interpretation should be chosen in part on the basis of how much agreement about the content and application of the law they generate between different interpreters. There is long-running debate between textualists and purposivists over methodology in statutory interpretation. Textualists tend to favor interpretive methodologies that require that interpreters consider only the statutory text whereas purposivists favor broader inquiry in the aims of the statute that may involve consideration of other materials such as legislative history. People interpreting legal texts rely on intuitive judgments (moral, legal, or otherwise). A crucial question for any given domain of law is the extent to which actors within a legal system converge in their intuitive judgments. My argument yields an argument in favor of textualist methodology in areas of law (e.g. constitutional law) in which pervasive moral disagreement generates stark differences in legal intuitions. But it counsels adoption of purposivist methodologies in areas of law in which there is wide convergence in judgment about the underlying normative issues (e.g. provisions of the tax code should be understood, whenever possible, in such a way that tax treatment reflects economic substance). In other words, formalistic interpretative methods are useful for increasing trust when legal actors do not agree on background principles, but may actually decrease legal certainty in areas in which there is broad agreement on the moral considerations at stake. The result is a modest relativism about interpretive method.

The argument will unfold in three stages. The first part will argue that rule by law is a convention because willingness to follow the law for its own sake depends on expectations about the behavior of other legal officials. The second part explores the role of trust between legal officials in maintaining the legal system. The third part traces implications of the role of trust in the legal system for legal interpretation. The three arguments build upon each other. It is possible to accept the first stages of the analysis while rejecting my normative conclusions. Likewise, the normative conclusions might be appealing for reasons other than those offered here.

8.1 Trust and the Rule of Law: Preliminary Matters

One might distinguish between two different ways in which social trust is important to the legal system. What I will call vertical trust refers to the relationship between legal officials and legal subjects. It concerns whether legal subjects trust legal officials to apply the laws fairly and impartially and whether legal officials trust that legal subjects will obey legally valid directives. Vertical trust is crucially important for perceptions of the legitimacy of the legal system and of the government and therefore in determining whether legal subjects follow the law. (Tyler 1990, 161–5).

Horizontal trust is concerned with the attitude legal officials take toward one another.[1] Highly trusting legal officials tend to believe that other officials can be trusted to apply the law fairly and impartially without extensive monitoring or heavy-handed sanctions. This does not mean that all legal officials agree on the content of the law in every instance, but instead that they expect other officials to make a good faith effort to get it right. A low trust system in this sense is one in which officials do not expect other officials to apply the law impartially but rather to make decisions on non-legal grounds, at least when they can avoid sanctions for doing so. The argument in this paper is concerned with horizontal trust in the legal system rather than vertical trust.[2]

It should be immediately conceded that a high trust legal system is not necessarily a good thing. High horizontal trust between legal officials enables the officials to better pursue their ends whether they are for good or for ill. Trust makes it easier for officials to implement oppressive legal regimes as well as benevolent ones. This might go some way toward explaining the historically common pattern for governments to be dominated by a minority, defined in some way—whether by ethnicity, language, or religion—that sets them apart from the governed masses. This presumably increases trust between government officials while lowering the odds that some branch of government will be captured by some part of the governed population. Most obviously, familial ties between the governing and the governed raise the risk that government officials will act in the interests of their family members rather than in those of the state.[3] To the extent that a government builds horizontal trust between legal officials by employing officials that are unrepresentative of the larger population, this will tend to reduce vertical trust.[4]

Horizontal trust is principally a concern for well-developed legal systems administered by legal specialists. Some degree of trust between legal subjects is necessary for such a system to emerge in the first place. There is an interesting literature, on the conventional roots of legal order that can be traced to David Hume (1886). This tradition suggests that much of the core of private law, especially property and contract, may evolve from repeated interactions between mostly self-interested agents who face a coordination problem. More recently, Gillian Hadfield and Barry Weingast (2012) have argued that the characteristics associated with the rule of law—generality, stability, openness, and impersonality—emerge from the conventions necessary to support a system of private decentralized enforcement of norms regulating collective punishment. My focus is somewhat different from theirs. I will analyze conventions concerning the application of the law by agents of the state rather than those concerning obedience to the law by legal subjects or creation of the law by either group.

The notion of trust employed in my argument is, in most respects, a thin one. It is at least primarily cognitive as opposed to non-cognitive or affective.[5] This means that trust is connected to the beliefs of the trusting party about the future behavior of the trusted party (Hardin 2006, 19; Sztompka 2000, 25–27). Trust is responsive to evidence about the trustworthiness of others. Trust in officials to follow the law might have an affective component in some instances, but it might be also displayed by people who take a rather cold-bloodedly calculating attitude toward the prediction of officials' future actions. Trust is part of a three-place relation between a party who trusts, a trusted party and a domain in which the trusted party is trusted (Domenicucci and Holton 2017, 149–60). The argument in this chapter will be concerned with trust in legal officials to follow the law. It is consistent with various cognitive theories of trust. For example, Russell Hardin's (2006, 19) encapsulated interest account of trust holds that a trusting party trusts a trusted party in some domain when the trusting party believes that the trusted party will act in the interest of the trusting party because the trusting party's interests are encapsulated in the interests of the trusted party. In this case, the way in which interests are encapsulated is via a shared normative commitment to following the law. Because this sort of trust involves reliance on normative commitment, the argument in this chapter is consistent with certain theories of trust that are more demanding than Hardin's. For example, Philip Nickel (2009, 353) defends a view of trust as risky reliance on what one morally expects another to do. On other words, trust involves a prediction that another will act according to a certain moral standard. Trust in officials to comply with their moral obligations to apply the law faithfully would fit Nickel's conception of trust as well as Hardin's.

Horizontal trust between legal officials is intermediate between trust in particular individuals and generalized social trust in the reliability of people in general. It is wider than trust in particular individuals because it concerns the attitude of individual officials toward other legal officials as a group. But it is not entirely generalized in that one might trust other officials to follow the law without in any way trusting their general moral judgment or their character in their personal lives. Likewise, one might trust other officials to follow the law while distrusting people in general. In short, the sort of trust at issue here exists within a particular domain and a particular group of people but does not require a personal relationship between the trusting party and the trusted parties beyond their participation in a common institution.

My argument concerns the behavior of legal officials. A legal official is an agent of the state who is charged with interpreting and applying the law. Judges are the most prominent type of legal official. However, legal officials also include prosecutors, government lawyers, executive branch officials, and various employees of government agencies. Legal officials consult legal sources and act on their interpretations of these materials. They have some degree of discretion when acting in their official capacity in interpreting and applying the law. Of course, most legal officials operate within a hierarchy in which higher-level officials may review the determinations of lower level officials and countermand their orders on this basis. At the lowest levels of such hierarchies, officials are not expected to exercise much personal judgment about what the law requires and instead follow directives from their superiors. At higher levels a greater degree of personal judgement is often required.

For ease of presentation, I will often speak as if what the law requires is either relatively determinate, in which case legal officials must decide whether to apply the law, or indeterminate, in which case they may act on non-legal considerations. This is an oversimplification. Legal determinacy is not all or nothing. There are cases in which some answers seem legally better than others but it may not be entirely clear which answer is correct. For example, a common law judge might be faced with a case in which no prior case is wholly analogous and the nearest precedents point in opposite directions. In such instances, the legally correct decision will depend on how to understand the rule set out in these cases and on which precedents are most similar to the facts of the instant case. Because reasonable minds might differ as to how to weigh conflicting considerations, it might be better to speak of some answers being legally better than others without one being definitively correct and the others incorrect. A given case could be resolved in many different ways with A, B, C, D, and E each being a ruling with supporting legal reasoning. I might prefer A, but count B and C as legally plausible answers that another competent lawyer might reach in good faith while thinking that D and E could only result from mistake, bias, or bad faith. This might well be the case even if A and D require a judgment for the plaintiff and B, C, and E require a judgment for the defendant. Agreement on outcome is therefore neither necessary nor sufficient for recognition that another person has reached a reasonable result while acting in good faith. For the purposes of this argument, what is most important is whether a legal judgment is good enough to count as a good faith attempt to get the law right rather than whether it is the best possible answer supported by the most compelling reasoning.

8.2 The Rule of Law as Convention

The rule of law depends on a convention that officials apply the law when the law directs them to do so rather than issuing directives and resolving disputes on some other ground. By this I mean that in situation type S_1, legal officials prefer to follow the law if other officials follow the law in situation type S_1 but would follow some other rule if others do not apply the law in situation type S_1. There are many reasons that an official might do A when the law requires B. The official might believe that the balance of non-legal moral considerations weighs in favor of not following the law.[6] The official might have reasons of self-interest, which could include anything from sheer laziness to out-and-out corruption, not to follow the law. The official might wish to seek favor with political authorities that prefer some result other than the legally prescribed one. Some of these considerations may be objectionable for reasons having nothing to do with the rule of law. But others may be morally weighty. A morally conscientious official will, from time to time, find that her private views about what is morally preferable diverge from the law.

Legal officials might take a range of attitudes toward the law. To simplify a bit, I will consider three types of general attitudes. An official who is faithful to the law makes a good faith attempt to determine what the law instructs her to do and treats this as a weighty, although defeasible, reason to act according to the law. The faithful official will typically apply the law as she perceives it regardless of external incentives to do so and will sometimes apply the law when it reaches results that differ from her all-things-considered moral judgment about the right result. When faced with a difficult legal question, she will go to great lengths to determine the proper legal result before concluding that the legal materials are indeterminate and that she must therefore rely on her own judgment. Even here, the faithful official will try to reach a result that coheres well with the rest of the law.

Of course, even legal officials who are committed to faithfully applying the law should deviate from the law in some circumstances. Following the law regardless of all other considerations is a sort of moral fanaticism. There are circumstances, even in basically just and decent legal systems, in which the prima facie obligation to apply the law is outweighed by other moral considerations. I do not wish to explore the issue of how wide or narrow this set of circumstances is. It suffices to say that if such circumstances are construed too broadly, they will undermine the convention that legal officials follow the law and so there must be some non-trivial range of circumstances in which the obligation to apply the law faithfully outweighs countervailing non-legal moral considerations.

A second type of official is the legal cynic. The legal cynic cares about the content of the law, but for purely instrumental reasons. The legal cynic is concerned to avoid sanction and perhaps to advance his career and will apply the law when necessary to achieve these ends. The legal cynic lacks, however, any internal motivation to determine the correct legal result or to apply the law faithfully. If he feels reasonably certain that he will not be sanctioned for failing to apply the law, he may make decisions on other grounds. The legal cynic may be public-spirited, self-interested, or some combination of the two. The cynic might be a careerist, concerned to receive good job evaluations, curry favor with political authorities or receive recognition for legal acumen. But the legal cynic might instead be someone genuinely motivated to do the most good in the world who does not see the law as a means to achieving that end.

This sort of cynic may have prudential reasons to follow the law since ignoring the law entirely could result in him being dismissed, demoted, sanctioned, or distrusted by his superiors and thus frustrate his ability to achieve his goals. Of course, being this sort of legal cynic might be an entirely appropriate response to a legal system that does not, in general, promote morally good ends.

A third sort of official is the legal nihilist.[7] The legal nihilist is like the legal cynic in having no intrinsic motivation to apply the law, but goes beyond this by ignoring the law altogether. This could be because the legal nihilist is skeptical that the law has any sort of determinant content whatsoever and therefore cannot require any particular result. Or the legal nihilist might believe that it makes no difference whether one applies the law or not. The legal nihilist might, for example, try to reach results that will please her superiors regardless of whether they are legal. Or perhaps she is committed to resolving disputes according to her broader moral views and finds that the law is simply irrelevant in working out what the best thing to do is. Legal nihilists may differ greatly from one another. The key commonality is that they only follow the law by coincidence.

All three types may exist within a single legal system. In general, the more faithful officials and the fewer legal nihilists in a legal system, the better it will function. The role of legal cynics is context dependent. In a system with many faithful officials, legal cynics are less likely to create trouble, as the cynics will be more likely to see themselves as having prudential reasons to apply the law. In a system with many legal nihilists, however, the cynics are less likely to apply the law since they will believe that reputational benefits for doing so are minimal and sanctions for failing to do so are unlikely. In a legal system with a mix of types, the behavior of legal cynics will depend in large part on how well they can be monitored and sanctioned. The presence of legal cynics stresses the legal system. Strong institutions can withstand a certain amount of stress. Too much stress will cause them to break down.

Dividing officials into ideal types is an oversimplification. The same officials might act as a faithful official in one context but not in another. For example, an official might faithfully apply the law in domains that seem morally defensible as a whole, but act as a legal cynic in a domain where the law seems morally perverse. More importantly, the behavior of legal officials might depend on their expectations about the behavior of other parties in the legal system. An official might act as a faithful official if she expects others to do so, but behave as a legal cynic if she perceives other officials as cynics or nihilists. In many cases this is perfectly reasonable.

A central function of law is to solve coordination problems for agents who have an interest in coordinating their actions with those of others but have difficulty in doing so when making choices individually. The law does this by guiding action, for example by requiring that drivers drive on the left side of the road rather than the right, and by prescribing punishment for those who break the rules. The latter is especially important in situations in which conventions are not self-enforcing and so establishing a rule is not sufficient to resolve the coordination problem. Many of the benefits of rule by law are only available if the law is applied at least somewhat regularly. The law cannot provide certainty or predictability if officials routinely ignore it. Legal subjects who realize that officials do not apply the law are unlikely to use the law to guide their own behavior. Rule by law is therefore a collective action problem. There are systemic benefits to using law to guide the behavior of legal officials but each official has their own competing non-legal reasons for action.

For morally responsible officials, applying the law is not a pure coordination convention. A pure coordination convention is one such as the convention to drive on the left side of the road in which agents are indifferent as to which rule to follow and care only that all follow the same rule. The rule of law is not like this. In a minimally decent legal system it is better that officials follow the law than that they act on non-legal reasons. So while the morally responsible official might look to whether other officials apply the law when deciding whether to apply the law herself, she will prefer the world in which all officials follow the law to the world in which no officials follow the law. In a system populated mainly by officials who prefer to follow the law if others do so as well, following the law will be a stable equilibrium. Of course, faithful officials faced with an environment in which few officials follow the law cannot simply will their way to the better equilibrium. It may be unwise for legal officials to apply the law in the face of non-legal reasons not to do so absent a belief that other officials behave similarly. There is little to be gained by being one of a few faithful officials in a legal system but much to be gained by having an entire legal system staffed by faithful officials.

In game theoretical terms, the situation faced by officials who value the rule of law resembles a stag hunt (see Skyrms 2012). In an example first introduced by Rousseau (1997, 163), hunters may either hunt stag together, which will only be successful if all hunters participate, or hunt hare individually, which each individual hunter can successfully do alone. The payoff for a successful stag hunt is greater than the payoff for a successful hare hunt. All hunters will do better if all cooperate in hunting stag together, but if some do not cooperate, the rest will do better to hunt hare alone. So if the hunters expect their fellows to do their part in the stag hunt, they should do so as well, but if they expect some other hunters to go after hare while letting the stag escape, they should hunt hare. Matters are more complex if the question of whether officials are to follow the law is more like a prisoner's dilemma. In this case, each official prefers to follow her own moral views when they conflict with the law but prefers that other officials faithfully follow the law.

The officials prefer the state of the world in which all officials follow the law to that in which no officials follow the law. But left to their own devices, they will each rule according to their own moral views. In this case, some mechanism may be necessary to sanction officials who do not faithfully apply the law so as to shift the motivations of officials. This will tend to shift the strategic situation from a prisoner's dilemma to the stag hunt. Sanctions are less important if legal officials are intrinsically motivated to promote the rule of law. One benefit of a legal culture with a strong commitment to the rule of law is that legal officials who intrinsically care about the rule of law are more likely to see themselves as in a stag hunt than in a prisoner's dilemma and therefore more likely to follow the law so long as they expect others to do so as well.[8]

If the foregoing analysis is correct, the attitude that a legal official takes toward the law will depend in part on their expectations about the behavior of other officials in the legal system. Legal officials are not likely to apply the law for its own sake unless they believe that other officials apply the law with a certain degree of frequency. Trust in the good faith of other officials in the legal system is therefore of great importance. This will depend both on whether officials perceive others to be applying the law impartially and on whether officials trust the moral and prudential judgment of other officials. High trust in other officials encourages faithful application of the law, which in turn encourages these other officials to follow the law. High trust and high compliance with the law is therefore likely to be a stable equilibrium while low trust and low compliance is also likely to be stable. Partner choice over repeated interactions is sometimes effective in spreading pro-social norms (Baumard, Andre, and Sperber 2013). But legal officials typically do not have control over which officials they will interact with. Oversight by faithful officials may push cynical officials to follow the law, but in a low trust environment, unlawful conduct may be so common that sanctions cannot be deployed against enough officials to change the legal culture.[9] This might go some way to explaining why some governments seem remarkably law abiding while others seem pervasively lawless despite superficially similar laws and institutional arrangements.

Perceptions of fellow officials are of great importance. For several reasons, whether officials are making a good faith effort to follow the law is only partially observable. First, officials have limited time to monitor the behavior of other officials, especially those for whom they have no formal responsibilities. Second, legal officials are not always candid about the true reasons for their actions. A skillful lawyer can often find an explanation for a dubious decision that has at least a surface level of plausibility, especially to those who have not carefully studied the underlying legal materials. Even in well-functioning legal systems, judges sometimes give pretextual reasons for their decisions (Kolber 2018). Shrewd cynics and nihilists will usually find ways to cloak their actions so as not to appear too egregious. Faithful officials will also be inclined to offer pretextual reasons for their decisions in those rare cases in which they deviate from what the law requires in order to protect the reputation of the legal system. Third, it can be difficult to distinguish good faith mistakes from officials who are in some sense not really trying to get the law right. This is especially so where the law is not clear or where the facts are complex. Fourth, faithful officials might have reasonable disagreements about whether a particular case is one in which officials ought to deviate from what the law requires.[10]

All of this suggests that officials have imperfect information about the extent to which others are attempting to follow the law faithfully and are not able to signal such a disposition to each other with perfect clarity. Officials will tend to conclude that other officials are applying the law faithfully insofar as that they agree with their legal judgments, find that they give plausible reasons for their legal conclusions and do not appear to overstep their authority. Because legal officials have only limited insight into the motives of other officials and may have different conceptions of the scope of reasonable disagreement between faithful officials, significant disagreement about legal outcomes tends to lower trust between officials. Disagreement in legal judgment among officials thus discourages faithful application of the law and tempts officials to give legal explanations that do not reflect their underlying reasoning.

An implication of this argument is that agreement on the content of the law among legal officials is desirable for reasons that do not depend on agreement being a sign of correctness. Of course, this is not the only reason to care about agreement on legal results. Convergence in legal judgment is often evidence of moral merit. And convergence in judgment makes legal systems more efficacious in guiding the action of legal subjects and resolving disputes in a predictable and expeditious manner. Promoting agreement between legal officials is only one virtue of a legal rule and must be weighed against other considerations. "Always find for Defendant against Plaintiff" is a rule that is simple to apply and could, in principle, generate universal agreement on the correct outcome of civil cases. But because it is entirely divorced from the point of having civil adjudication at all, it is a non-starter as a decision rule. It is self-undermining, because the sheer irrationality of the rule would encourage officials to find pretexts to avoid situations in which it should be applied or to ignore the rule altogether. Agreement should therefore be a criterion to decide between legal norms that are otherwise plausible on other grounds, especially when there do not otherwise appear to be decisive considerations to distinguish between them. As will be argued later, theories of statutory interpretation provide a plausible example.

To summarize, legal officials often face situations in which they must choose between applying the law and pursuing other objectives. For many officials, willingness to apply the law depends on their expectations of other officials in the legal system. Trust in the lawful conduct of other officials makes faithful application of the laws more likely which in turn reinforces trust. Distrust encourages a cynical approach to the law, which spreads distrust. This means that it is of great importance to achieve and maintain a high trust equilibrium in the legal system. Faithfulness to the law is only partially observable. Legal officials are likely to take agreement with their legal judgment as strong evidence of faithfulness to the law. This gives us reason to prefer legal rules that tend to create convergence in judgment between officials to rules that lead to disagreement between officials aside from any epistemic value of agreement. In other words, it is good for legal officials to agree about how to apply the law apart from whether their judgment converges on the best result.

8.3 Building Trust between Legal Officials

The foregoing argument suggests that trust between legal officials is important to a well-functioning legal system. A low trust legal system will necessarily rely more heavily on monitoring and incentives for good legal performance. Such legal systems can function well if they are carefully designed and well-administered. All else equal, however, a high trust legal system will both be more effective, efficient, and stable. Low trust systems are at greater risk of unravelling if the threat of sanctions becomes insufficient to motivate officials or if the system of sanctioning becomes too capricious because the higher level officials administering it are insufficiently concerned with fidelity to the law as opposed to disciplining officials who displease them for other reasons.

A high trust legal system has other benefits as well. Judges in a high trust system are more likely to be transparent about the true reasons for their decisions and less likely to make rulings on pretextual grounds or otherwise obfuscate the reasons for their decisions. Appellate tribunals are more likely to defer to fact-finders if they believe that the fact-finders' determinations are based on a good faith effort to get things right and that the reasons they give in their rulings reflect the actual reasons for their decisions. The law in a high trust system is more likely to be stable and thus more likely to be predictable. And a high trust system is more likely to respond effectively to changing circumstances because the officials in the system will find it easier to coordinate on responses that all accept as authoritative.

Social trust is important to the rule of law in a second way. In a complex legal system, convergence on shared understandings of how to apply the law to particular facts depends on shared understandings about how to translate legal materials—statutes, case law, administrative regulation, and so on—into legal content. Some such understandings are based on formal constitutional or statutory rules, such as the rule that the US Constitution is superior to other sources of law. Others emerge from judicial practice. A great deal of interpretive work is done by informal rules, sometimes called canons of statutory interpretation that judges use to resolve difficult interpretive questions (Baude and Sachs 2017). For example, the canon against surplusage provides that when considering two interpretations, one should prefer an interpretation that renders all words necessary to the meaning of the statute to an interpretation that renders some words duplicative or superfluous (Scalia and Garner 2012, 440). Canons help judges to agree on interpretations of ambiguous statutes and give prospective guidance to legislatures about how their legislation will be construed by courts.[11] Will Baude and Steve Sachs (2017, 1084) argue that canons can be divided into linguistic canons that reflect standard linguistic practice and legal canons that are rules of a legal system. The former are useful for interpretation of both legal and non-legal texts since they reflect the practices of typical writers in a given language while the latter might well violate rules of standard English usage and are in fact a substantive law of interpretation created by judges. What counts as a canon is dependent on what judges accept as a canon. As Victoria Nourse and Anita Krishnakumar (2018, 188) argue, "the basic thread connecting the canons is (or should be) established convention. Longevity or historical pedigree, and perhaps a connection to the Constitution, can help demonstrate established convention, but ... the real, indispensable measure for such convention must be regular Supreme Court use across ideological divides." The disposition to accept rules adopted by one's ideological opponents depends in part on trust that one's opponents will apply the rules fairly when they go against their preferred outcomes. Trust across ideological lines is therefore important in creating the tacit understandings that make legal interpretation more stable.

Various features of the design of legal systems and the substance of legal doctrine serve to minimize the scope for disagreement on potentially controversial interpretive questions. I will discuss two. One strategy to conserve trust in the legal system is to make procedure the primary focus of legal rules and delegate context-specific factual judgments and decisions on controversial normative matters to decision-makers with somewhat narrow institutional roles. For example, a wide range of questions in civil and criminal trials are delegated to unaccountable juries (or trial judges) whereas appeals courts largely review whether the trial court has followed the proper procedure. As a result, the substance of appellate cases in the US legal system focuses very heavily on procedural matters such as jurisdiction and rules of evidence. This focuses appellate judges on legal questions concerning fair procedures about which there is more likely to be broad agreement on most underlying normative principles. This division of labor might be dubious from an epistemic point of view as it puts important decisions in the hands of lay jurors who may not be especially well prepared to sort through complex fact patterns involving complicated business transactions or intricate financial frauds. By contrast, appellate judges are typically asked to consider not whether a defendant is guilty or not guilty or whether a defendant's conduct was reasonable or unreasonable but only whether a reasonable jury might have found it so. In theory at least, this means that the most difficult questions in these areas should be left to juries and trial judges while appellate judges decide only whether the lower court's decision fell below the threshold of reasonable disagreement.[12]

Similarly, judicial review of administrative action focuses heavily on procedural questions. Administrative agencies are given considerable discretion to make substantive decisions so long as they follow the proper procedures and do not exceed their statutory authority. As with jurors, judges are typically asked to decide whether agency action has gone too far rather than whether the action was, all things considered, the best thing to do. When substantive matters are considered, they are often done in a way that is deferential to the initial decision-maker such as when agency decisions are reviewed under the arbitrary and capricious standard (Administrative Procedure Act, 5 U.S.C. § 706(2)(A)) or when agency interpretations of statutes are given deference under *Chevron v. Natural Resources Defense Council*, 467 U.S. 837 (1984). Part of the justification of *Chevron* is clearly epistemic: agencies receive deference in areas in which they are expert as long as they stay within the scope of plausible interpretations of a statute. But a side effect of this approach is that it potentially removes a number of politically controversial interpretive questions from the remit of appellate courts by adopting a "tie goes to the agency" approach to hard interpretive questions.[13] Of course, heated disagreement might still emerge when considering whether an agency's decision is based on a permissible construction of the statute. But here the inquiry is whether the agency has given a plausible reading, not whether it has given the best one. The approach may tend to diminish vertical trust by making administrative agencies less accountable, but increase horizontal trust since it spares judges the necessity of reaching agreement on a significant class of hard legal questions.

A second strategy for building horizontal trust is to design rules for the selection, training, and promotion of legal officials that inculcate shared understandings about the law. This is most easily done by maintaining a professional staff of legal officials who work within the same system for an entire career. Such officials would receive similar educations, which would provide them with a similar knowledge base, inculcate similar cultural norms, and allow future officials to develop social relationships with one another. They would be subject to similar standards for hiring and promotion and would play the leading role in evaluating each other's work. In many nations, although not in the United States, judges are selected at a relatively young age and hired into a meritocratic bureaucracy, in which the most esteemed judges are promoted from the lowest level courts to high level courts over the course of their career. Commonality of experience and strong career incentives to appear favorably in the eyes of other judges probably contribute to higher levels of horizontal trust. But there is an important trade-off here. The very factors that build trust between members of the legal system tend to make it unrepresentative of the larger population and poorly responsive to public sentiment. For this reason, there is a danger that institutions that build horizontal trust may undermine vertical trust.

8.4 Trust and Statutory Interpretation

The first part of the argument has established that trust between legal officials is important to the rule of law and that agreement between officials is valuable in that it enhances trust. This section will explore some implications of this conclusion for debates about legal methodology. I will argue that the desideratum of agreement between legal officials can be used in selecting methods of statutory interpretation. This is an unusual approach. More typical approaches to interpretive methodology usually involve (a) arguing that a methodology captures the meaning of statutes better than its rivals (Katzmann 2014, 4–5), (b) arguing that a methodology captures the intentions of the legislature better than its rivals (Fallon 2014, 686), or (c) identifying some extrinsic value such as democratic legitimacy, legislative supremacy, or transparency to the public and argue that the methodology better serves this end (Dworkin 1986). My argument is most similar to the third approach, but rather than being grounded in an expensive conception of the moral aims of law, appeals only to a fairly minimal conception of the rule of law. This minimal conception depends only on the proposition that it is better for legal officials to apply the law for its own sake absent unusually strong moral considerations to the contrary. For this reason, it might find support from people who have deep disagreements about other aspects of legal methodology.

There is a long running debate between proponents of textualist and purposivist approaches to statutory interpretation. How to define these terms is controversial. In general, textualists prefer interpretation in terms of plain meaning, oppose consultation of legislative history, and prefer to resolve ambiguities through use of canons of interpretation rather than speculation about legislative motives. Purposivist interpretation construes statutory language in light of the purposes that might reasonably be attributed to the legislature. In a classic statement of the "legal process theory" of statutory interpretation, Henry Hart and Albert Sacks (1994, 1374) argue that

> [I]n interpreting a statute a court should: 1. Decide what purpose ought to be attributed to the statute and to any subordinate provision of it which may be involved; and then 2. Interpret the words of

> the statute immediately in question so as to carry out the purpose as best it can, making sure, however, that it does not give the words either—(a) a meaning they will not bear, of (b) a meaning which would violate any established policy of clear statement.

The gist of this is that the plain meaning of statutory terms is a constraint on permissible interpretations, but when choosing between plausible interpretations, courts should prefer an interpretation that coheres with the overall aims of the statute even if that interpretation might seem less preferable on purely linguistic grounds. Textualists disagree. John Manning (2006, 110) suggests, "textualism means that in resolving ambiguity, interpreters should give precedence to semantic context (evidence about the way reasonable people use words) rather than policy context (evidence about the way reasonable people would solve problems)." Caleb Nelson (2005, 351) argues that underlying this difference is a preference for rules on the part of textualists and for standards on the part of purposivists. In other words, textualists prefer bright line rules applied in a somewhat formalistic way whereas purposivists prefer standards that are more open-ended.

There is a vast literature on the advantages and disadvantages of each approach. Textualists tend to suggest that their approach is preferable on the one hand in placing greater constraints on judges who might be inclined to read their only policy preferences into the law and on the other in making the law more understandable and predictable for citizens trying to understand their legal position by reading statutes (Scalia and Garner 2012, xxviii, xxix). Arguments for textualism range from the claim that purposivist judging usurps the role of the legislature (Manning 1997), the argument that judges are better positioned to apply textualist than purposivist methodology (Vermeule 1998), and the argument that purposivist method undermines that rule of law by making the meaning of statutes opaque for citizens attempting to determine their rights and duties (Scalia 1989). Purposivists suggest that textualist methodology tends to frustrate the aims of legislatures (Eskridge 2013, 560–7), is apt to be unworkable in the sort of hard cases in which interpretive methodology is likely to be important (Eskridge 2013, 583–7), and deprives judges of valuable contextual information such as legislative history (Katzmann 2014, 35–39). I will not try to resolve this debate. Instead, I would like to suggest that different methodological approaches may be appropriate in different areas of the law[14] and that the importance of agreement on legal outcomes can help to determine which approach is more appropriate in a given context.

Does textualist methodology lead to greater convergence among interpreters on the content and proper application of the law or does purposive methodology generate greater agreement? There are things to be said in favor of each view.[15] Textualists might point to the way in which their methodology restricts the scope of considerations that can be brought to bear on statutory interpretation. This both limits the extent that judges can appeal to normatively controversial purposes and the extent to which they can "cherry pick" favorable legislative history. Purposivists might argue that textualism fares poorly when confronted with ambiguous texts and needlessly produces hard cases by removing some of the tools judges might use to resolve ambiguities. Moreover, the canons of interpretation that textualists believe should resolve ambiguities sometimes yield unequivocal or even contradictory results (Llewellyn 1950, 399).

The extent to which textualism or purposivism leads to greater agreement on the content of the law is likely to be domain specific. In areas in which there is broad agreement on the background normative considerations, purposivism may have an advantage. In such areas, legal interpreters are likely to have similar intuitions about the ways to interpret provisions in light of the underlying aims of the statute.[16] It also is more likely to be the case that the statute in question reflects a normatively coherent perspective rather than an unprincipled compromise between mutually inconsistent viewpoints. Purposive considerations and policy reasoning more generally can help interpreters to come to similar conclusions even when the text is semantically or syntactically ambiguous or when different parts of the same statute appear to have different implications.

Where there is broad agreement on the background objectives of the law, legal officials should develop shared understandings about the ways in which laws are to be interpreted in this domain. This is not a suggestion that judges develop shared understandings that undermine the values implicit in the relevant statutory schemes. The idea is that where the shared understandings are consistent with the statutory scheme, they might render more purposive interpretation appropriate. I want to remain neutral about whether the norms governing interpretation in a given legal system are a part of a law of that legal system or merely a set of extra-legal conventions concerning the extraction of legal content from legal materials. It may be that some fall into the former category and some in the latter (Baude and Sachs 2017, 1084). The key point is that these norms should be crafted in part with an eye toward helping legal officials to converge on the same interpretation of legal materials.

Matters are different when there is deep normative disagreement about the relevant policy considerations. Here, interpreters are likely to have different intuitive reactions to the way in which purposes have bearing on the meaning of a statute. Of course, judges are capable of interpreting statutes in light of purposes that they find normatively objectionable. But it is generally much easier to reason from a position with which one agrees than from one with which one disagrees. And it is easier to imaginatively reconstruct the intentions of parties whose aims one broadly shares. When there is pervasive underlying normative disagreement, it may be advantageous to restrict interpreters to consideration of purposes found on the face of the statute. Although textual considerations may not always be decisive, in normatively contested areas of law they will tend to be less divisive than purposive considerations. A formalistic approach to statutory interpretation can be useful precisely where more open-ended inquiry is likely to leave judges with differing ideologies at loggerheads.

Income tax law provides an example of the first type of case. Although tax law is based on a voluminous statutory code reinforced by an even larger number of regulations, it is an area in which agreement on the underlying policy animating much of the code can help to resolve statutory ambiguities. The underlying idea is that as Lord McNaughton once put it, "an income tax is ... a tax on income" (*London CC v Attorney General* [1901] A.C. 26 HL, 35). In light of this aim, the tax code should be interpreted to the extent possible such that tax is imposed on all and only those items that are the taxpayer's income from an economic point of view. This does not resolve all possible ambiguities because there are still hard cases that turn on whether a receipt is an item of income or not or if so whether it is income to the taxpayer or to some other party. But it does give us reason to prefer interpretations that make sense in light of economic substance to ones that would cause tax treatment to deviate from the underlying economic reality. To illustrate the differences in possible approaches, consider a pair of cases from around the same time in the United States and United Kingdom. In *Gregory v Helvering*, 293 U.S. 465 (1935), Evelyn Gregory owned shares in a company, United Mortgage Holdings ("United") that held 1,000 shares of Monitor Securities Corporation ("Monitor"). If United sold the shares of Monitor and distributed the proceeds to Gregory, the amount distributed would be taxed as a dividend. Instead, Gregory, formed a new corporation, Averill, and transferred the Monitor shares to Averill. She then liquidated Averill, distributed the Monitor shares to herself, sold the Monitor shares, and claimed the proceeds to be taxable as a capital gain (*Gregory v. Helvering*, 467). Gregory claimed that the transaction was a "'reorganization' under Section 112(g) of the Revenue Act of 1928" (*Gregory v Helvering*, 467). Although Gregory's transaction seemed to fall under the literal meaning of Section 112(g) insofar as she was in control of both the transferring corporation and the recipient corporation, the US Supreme Court, affirming a Second Circuit Court of Appeals opinion authored by Judge Learned Hard, (*Helvering v. Gregory*, 69 F.2d 809 (1934)), ruled that Gregory should be taxed as if she were paid a dividend by United. As Justice Sutherland put it, Gregory's transaction was "an operation having no business or corporate purpose ... [the] accomplishment of which was the consummation of a preconceived plan, not to reorganize a business or any part of a business, but to transfer a parcel of corporate shares to the petitioner." (*Gregory v Helvering*, 469). The upshot of this approach is that courts should consider the economic substance of a transaction in light of the purpose of the relevant statutory provision and not necessarily uphold transactions merely because they take a form that plausibly falls within the meaning of a formalistic interpretation of the statutory language.

The UK approach at this time was quite different. In *IRC v Duke of Westminster* [1936] AC 1, the Duke of Westminster signed covenants to provide annuities to several long-time servants. In a separate letter, the Duke's solicitor explained that the servants would be expected to accept a wage reduced by the amount of the annuity. However, there was no obligation for the servants to stay in the Duke's employment in order to receive the annuity. Under UK law at the time, an annuity was generally income of the recipient for tax purposes and could be set against the payer's taxable income. Wages paid to personal servants, however, could not be set against the employer's taxable income. The Duke, an extraordinarily wealthy aristocrat taxed at a very high marginal rate, claimed that he should not be taxed on the value of annuities. The Commissioners of Inland Revenue disagreed. A divided House of Lords held that the Duke was not liable for tax on the annuities. The majority emphatically rejected the notion that taxation should follow the economic substance of the transaction. Lord Russell of Killowen stated, "I view with disfavour the doctrine that in taxation cases the subject is to be taxed if, in accordance with a Court's view of what it considers the substance of the transaction, the Court thinks that the case falls within the contemplation or spirit of the statute. The subject is not taxable by inference or by analogy, but only by the plain words of a statute applicable to the facts and circumstances of his case" (*IRC v Duke of Westminster*, 24).

The reasoning in *Gregory v. Helvering*, if applied to the facts of the *Duke of Westminster*, would make for an easier case. Here, the formalistic approach—asking whether the annuity is a separate agreement from the employment agreement—leads to a close case, whereas the appeal to economic substance considered in light of the purposes of the statute—asking whether the Duke enjoyed the benefit of the income or was simply making a disinterested gift—yields a more determinate result. Although matters may not have been so when *Duke of Westminster* was decided, there is now broad agreement that income taxes should be imposed on economic income enjoyed by the taxpayer to the extent that this is administratively feasible.[17] This agreement tends to cut across ideological lines, including, for example, supporters and opponents of progressive taxation. In this way, overarching policy considerations can help interpreters agree on how to apply the technical provisions of the tax code to complex fact patterns.

By contrast, textualism seems better able to promote agreement in areas in which there is deep normative disagreement on the relative underlying policy considerations and where purposivist methodology is likely to push interpreters with different ideological perspectives apart. This suggests that textualist approaches should be preferred in areas such as constitutional law in which there is deep disagreement about foundational normative matters. Which areas are ideological flashpoints varies by legal system and varies over time within a single legal system. In general, areas of regulatory law that balance competing considerations, environmental protection, and economic growth for example, are more likely to be sites of normative discord than areas, (antitrust might be such an area), in which disagreement centers more on means than on ends. In the former areas, a more formal approach to statutory interpretation might yield as much agreement as possible given the underlying ideological tensions.[18]

8.5 Conclusion

In order for the legal system to function effectively, officials must sometimes apply the law because it is the law. Their disposition to do so depends in part upon trust in other officials to act similarly. Disagreement over the content and proper application of legal rules tends to undermine trust between officials and thus their motivation to follow the law. For this reason, promoting convergence in judgment should be an aim of legal methodology even aside from any reason to think that this convergence of judgment tracks substantively desirable results. For hard issues, such as the best approach to statutory interpretation, the question of which method best promotes convergence in judgment can be used to choose legal methodology where other considerations are equivocal or too controversial to secure broad agreement. Purposivism is generally a better tool for securing agreement about how to construe ambiguous passages in statutes where there is rough normative consensus about the higher-level considerations of policy. Textualism is typically more attractive when there is deep disagreement about the background normative principles. The appropriate balance between the two approaches will vary across legal systems. Which methods promote convergence in legal judgment depends both on the institutional design and culture of a legal system and on broader social and political factors. Conventions are often path dependent and every legal system must work out its own common understandings.

Notes

* The author would like to thank the editors for helpful comments as well as participants in the Bowling Green State University Conference on Social Trust, in staff research seminars at the University of Surrey School of Law and at the University of Bergen Faculty of Law, and in the 2020 Tax Research Network Conference. The author also wishes to thank Benita R. Mathew for research assistance.

1. "Horizontal trust" sometimes refers to the bonds of trust between citizens (Lenard 2015, 353). The terminology seems applicable here as well since the reciprocal relationships among citizens and among legal officials contrasts with the hierarchical relationship between legal officials and citizens.
2. A final sense of trust is the trust the legal system places in legal officials when giving them discretion to interpret, construct or create the law (Shapiro 2011, 331–52). This is not what I mean by trust here. Rather than the attitude of the legal system toward officials, I am concerned with the attitude of legal officials toward one another.
3. The Ottoman Empire and Mamluk Egypt addressed this problem by conscripting or buying children from outside the governing class to form the next generation of government officials so that officials would have no family ties outside the state and could not aspire to pass on their political power to their own children (Turchin and Nefedov 2009, 24–25).
4. As Andreas Bergh, Christian Bjørnskov, and Kevin Vallier (2021) point out elsewhere in this volume, although trust in the legal system is typically associated with social trust in the society as a whole, this linkage may be broken if agents of the legal system are seen as unrepresentative of the larger society.
5. For the distinction between cognitive and non-cognitive theories of trust, see Becker (1996) and Jones (1996).
6. For purposes of exposition, I put my argument in terms that suggest a positivist view of the law. More specifically, I appeal to a distinction between legal reasons and non-legal moral reasons for action. Legal positivism is the view that whether a norm is legally valid depends on its sources and not on its merits (Gardner 2001, 199). In other words, whether a given rule is part of the law depends on whether it has been created according to the rules of the legal system and not on whether it is morally desirable. This leaves open the question of whether the law might sometimes require legal officials to exercise their moral judgment by incorporating moral standards and the question of whether legal officials morally ought to follow the law when the law gives directives that conflict with the official's own moral judgment. It is possible that my argument could be reconstructed in anti-positivist terms, although I will not attempt to do so here. For Dworkinians, all types of moral considerations could, in principle, be relevant to the ways in which legal materials create legal content (Dworkin 1986). It is less clear for Dworkinians than for positivists, therefore, whether a given normative consideration gives rise to legal reasons or non-legal moral reasons.
7. The label is inspired by Russian Prime Minister Dmitri Medvedev, a corporate lawyer by training, who complained a decade ago that Russia was a land of "legal nihilism" (Smolchenko 2008, 1).
8. Once the parties have committed to following some legal rule, the strategic situation may shift to a partial conflict coordination game, sometimes known as "The Battle of the Sexes," in which two parties prefer to agree on some outcome, but disagree on which of two preferable outcomes is preferable (Gaus 2011, 458; Waldron 1999, 103–4). This differs from a stag hunt because each party prefers agreement to disagreement under all circumstances.
9. In some cases, the best option may be to dismiss officials en masse and start over. To take an extreme example, the Republic of Georgia was without traffic police for several months in 2004 while new officers were trained after the government fired all traffic police (Light 2014, 325).

10. Some judges take their jobs to be primarily to resolve disputes in a manner that is fair to litigants and provide appropriate incentives for future conduct rather than to apply a body of pre-existing legal rules. For example, Judge Richard Posner described his own method of judging by saying that "I pay very little attention to legal rules, statutes, constitutional provisions. . . A case is just a dispute. The first thing you do is ask yourself—forget about the law—what is a sensible resolution of this dispute?" (Liptak 2017).
11. This guidance is imperfect. Surveys of congressional staff responsible for legislative drafting show that staff are aware of only some of the canons cited by judges (Gluck and Bressman 2013, 933–6).
12. In practice, judicial discomfort with delegating decisions to juries in certain contexts sometimes leads judges to try to avoid sending cases to trial or to take a more active role in policing the outcome of jury deliberations than might be expected from a straightforward reading of the doctrine.
13. This justification is controversial. For example, Justice Kavanaugh (2016, 2137–8) argues that *Chevron* generates uncertainty because judges have different standards for how ambiguous a statute must be before deference is required with some judges treating 90-10 issues as ambiguous while other require that an issue be closer than 65-35.
14. Frederick Schauer (1988, 547) has made a similar suggestion about the role of formalism in the legal system.
15. Skeptics doubt that differences in theoretical approaches to statutory interpretation have any large influence on results. For example, an empirical study by Frank Cross (2007, 1991–5) found that convergence upon textualist and purposivist methodologies does not lead to consensus among judges about case outcomes.
16. For a perceptive discussion of the role of intuition in legal judgment, see Crowe (2019, 77–84).
17. UK tax law has also moved away from the *Duke of Westminster* approach in the direction of *Gregory v. Helvering*, although it is fair to say that it remains more formalistic than the US approach to tax law.
18. Similar considerations might count in favor of the plain meaning rule (Schauer, 1990, 231–2; Schauer 1992, 724).

References

Baude, William and Stephen E Sachs. "The Law of Interpretation." *Harvard Law Review* 130, no. 4 (February 2017): 1079–147.

Baumard, Nicolas, Jean-Baptiste Andre, and Dan Sperber. "A Mutualistic Approach to Morality: the Evolution of Fairness by Partner Choice." *Behavioral and Brain Sciences* 36, no. 1 (February 2013): 59–78.

Becker, Lawrence C. "Trust as Non-Cognitive Security about Motives." *Ethics* 107, no. 1 (1996): 43–61.

Bergh, Andreas, Christian Bjørnskov, and Kevin Vallier. "Social and Legal Trust: The Case of Africa." in *Social Trust*, edited by Kevin Vallier and Michael Weber, Routledge, 2021.

Cross, Frank B. "The Significance of Statutory Interpretive Methodologies." *Notre Dame Law Review* 82 (2007): 1971–2004.

Crowe, Jonathan. "Not-So-Easy Cases." *Statute Law Review* 40, no. 1 (February 2019): 75–86.

Domenicucci, Jacopo and Richard Holton, "Trust as a Two-Place Relation." in *The Philosophy of Trust*, edited by Paul Faulkner and Thomas Simpson, 149–160. Oxford: Oxford University Press, 2017.

Dworkin, Ronald. *Law's Empire*. Cambridge: Harvard University Press, 1986.

Eskridge Jr., William N. "The New Textualism and Normative Canons." Review of *Reading Law: The Interpretation of Legal Texts*, by Antonin Scalia and Bryan A Garner. *Columbia Law Review* 113 (2013): 531–92.

Fallon Jr., Richard H. "Three Symmetries between Textualist and Purposivist Theories of Statutory Interpretation—and the Irreducible Roles of Values and Judgment within Both." *Cornell Law Review* 99, no. 4 (May 2014): 685–734.

Gardner, John. "Legal Positivism: 5½ Myths." *The American Journal of Jurisprudence* 46, no. 1 (June 2001): 199–227.

Gaus, Gerald, *The Order of Public Reason: A Theory of Freedom and Morality in a Diverse and Bounded World*. Cambridge: Cambridge University Press, 2011.

Gluck, Abbe R. and Lisa Schultz Bressman. "Statutory Interpretation from the Inside—An Empirical Study of Congressional Drafting, Delegation, and the Canons: Part I." *Stanford Law Review* 65, no. 5 (May 2013): 901–1025.

Hadfield, Gillian K. and Barry R. Weingast. "What is Law? A Coordination Model of the Characteristics of Legal Order." *Journal of Legal Analysis* 4, no. 1 (2012): 1–44.

Hardin, Russell. *Trust*. Cambridge: Polity Press, 2006.

Hart, Henry M. and Albert M. Sacks. *The Legal Process: Basic Problems in the Making and Application of Law*. Edited by William N. Eskridge and Philip P. Frickey. Westbury, NY: Foundation Press, 1994.

Hume, David. *A Treatise of Human Nature*. Edited by L. A. Selby-Bigge. Oxford: Clarendon Press, 1886.

Jones, Karen. "Trust as an Affective Attitude." *Ethics* 107, no. 1 (October 1996): 4–25.

Katzmann, Robert A. *Judging Statutes*. New York: Oxford University Press, 2014.

Kavanaugh, Brett M. "Review of *Judging Statutes* by Robert A. Katzmann." *Harvard Law Review* 129, no. 8 (June 2016): 2118–63.

Kolber, Adam. "Supreme Judicial Bullshit." *Arizona State Law Journal* 50, no. 1 (Spring 2018): 141–78.

Lenard, Patti Tamara. "The Political Philosophy of Trust and Distrust in Democracies and Beyond." *The Monist* 98, no. 4 (October 2015): 353–9.

Light, Matthew. "Police reforms in the Republic of Georgia: The Convergence of Domestic and Foreign Policy in an Anti-corruption Drive." *Policing and Society* 24, no. 3 (2014): 318–45.

Liptak, Adam. "An Exit Interview with Richard Posner, Judicial Provocateur." N.Y. Times (New York, NY) September 11, 2017, https://www.nytimes.com/2017/09/11/us/politics/judge-richard-posnerretirement.html.

Llewellyn, Karl N. "Remarks on the Theory of Appellate Decision and the Rules or Canons of About How Statutes are to be Construed." *Vanderbilt Law Review* 3, no. 3 (1950): 395–405.

Manning, John. "Textualism as a Nondelagation Doctrine." *Columbia Law Review* 97, no. 3 (April 1997): 673–737.

Manning, John F. "What Divides Textualists from Purposivists?" *Columbia Law Review* 106, no. 1 (January 2006): 70–111.

Nelson, Caleb. "What is Textualism?" *Virginia Law Review* 91, no. 2 (April 2005): 347–418.

Nickel, Philip J. "Trust, Staking, and Expectations." *Journal for the Theory of Social Behaviour* 39, no. 3 (August 2009): 345–62.
Nourse, Victoria F. and Anita S. Krishnakumar. "Canon Wars." *Texas Law Review* 97, no. 1 (November 2018): 163–91.
Rousseau, Jean-Jacques. *Discourse on Inequality (1754) reprinted in Rousseau: The Discourses and Other Early Political Writing*. Edited and translated by Victor Gourevitch. New York: Cambridge University Press, 1997.
Scalia, Antonin. "The Rule of Law as a Law of Rules." *University of Chicago Law Review* 56, no. 4 (Autumn 1989): 1175–88.
Scalia, Antonin and Bryan A. Garner. *Reading Law: The Interpretation of Legal Texts*. St. Paul, MN: West Publishing Company, 2012.
Schauer, Frederick. "Formalism." *Yale Law Journal* 97, no. 4 (March 1988): 509–48.
Schauer, Frederick. "Statutory Construction and the Coordinating Function of Plain Meaning." *Supreme Court Review* 7 (1990): 231–56.
Schauer, Frederick. "The Practice and Problems of Plain Meaning: A Response to Aleinikoff and Shaw." *Vanderbilt Law Review* 45, no. 3 (April 1992): 715–41.
Shapiro, Scott. *Legality*. Cambridge: Harvard University Press, 2011.
Skyrms, Brian. *The Stag Hunt and the Evolution of Social Structure*. New York: Cambridge University Press, 2012.
Smolchenko, Anna. "Medvedev Address Hints at Change." *Moscow Times* (Moscow, Russia), January 23, 2008.
Sztompka, Piotr. *Trust: A Sociological Theory*. Cambridge: Cambridge University Press, 2000.
Turchin, Peter and Sergey A. Nefedov. *Secular Cycles*. Princeton: Princeton University Press, 2009.
Tyler, Tom R. *Why People Obey the Law*. New Haven: Yale University Press, 1990.
Vermeule, Adrian. "Legislative History and the Limits of Judicial Competence: The Untold Story of Holy Trinity Church." *Stanford Law Review* 50, no. 6 (July 1998): 1833–96.
Waldron, Jeremy. *Law and Disagreement*. New York: Oxford University Press, 1999.

9 Social Trust and Mistrust of Parental Care

Amy Mullin

9.1 Introduction

We often focus on the extent to which, in trusting others, we risk personal betrayal. Trust always involves vulnerability, or susceptibility to harm, whether or not we reflect upon it. We worry that our own interests may be negatively affected by inappropriate trust. In this essay, I focus instead on the risks to which a third party is subjected and what responsibilities we have regarding our trust in others to care for a vulnerable third party. More particularly, I am interested in the responsibilities a society can have with respect to their trust in parents to care for children. Since young children are typically extremely trusting and largely incapable of protecting themselves, there are real risks to them when society trusts parents inappropriately. In order to trust appropriately, whether as professionals charged with specific responsibility for children, or merely as shared members of a particular society, people need to be informed about what children need, how parents may fail to meet those needs, and how biases about who is trustworthy and who is not may lead to inappropriate trust and mistrust. In what follows, I explain what I mean by simple interpersonal trust, discuss how this understanding of trust can be applied to situations in which society trusts parents to care for children, and explore not only how we can draw the borders of a society in a particular instance, but also how that society can best function in order to trust parents appropriately.

9.2 Interpersonal Trust: Simple Cases

What does it mean for trust to be appropriate? To answer this question, and to make sense of the risks involved in trusting individuals or groups to care adequately for a third party, we must first explore what is involved in normative interpersonal trust,[1] how it differs from mere reliance, and what constitutes a betrayal of trust in ordinary interpersonal cases.

In an ordinary case, a vulnerable party trusts an individual or group who can directly advance or harm their interests. Often when we trust we are not aware that we are doing so, because we have not reflected on the matter and our trust does not rise to the level of belief. The vulnerable party may simply assume that the ones trusted will do as expected, but in order for this to count as trust, it matters *why* the vulnerable party expects the entity trusted to advance, or at least not intentionally undermine, their interests, or some subset of them. If the vulnerable party has observed others behaving in a predictable manner, and has no interest in why, then they are simply relying on that behavior to be consistent. For instance, Max wants to sell banners that fans of a soccer team can wave to support their favorite team. Max has invested in manufacturing a large number of banners, is set to sell them outside a stadium, and expects that 10% of fans of the home team will purchase banners, and 20% of the more emotionally invested fans of the visiting team. Max does not care about soccer and has no idea why people would be silly enough to buy the banners, but relies upon their purchase. Should the fans of either the home team or the visiting team purchase fewer banners, Max would be disappointed and face a significant business loss. This means that Max is vulnerable with respect to the actions of the sports fans. However, since he is not interested in their motives, let alone approving of them, he would not feel betrayed by them. He does not trust them but instead merely relies on their behavior.

In contrast, Elena expects other members of her community to care about the local public library because it is an important community resource. She has organized a protest against cutbacks to libraries at the state level, and is confident that many people will join her protest. She also plans to work with members of her community to fundraise to support local libraries. When others do not join Elena in either the protest or the fundraising, she feels not only disappointed that her prediction was wrong and the situation will not go as she wants, but also betrayed by the apathy of people who live in her town, and especially by specific people she had identified as sharing her goals. Without necessarily thinking about it too much, Elena assumed that they shared her valuing of the local library, and her sense that it was an important community resource, not only as a way of making reading free, but also as a community center offering classes for seniors to improve their internet searches, and story time for toddlers and preschoolers. She trusted them to value public libraries for the same reasons she does and be willing to act to protect them.

Most basically, interpersonal trust involves assumptions about what other people care about and what they are capable of doing. Sometimes these assumptions will rise to the level of belief, but often they will not. People may only become aware of what they had assumed when they are confronted with a reality that does not meet their expectations. For instance, I may only realize that I trusted other members of my gym not to steal my street clothes, left in an unlocked locker while I worked out, when one of them steals from me and I feel betrayed. When we trust, we assume that the people we trust are capable of doing what we expect them to do. If Alex hopes that people he knows will join him in a political protest, but is aware they are disorganized and overcommitted, and often do not keep their promises, he does not trust them. Even though his acquaintances share Alex's political values, they are not competent when it comes to acting on the basis of what they pledge to do.

As the examples above suggest, when we trust, in addition to competence we assume that people share our values in a specific area. This is in keeping with D'Cruz' point that "Trust extends agency and affords reassurance in the relevant domain. The fundamental notion of trust is 'X trusts Y in domain of interaction D'" (2018, 243). The domains could be one or many. In this essay, I focus primarily on trust that is limited to a particular arena or domain, as defined by a social role or a specific undertaking. Moreover, when we trust someone within a particular domain, we expect them to behave for motives that we approve and share. For example, if Elena expects people to join her political protest but to do so cynically, as a way of currying her favor, then she does not trust them. I therefore differ from Hawley's account of trust, which links trust to people's competence to do something and having made a commitment (implicit or explicit) to do it: "To trust someone to do something is to believe that she has a commitment to doing it, and to rely upon her to meet that commitment" (Hawley 2014, 10). On my account, it is not enough that a person capable of doing X has made a commitment to do it. It also matters why we think they made that commitment. If they committed to doing something we want, but we believe or assume their reason is not one we share, especially if we disapprove of their reason, but even if we regard it as simply odd, then we do not trust them. If Elena's acquaintances are going to join her protest as a chance to gain personal notoriety, she may believe she can count on them to join her, but fail to trust them because she disapproves of or is bewildered by their reason. She can rely on them but does not trust them. Trust requires that those who are trusted act on the basis of social norms shared by the vulnerable party. However, we can trust people even when our values differ significantly. So long as what we are trusting them to do concerns the domain in which our values overlap, as well as dealing with actions we judge them competent to carry out, then we trust.

Annette Baier (1986) is an important theorist of interpersonal trust. My view has been shaped by and overlaps with hers in that she outlines trust as involving attitudes about others' competence and motivation. However, in her account the motivation we expect of those we trust is one of goodwill, either directly toward the person who trusts, or toward something or someone that person cares about. Certainly, many cases of interpersonal trust involve the vulnerable party assuming that the person who is trusted has goodwill toward them. For instance, if we trust a friend to care about us and come visit when we are recovering from a surgery, we expect that friend to have goodwill toward us. Similarly, when we trust an intimate partner to look out for our interests while we are recovering from our surgery, we expect them to bear us goodwill. However, we actually expect something more specific from friends and partners than mere goodwill—we expect the kind of care and consideration that is the norm in friendship and romantic partnerships.

While this might make it seem that Baier was right, I think she is wrong to believe that goodwill is always what vulnerable parties expect from those they trust. I think instead they expect the person or group they trust to share a commitment to a particular social norm, often but not always connected with a social role.[2] Sometimes the social norm might include bearing goodwill toward the vulnerable party. But sometimes it will not. For instance, I expect other members of my community to let the flowers in our park grow, and not uproot and take them home for their own gardens or cut and take them to put in a vase. I don't expect this behavior because I think those members of my community have goodwill toward me, or are even aware of my existence, but because I think they value being able to walk in a beautiful setting with flourishing plant life, and intend to do their part in preserving the park as just such a place. While this could be characterized as "goodwill" toward lovely parks, I think it is more accurately described as caring about having access to beautiful parks and wanting other people to care too. Perhaps the inaptness of thinking about "goodwill" in this context is made even more clear if we think about other members of our town wanting to be confident they can use public sidewalks without slipping on household garbage. They don't have goodwill toward the sidewalks. Instead they value being able to walk around our town easily and assume that others will share the norm of keeping sidewalks clean of detritus for this reason.

Another example, related to competitive activities, can suggest that trust can even be compatible with some ill will or at least competitive animus. When I play softball, I expect that the members of the other team will play fairly and care about winning in accordance with the rules. I believe they may steal a base, because that's part of the game, but I don't think they will come in my team's dugout and steal my equipment. Even if I think they feel resentment toward me and my team (perhaps we have had an easier route to softball success, and have sponsors who pay for our training and equipment, and they do not), I trust them to care about softball and want to play—and beat my team—according to its rules.

9.3 Third Party Risk, Appropriate Trust, and Morally Valuable Trust

Since trust involves assuming that the one trusted is competent to act as expected, and assuming (or believing) that those who trust and those who are trusted share a commitment to a social norm governing the realm in which the behavior is expected to occur, this lets us know what makes for appropriate trust. Trust is appropriate when the assumptions about competence and the social norm in question are warranted. But what makes these assumptions warranted? After all, if we had ample information about the trusted party's competence and motivations, we would not need to trust but could instead simply have well founded beliefs about what they will do and why.

In order to understand whether or not the assumptions are warranted, we need to know more about what is risked, and hence what is at stake. Hawley (2017) writes that:

> Some people are cautious about trusting, whilst others are quicker to trust: these differences may be due to varying past experiences (including experiences of injustice), to varying significance of the stakes, or just to differences in personality .... Trust typically involves risk, and we are familiar with the idea that people vary in their levels of risk aversion, so this should come as no surprise. Indeed, within certain limits, we can regard quite a large range of different attitudes to trust as both morally and rationally acceptable. (77)

However, while Hawley is surely right that one of the factors that affects whether or not trust is morally or rationally acceptable is the stakes involved, we also need to know *who* faces the risks, as it is often the case that a vulnerable third party will be more harmed by behavior that violates trust than the trusting party. The basic principle at operation here is what I call the *Third Party Risk Rule*: when risks are more than minimal and those who trust are not the only or main people to be vulnerable to betrayal, but instead some third party faces the bulk of the risk, then trust is less appropriate than when those who trust bear the overwhelming majority of the risk. In cases of trust that involve substantial Third Party Risk, moreover, those who trust have additional responsibility to take steps to become aware of reasons that would undermine confidence in the trusted party's competence and/or motivation to do what is expected for the reasons expected.

This might make it seem as if it will always be wrong to trust when Third Party Risk is involved, and that in those instances, instead of trusting, people should always or typically investigate and then make a well-founded judgment about what an individual or group can be expected to do and how this might affect vulnerable third parties. However, this cannot possibly be the case, for three reasons. First and perhaps most importantly, it would forestall needed action in many instances in which there is insufficient time or resources to investigate others' motives and competence. For example, imagine I am one of four parent volunteers accompanying a class of eight-year-old children on a trip to a local farm. Yasmine, one of the children in the group I am chaperoning suddenly takes off, running away from the others. I want to run after Yasmine but cannot do so without leaving behind the other children in my group. I notice another parent volunteer and cast him a frantic look asking him to watch over the other children in my group while I chase the runaway. I trust him and have no time to verify his competence and our shared social norms around what children need, what dangers might present themselves, and what adults can appropriately do in looking after them at a farm. So long as I am not overlooking an alternative that would subject the rest of the children in my group to even less risk while I run after Yasmine, it seems appropriate to trust, and certainly it would be wrong for me to investigate the trustworthiness of alternative parent child minders while leaving Yasmine to sprint away.

Second, routinely withholding trust when it comes to matters that impact children until their caregivers have been investigated and emerge as trustworthy would mandate intrusive surveillance of other people in contexts, such as their behavior in their own homes, in which it is reasonable for them to expect some privacy. Moreover, this surveillance would need to be undertaken in a manner that may be counter to developing and sustaining intimacy among people, such as members of a family, living together (Brighouse and Swift 2006). If we feel that our actions are or potentially are being viewed by others, or can be viewed by them later, such as if our interactions with children in our homes are videotaped, then it could be hard to share our honest enthusiasms, grumpy moods, and periods of silly play with those children. Yet without disclosing who we really are, with respect to a wide range of our character traits and interests, it is difficult for true intimacy to develop.

Third, we have good reason to be concerned that surveillance of others would be unevenly applied, and that prejudice and discrimination would factor into whose family life, or other private conduct, would be subject to scrutiny. For instance, Benjamin Levi and Greg Loeben (2004) have shown that when a girl is suspected of being abused, this suspicion is less likely to be reported. In addition, when a woman is suspected of being an abuser, this is less likely to be reported (2004, 279). Instead we will need to develop mechanisms that come short of extensive investigation into someone's behavior in all cases involving Third Party Risk, but still take account of the difference between appropriate trusting when one's own interests are primarily at stake and appropriate trusting in instances of Third Party Risk.

In order to make this situation more concrete, I turn in the next section to more detailed discussion of parental care, but first, I want to be clear that saying that trust is appropriate is not the same as saying that it is either morally justified or that it would be immoral to betray that trust. One situation in which trust is generally *appropriate* is when risks to oneself and others are not high, and there are no reasons to which the trusting party has access that undermine assumptions about the competence and motivation of those they trust to behave as expected (for reasons shared by those who trust). Even when risks are low, if those who trust are aware, or should be, that those they trust are unlikely to act as expected, trust is not appropriate, even if, for some other reasons, people think it would be good to act as if they were trusting. However, even when trust is appropriate, if those who trust are expecting the ones they trust to do something that might advance the trusting party's interests but be immoral or amoral, then that trust is not *morally* justified. For instance, there are norms governing the behavior of dinner party guests, that include not bringing along uninvited guests, bringing a gift for the party's hosts, being on time, not staying too late, and so forth. Raphael might expect Michelle, when invited to a dinner party at Raphael's house, to bring wine, because this is a traditional dinner party gift, but Michelle might disapprove of alcohol and bring flowers instead. Even if Raphael had been counting on serving Michelle's anticipated wine to dinner guests, she has done nothing wrong in bringing the flowers. This is because the expectation that a guest brings wine to a host's home in appreciation of a dinner invitation is *amoral* rather than moral and so Raphael's trust may be appropriate without being morally justified. Even in instances like this one in which the social norm concerns amoral behavior, Raphael's expectation that Michelle will conform to that norm could subject Raphael to some loss, such as embarrassment when he doesn't have enough wine to serve to guests. However, if Michelle's behavior falls within a range of reasonable expectations associated with the norm in question, as when she brings flowers rather than wine, it seems wrong to say that she has violated that norm, or has failed to live up to Raphael's trust.

Sometimes the social norm in question will be *immoral* rather than amoral. For instance, Patrick might expect Zach to join in his nasty gossip about other coworkers. When Zach refuses to do so, Patrick might feel betrayed, but Zach's refusal could easily reflect taking a moral stance, and so being untrustworthy in this instance would be a good thing. While one could define "appropriate trust" as only that trust which is not only warranted, when considering vulnerability, risk, and available information, *but also* morally justified, I think it is more straightforward to recognize that these two different ways in which trust may fail are quite distinct, and hence to use different terms to denote the different kinds of failure.[3] Trust may fail to be appropriate and it may fail to be morally justified. Of course, it may fail in both ways.

9.4 Trust and Parental Care

I turn now to a particular kind of trust that subjects third parties to significant risks and sometimes subjects the party that trusts to only minor risk, and that is when society trusts parents to care adequately for children. In my discussion of simple interpersonal trust, I mentioned trusting other people against whom one plays softball. However, softball is a game with a long history, and many codified rules. Many of the pursuits we engage in and norms we trust people to follow are not so detailed and the expectations are not explicitly laid out. Friendship is one example of a more open-ended practice and accordingly the social norms governing friendship can be fuzzy at the edges. Parental care, by which I mean care provided by people who are invested with significant long-term responsibility for a child's survival and development, is another.

Clearly in parental care we expect parents[4] to strive to meet the needs of their children and to seek help if they cannot meet them on their own. We expect parents to try to keep their children alive, protect them from unnecessary pain and suffering, and help them develop the basic skills and capacities they will eventually need to function as adults in their societies. Different parents will have varying ideas as to what those skills and capacities are, but we would expect parents in industrialized democracies to aim to have literate and numerate children, when the children seem capable. We would expect parents to help their children develop some self-control, and hence to resist temptation, at least occasionally. We could agree that parents should aim to have children who are capable of rewarding personal relationships with others, both within the family and outside it. Some parents might regard the ability to appreciate literature and music as an important basic capacity, and others might think that all children should be taught to use technology fluently and learn how to code, but we recognize that there is room for disagreement on those fronts, and would not consider parents who do not aim to develop one or another of those capacities as abusive or neglectful, even if we might disagree with some of their decisions.

While some parental decisions and actions might be at the fuzzy borderline, with some people thinking parents who take their children to church, synagogue, or mosque are harming them, and other people thinking parents who do not do so are harmful, there has to be substantial agreement within a community about the nature of children's basic needs in order for there to be a common concept of child maltreatment. In other words, there has to be a substantially shared social norm around adequate parenting in order for a community to think it has some responsibility to ensure that children are neither abused nor neglected, and to act to improve the children's lives when either of these are detected. Without social norms, there is no room for trust and also no room for shared responsibility for intervention when trust is betrayed.

In fact, some research shows that community homogeneity and intracommunity trust are correlated (Laurence, Schmid and Hewstone 2019). In a homogeneous community, attitudes toward out groups do not affect trust in one's neighbors, a level of trust which tends to be high. Interestingly, in a diverse community, neighborhood trust can also be high, but if groups located outside one's community are seen as a threat, then trust in one's neighbors, many of whom may belong in complicated ways to those groups, tends to be lower. If we accept my account of the nature of interpersonal trust, this would be expected, as we only trust people when we expect, assume or believe that they share social norms with us. When we view others as outsiders and threats, we are much less likely to share social norms, and hence less likely to trust those others. Of course, we can trust others in areas in which we think they share our social norms, fail to trust them in realms in which we are unsure whether or not they share our values, and distrust them in circumstances in which we find their values very different from our own. Therefore, my account of the nature of interpersonal trust would suggest that we would do better to specify the area(s) in which we trust others, including our neighbors, rather than talking in a more blanket fashion about high or low levels of community trust.[5]

If only those with some shared social norms can appropriately trust one another, then this raises two questions. First, how are we to understand social norms around child abuse and child neglect? Second, what demarcates a society or community with responsibility to trust appropriately and intervene when trust is betrayed? The answer to the second question will be shaped by the answer to the first, but will also depend upon how institutions have been set up to handle cases of suspected child maltreatment.

9.5 Trust and Child Maltreatment

As mentioned above, in order to trust parental care of children, we need to understand what adequate parents should strive to provide to their children, and the level of competence they need to possess. To reiterate, this is because trust involves both an assumption of competence, and an assumption about the one trusted being motivated to accord with a social norm. Yet how demanding is this norm? David Gil (1975) counts as abuse any circumstances that fail to serve children's best interests, including not facilitating their optimal development. However, it would be unduly demanding to characterize any discrepancy between ideal care and the actual level of treatment a child receives as maltreatment. This would also require an unusual level of agreement among the members of a community with respect to what we should consider to be ideal care for children.

Instead I defend an approach based on adequate care which in turn is understood in terms of care required to meet a child's basic needs. Children need first and foremost to have their immediate needs met: they need food, shelter, defense against those who seek to harm them, and protection from agents of harm that do not seek to harm them, but might nonetheless do so as innocent victims of war, traffic accidents, or calamitous climate and weather conditions. They need medical aid when they are injured or ill, and preventative measures (such as vaccines), to keep them healthy. They need emotionally close intimate relationships that enable them to learn to trust others, to understand their own and others' emotions, and to develop the ability to have positive social interactions with others in the future (Mullin 2014). They need to develop the capacities necessary for them to self-govern in the service of personally meaningful goals, which is how I understand autonomy (Mullin 2007). These include capacities of self-control, the ability to imagine alternatives, and the ability to care stably about some things, whether these things are people, experiences, possessions, or ways of living. Finally, they need to develop their understanding of the world and their intellectual capacities so as to be able to make social contributions, both economically rewarded and otherwise. If children do not receive the care required to meet their immediate needs and enable their basic development, and this shortfall is due to human action, whether individual or collective, then they are being maltreated.

When children are maltreated, whether abused or neglected, they suffer considerably, both physically and emotionally, in the short term. This alone gives us reason to be very concerned by the scope of child maltreatment. However, there is ample evidence that the long-term effects on children's development and life prospects are substantially negative, even while some can go on to do well (Widom 2014, 240). The documented negative long-term effects include lower educational attainment, reduced prospects for employment, increased engagement in violence, and increased physical and mental health problems (Widom 2014). As a result, the risks to vulnerable parties are very high when a society trusts parents to care for children.

If members of a society expect parents to care for children, and believe or assume that children will not be mistreated, this is not yet sufficient for trust. Members of that society must also believe or assume that parents aim to meet children's needs out of concern for children and valuing their well-being and development. This is because trust involves not only the expectation that the trusted entity, in this case parents, and other long-term caregivers of children, are competent to do what they are trusted to do, but also are motivated to do it in virtue of a norm, in this case a norm around parental care for children, that their wider society shares. Norms for parental care stipulate not only what parents and other long-term caregivers with significant responsibility for children's care, should do, but also why. If parents strove to meet and succeeded in meeting children's needs, but did so purely out of fear of negative consequences, or solely in order to receive pecuniary rewards, this would not meet typical norms for parental care. Parents are expected not only to care for their children in the sense of meeting their basic needs, or making all reasonable efforts to do so, but also to care for children, in the sense of caring about them and valuing them.

9.6 What Demarcates the "Society" Responsible to Oversee Parental Care?

Thus far I have been speaking generically of a society that trusts parents to care for children. But what sets the borders of a particular society? We could claim that all adults have a responsibility, considerably attenuated in the case of significant geographical distance and barriers to intervention, to set up social systems that aim to meet children's needs, and support, supplement, or replace parental care when required. However, this would be an understanding of responsibility that would do little to direct attention to what needs to be done and who needs to do it. Instead, it makes more sense to identify the borders of a particular society, in the case of parental care and child welfare, with the community that has rules and processes with respect to child welfare and child maltreatment—that sets up and funds and oversees child protection agencies, and in whose courts legal proceedings relating to child abuse or neglect are heard.

Does this mean that we have no business trusting or monitoring the behavior of parents outside those borders? Not exactly. We can use international mechanisms, including membership in the United Nations (UN), to work toward developing documents such as the UN Convention (1989) on the Rights of the Child. We can also turn to organizations that track relevant data and develop policies around children and families, as in not only the UN but also the Organization for Economic Cooperation and Development (OECD) (2019) with its Child Well Being Portal and Family Database. But primarily, what makes us members of a society with a responsibility for particular children's care, and for setting up mechanisms for monitoring failures of care, and providing supports for families and remedies for maltreated children, are actual institutions and practices of funding, monitoring, and legislating.

This can sound circular—what makes a group of people responsible for regulating and monitoring children's care, and seeking to provide supports to families and children in need, is precisely the fact that there are such mechanisms in place. How then, would initial responsibility ever be generated? Initial responsibility would be generated by a general obligation to help meet the needs of vulnerable people so long as one has the capacity to help. This is one of the most important principles of an ethics of care (see for instance Kittay 2011), but is also a tenet that can be supported by other approaches to moral theory, such as utilitarianism. If we can demonstrate that failing to meet needs for care causes suffering, and meeting them produces well-being, as seems reasonable to assume, then utilitarian approaches would harmonize in important respects with the ethics of care on this front.

Responses to need can be individual, as when someone stops to help the victim of a mugging, or collective, as when members of a society work together to develop a system to address children's needs. While it is true that societies allocate primary responsibility for children's care to their parents, Robert Goodin argues that social responsibility to meet vulnerable people's needs includes responsibility to assist those allocated primary responsibility, to set up collective mechanisms to respond to need, and to monitor the failures of others, like parents, to meet their primary responsibility to care adequately for children (Goodin 1985, 779). Otherwise we put unduly high burdens on some people with primary responsibility, such as parents in difficult circumstances, and fail adequately to meet the needs of those whose assigned primary caregivers cannot or will not meet their needs.

Different societies will vary with respect to how well their members can work together at a distance, and how much agreement they have in defining child maltreatment and intervening. Given that the United Nations Convention on the Rights of the Child is the most ratified human rights treaty in history (UNICEF 2019), there is considerable international agreement on the core principles of the Convention, including the ideas that children should not experience discrimination, that their best interests should be a primary consideration in interactions with them, that they have rights to life and development, and that their perspectives should be respected, even while different nations reserve the right to disagree with particular sections of the Convention (Canadian Bar Association 2019).

However, different states have different definitions of child maltreatment,[6] and different institutions and social actors are assigned to do the work of educating the public, detecting maltreatment, providing support to families at risk, and finding alternate care for children. Most of this work occurs at the local, municipal, level which means that we can find the communities that trust parents to care adequately for children primarily at this level. This makes sense, as trust requires shared social norms, and social norms are typically most closely shared at the local level. When the community that trusts parents to care for children is found at the local level, this also means that its members are more likely, because of other shared norms, to understand parents' behavior and motivations, and also to understand what kinds of interventions could be productive, and which might even be welcomed.

Research on large scale interventions to prevent and address child maltreatment in the United States suggests that it is most productive to locate the society that is responsible to appropriately trust parents to care for children with the level of the local community. Strong Communities for Children, undertaken in Greenville, South Carolina (hereafter Strong

Communities), was a multiyear research and social action project that made local communities, such as neighborhoods, the focus of a strategy to keep children safe, and minimize both child neglect and child abuse (Melton 2014). Rather than investing in more child protection workers hired to investigate cases of suspected child maltreatment reported by the community, Strong Communities focused on supporting families with young children (roughly up to 6 years of age) by means of community outreach workers, and networks of individual volunteers, schools, family health clinics, churches, social groups, businesses, and public service agencies (334–5). The strategy Strong Communities used was to create local Family Activity Centers that offered play groups and the ability to chat with family advocates, and the message was that members of the community should do more to get to know and support one another. In less than 5 years, in a community with roughly 90,000 adults, there were 5,000 individual volunteers in Strong Communities, along with 188 businesses; 213 religious organizations, and 85 voluntary organizations (335).

The impact of Strong Communities was extensively researched, with neighborhoods that were part of the initiative compared to similar neighborhoods that were not, and by multiple measures, child maltreatment was significantly reduced. These measures include emergency room visits due to child maltreatment, parental reports of stress and community support, and substantiated reports of child maltreatment, which declined in the Strong Communities service areas but increased in the other communities (336–7). More children received adequate care without families always having to ask for help, and families that were already involved in the child protection system benefited as well. These results are also consonant with research that suggests that children who have experienced maltreatment, but live in cohesive communities, are more resilient (Widom 2014, 235). Cohesive communities share social norms, and as a result are more likely to be able to rebuild trust, and in particular to help children regain their ability to trust.

In Strong Communities, the targeted service areas were diverse, and the volunteer base was even more diverse (336), but they developed shared social norms about the goal of preventing and addressing child maltreatment primarily by supporting families. Nonetheless, it might appear that the connection between trust and shared social norms mean that a society will inevitably ride roughshod over members of minority cultures, and impose majority expectations with respect to how to appropriately meet children's needs. Much will depend on how open a community's members are to learning about minority cultures present within them, and whether they are open to contact that allows them to discover that there will be both overlaps and disjuncts when it comes to social norms. Strong Communities was committed to noticing what was happening in the families in one's community and caring about it, and it encouraged contact, with volunteer firefighters visiting community members to let them know about meetings, and families pledging to learn the names of all the children who lived nearby (335). However, as important as it is to be open to learning that members of minority cultures have distinct ways of arriving at commonly shared goals, a responsibility to ensure that children receive needed care means that sometimes the community will need to reject the views of some of their members, such as those who have religious reasons to withhold all medical care from their children, and whose children die as a result from infections easily treated with antibiotics (Hughes 2004). This means that a community must be attentive to what is happening in and to the families within it, so as to be able to notice and respond to situations in which providing family support is not enough to ensure that children are not maltreated. Communities must therefore be open to distrust.

9.7 Appropriate Trust and Private–Public Partnerships

I have said that, in keeping with the Third Party Risk Rule, trust is generally appropriate when risks to vulnerable third parties are low and there is no information to which those who trust have access (or should have access) that would undermine their faith in the competence and motivation of those they trust to behave in expected ways for reasons they share. Obviously when we are talking about a society's trust in parents to care adequately for children, the risks to vulnerable third parties are high. When that is the case, there will frequently be information available that would, if known and attended to, undermine a community's faith in some parents' competence and motivation. However, when families live in private homes, there can be little opportunity for private citizens to acquire the information that would indicate that trust is inappropriate, and that children are being abused, neglected, or at risk of maltreatment.

In addition, because people are less likely to live communally and in extended families than in the past, many adults in contemporary industrialized democracies do not have a good sense of children's needs, particularly when it comes to their development. Almost all adults would be well aware that subjecting children to violence is abusive, and that it is abusive for adults to conduct sexual relationships with young children. Again, almost all would agree that depriving children of food, shelter, and medical care is neglectful, if there are opportunities to provide them with these necessities. However, people without much regular contact with children will be less aware of their emotional needs, and hence of the nature of emotional abuse and neglect. Indeed, many governments, including half of the states in the United States, do not mandate reporting of emotional abuse or neglect (Sedlak and Ellis 2014, 4). Moreover, to the extent that adults have not reflected upon what is required for children to develop the skills, habits, and capacities required for a wide variety of productive lives in their communities, or when children are likely to do so, forms of child maltreatment that negatively impact children's development are less likely to be understood or detected by many adults.

This is why community undertakings in the area of child maltreatment will ideally involve government, in order to ensure that they have the power to intervene when parents resist more informal attempts at community oversight. It is also why they must involve education, of a sort that need not occur in public schools, but ideally would. It is not only parents who should know what children need, how they develop, and what harms them, but all of the capable adults in a society. While we might seek to pay social workers or caregivers to provide oversight of or supplement parental care, it would presumably be up to government bodies to regulate and pay them, and those paid would need to be well educated about children's needs and development. If we want to decrease the likelihood that children are abused or neglected, a community in which all members are educated about human development would be an excellent option, as children and youth would learn about children's needs before they became parents, and all adult members of a community who were raised within it would know how to recognize failures of care. It is only when a community is properly informed that it may fulfill its role of trusting appropriately, by becoming aware that many children are maltreated, and that this can be because their families need more support.

When a community is well informed about children, their needs, and the extent to which those needs often go unmet, this can also motivate a commitment to making that community into a place that cares about families and intervenes when necessary to support them and ensure children's needs are met. When public health officials and social workers engage with schools, religious institutions, individual volunteers, and community groups to get to know children and families and understand how they are striving to meet children's needs, they are more likely to be effective at noticing and responding to child maltreatment and warning signs that it may be on the horizon. Adults in a community can do far more than report instances of suspected neglect and abuse to social workers who investigate. They can also be resources in meeting children's needs themselves, and directing parents in stressful circumstances to sources of support, both informal and publicly directed and funded.

This kind of public–private partnership is an alternative to taking a naively trusting attitude toward parents with responsibility for children's care. It is also an alternative to therapeutic trust, which aims to increase people's trustworthiness by trusting them, or acting as if one does (Horsburgh 1960). However, reasons to engage in therapeutic trust of this instrumental nature, by citing factors such as the benefits of living in a more trusting and trustworthy society, are rarely decisive factors to trust any given group or individual. As Hieronymi notes: "reasons that show trust useful, valuable, important, or required are not the reasons for which one trusts a particular person to do a particular thing" (2008, 235). Instead people typically trust others because they think them competent to do what they are expected to do and motivated by commitment to a shared social norm in doing so.

Moreover, Third Party Risks are too high, and carried by vulnerable children, to merely hope that parents will respond positively to being trusted. Hedman (2000) argues that as a society we should both support and trust parents, and that parents are more likely to be able to function well when their communities share a sense of responsibility for meeting children's needs. This aspect of his argument fits with my view, and with the evidence discussed above about the role for communities in preventing child maltreatment. However, Hedman opposes the majority of government interventions intended to protect children, as he regards them as likely to diminish more local and informal community supportive activities. He also recommends a significantly reduced role for social workers involved in child protection. By contrast, I see no reason to think that government policies and activities must be in this kind of tension with activities undertaken in more informal associations. I also consider it irresponsible to simply trust informal organizations in local communities to notice and appropriately respond to all instances of child maltreatment, particularly without the power to investigate. Moreover, as the research discussed above suggests, local communities are most effective in addressing child maltreatment when those communities form partnerships between volunteers, businesses, religious organizations, social workers, and public health agencies.

Trusting the volunteer sector alone to prevent and address child maltreatment involves too high a level of Third Party Risk. Given data about child maltreatment, this is difficult to justify. Even when we refer only to substantiated cases of child victimization, in 2011 in the United States there were 93 children who were maltreated for every 10,000 in a community (Sedlak and Ellis 2014, 7). The National Incidence Study of child maltreatment, which includes not only children whose families were investigated by child protective services, but also other maltreated children referred to community professionals, report 39.5 maltreated children per every 1,000 in the United States in 2005–6 (Sedlak and Ellis 2014, 8–9). Given that this data is for a country whose inhabitants are, on a global scale, relatively wealthy, with few of them subjected to the kinds of major disruption posed by war and climate catastrophe, it is likely that globally the incidence of child maltreatment is much higher. Of course, the mere fact that volunteers are partnered with businesses, religious organizations, social workers, and public agencies is not enough to guarantee that children will be less likely to suffer from failures of care.

Overworked and underpaid social workers and staff at public agencies may easily miss signs of such failure. However, awareness of the range of community members involved might on its own prompt greater vigilance, and provide children with more protection.

9.8 Impact on Children's Trust When They Are Maltreated

As I have shown above, when a community trusts parents to care for children and this trust is misplaced, children are impacted both immediately and long-term, in myriad deeply unfortunate ways. I wish to turn now to the impact of this misplaced social trust in parental care on children's own ability to trust appropriately. Psychological research has shown that when children are maltreated, "In addition to disrupting the ability to make wise decisions about the trustworthiness of others, betrayed children may end up with a general bias such that they are either overly trusting adults or, alternatively, they are unwilling to trust others, even those they should" (Gobyn and Freyd 2013, 505). Maltreated children sometimes trust adults indiscriminately, a strategy that makes some sense given their need to forge connections to find someone who will help meet their needs. As the research has shown, this excessive trust can continue into adulthood. Presumably they would then have unjustified trust in parents to meet children's needs, even though they experienced the kind of maltreatment that shows this trust can be unwarranted.

Alternatively, if they are unwilling to trust even those they should, this could mean they do not engage in social practices whenever they can avoid them, and this would contribute to a community with less close affiliation. As we have seen, this can undermine the ability of a community to be aware of what is happening to the families within it, to notice when maltreatment is occurring, and to productively intervene in order to prevent it by supporting families, supplementing parental care when parents cannot meet all their children's basic needs, or finding alternative care for children. Thus, child maltreatment is not only enabled by misplaced trust, but also makes it more difficult for the adults those children become to trust appropriately, in a potentially vicious cycle, depending on the extent of child maltreatment in any given community. When a community is either insufficiently attentive to child maltreatment, or does not consider children's care to be an important community responsibility, many of the children being raised within it may experience levels of abuse or neglect that leave them unduly mistrustful or excessively trusting. Fortunately, however, children who are properly cared for are likely to learn to trust appropriately, and this can launch a virtuous cycle in which they aim to ensure that the next generations of children also have their needs met, by trustworthy parents who are both overseen and supported by their local community.

9.9 Conclusion

In summary, there are very high Third Party Risks when a society trusts parents to care for children. This means that a community has a responsibility to seek out information that suggests when trust in parents to care adequately for their children is not appropriate. However, I also argued that it will not be possible to eliminate a need to trust by engaging in extensive surveillance of parental behavior for several reasons. These include the need to trust in situations that require action when there is no opportunity to investigate prior to acting, the need for some freedom from surveillance in order to develop and maintain family intimacy, and concern about prejudice playing a role in those who are selected for surveillance.

Instead, the proper response to the Third Party Risk problem is for local communities to form public–private partnerships aimed at a shared sense of responsibility for meeting children's needs, that include means for becoming aware of families living in significant stress, and situations in which children are either already being maltreated, or at risk of being so. Local communities are well situated to understand the families living within them, and to offer support in ways that can be welcomed. This kind of approach, as exemplified by the Strong Communities initiative, is more likely to lead to appropriate trust, even in instances of high Third Party Risk, where that risk is carried by the vulnerable children of that community. These children, when not subject to maltreatment, learn to trust appropriately themselves, both while they are children and when they become adults, in a virtuous circle that can build, rebuild and maintain the kinds of trust needed for flourishing communities.

Notes

1. The word "trust" can be used in a variety of ways, but most philosophers are interested in the kind of interpersonal trust that is directed to people who are held responsible, to varying extents, for their actions. I associate this with holding the ones trusted to be competent to engage in the activities they are trusted to carry out, and motivated by a norm that is shared by the person who trusts. When someone fails to live up to another's trust, the one who trusted will often feel resentful or betrayed. Holton (1994) discusses this kind of interpersonal trust and connects it to Strawson's (1974) account of people as appropriate targets of reactive attitudes. Unless otherwise indicated, when I use "trust" in this paper, I am referring to normative trust directed at persons.
2. Vallier offers a detailed account of social norms, moral rules, and trust in the first chapter of his *Must Politics Be War?* (2019). These norms can involve social roles, but can also be broader.
3. Hawley suggests that in interpersonal cases in which we expect somebody else to do what we want them to do, we either *rely* on their behavior (when we do not think about or do not care about their motives) or *trust or distrust* them because of the connection between morality and trust. For instance, she writes that: "Distrust embodies a moral criticism, involving

attitudes such as resentment, and may have a distinctive emotional colour." (2017, 71). It is possible that Hawley is using "moral" here as a synonym for "normative" but I think it is important to distinguish between moral norms and other norms.

4. I use the term "parent" to refer in this essay only to people who regularly do the work involved in caring for a child's immediate needs and enabling its development, and not for those who may be biological parents (whether genetic, gestational, or both) who are not so involved. Typically, parents will be unpaid and will be recognized by their society as having primary responsibility for a child's care and authority to make decisions about that care so long as they meet the child's needs. There are circumstances in which grandparents may function as parents, and occasionally long-term paid childcare workers, such as nannies, may as well, although they are less likely to have the authority to make significant decisions that impact the child's welfare and development.
5. Dinesen and Sønderskov (2017) have published a well-researched critical review about the relationship between community homogeneity and social trust. However, their focus is on generalized social trust rather than the more particularized kind of social trust (in parents to care adequately for their children) that is the focus of this essay.
6. Sedlak and Ellis (2014) give examples of these differences in the United States. For instance, only about a half of the states recognize educational neglect or emotional neglect as types of child maltreatment (4).

References

Baier, Annette C. (1986) "Trust and Antitrust," *Ethics* 96: 231–60.

Brighouse, Harry and Adam Swift (2006) "Parents' Rights and the Value of the Family," *Ethics* 117: 80–108.

Canadian Bar Association (2019) UN Convention on the Rights of the Child. http://www.cba.org/Publications-Resources/Practice-Tools/Child-Rights-Toolkit/overarchingFramework/UN-Convention-on-the-Rights-of-the-Child

D'Cruz, Jason (2018) "Trust within Limits," *International Journal of Philosophical Studies* 26(2): 240–50.

Dinesen, Peter Thisted and Kim Mannemar Sønderskov (2017) "Ethnic Diversity and Social Trust: A Critical Review of the Literature and Suggestions for a Research Agenda," in *The Oxford Handbook of Social and Political Trust*, ed. Eric Uslaner. New York: Oxford University Press. DOI: 10.1093/oxfordhb/9780190274801.013.13

Gil, David (1975) "Unraveling Child Abuse," *American Journal of Orthopsychiatry* 45(3): 346–56.

Gobyn, Robyn L. and Jennifer J. Freyd (2013) '"The Impact of Betrayal Trauma on the Tendency to Trust," *Psychological Trauma: Theory, Research, Practice and Policy* 6(5): 505–11.

Goodin, Robert (1985) "Vulnerabilities and Responsibilities: An Ethical Defense of the Welfare State," *The American Political Science Review* 79(3): 775–87.

Hawley, Katherine (2014) "Trust, Distrust and Commitment," *Nous* 48(1): 1–20.

Hawley, Katherine (2017) "Trust, Distrust, and Epistemic Injustice," in *The Routledge Handbook of Epistemic Injustice*, eds. José Medina, Ian James Kidd and Gaile Margaret Pohlhaus. Routledge. Accessed on: 17 Jun 2019 https://www.routledgehandbooks.com/doi/10.4324/9781315212043.ch6

Hedman, Carl (2000) "Three Approaches to the Problem of Child Abuse and Neglect," *Journal of Social Philosophy* 31(3): 268–85.

Hieronymi, Pamela (2008) "The Reasons of Trust," *Australasian Journal of Philosophy* 86(2): 213–36.

Holton, Richard (1994) "Deciding to Trust, Coming to Believe," *Australasian Journal of Philosophy* 72: 63–76.

Horsburgh, H.J.N. (1960) "The Ethics of Trust", *Philosophical Quarterly* 10(41): 343–54.

Hughes, R. (2004) "The Death of Children by Faith-Based Medical Neglect," *Journal of Law and Religion* 20: 247–65.

Kittay, Eva Feder (2011) "The Ethics of Care, Dependency, and Disability," *Ratio Juris* 24(1): 49–58.

Laurence, James, Schmid, Katharine and Miles Hewstone (2019) "Ethnic Diversity, Ethnic Threat, and Social Cohesion," *Journal of Ethnic and Migration Studies* 45(3): 395–418.

Levi, Benjamin and Greg Loeben (2004) "Index of Suspicion: Feeling not Believing," *Theoretical Medicine* 25(4): 277–310.

Melton, Gary B (2014) "Strong Communities for Children: A Community-Wide Approach to Prevention of Child Maltreatment," in *Handbook of Child Maltreatment*, eds. J.E. Korbin and R.D. Krugman. The Netherlands: Springer, 329–39.

Mullin, Amy (2007) "Children, Autonomy and Care," *Journal of Social Philosophy* 38(4): 536–53.

Mullin, Amy (2014) "Children, Vulnerability and Emotional Harm," in *Vulnerability: New Essays in Ethics and Feminist Philosophy*, eds. C. Mackenzie, W. Rogers and S. Dodds. New York: Oxford University Press, 266–87.

Organization for Economic Cooperation and Development (OECD) (2019) Child Well-Being Portal http://www.oecd.org/social/family/child-well-being/

Organization for Economic Cooperation and Development (OECD) (2019) Family Database https://www.oecd.org/els/family/database.htm

Sedlak, Andrea J. and Raquel T. Ellis (2014) "Trends in Child Abuse Reporting" in *Handbook of Child Maltreatment*, eds. J.E. Korbin and R.D. Krugman. The Netherlands: Springer, 3–26.

Strawson, P.F. (1974) "Freedom and Resentment," in *Freedom and Resentment*, ed. P.F. Strawson. London: Methuen, 1–25.

UNICEF (2019) What Is the Convention on the Rights of the Child https://www.unicef.org/child-rights-convention/what-is-the-convention

United Nations (1989) Convention on the Rights of the Child https://www.ohchr.org/en/professionalinterest/pages/crc.aspx

Vallier, Kevin (2019) *Must Politics Be War?* New York: Oxford University Press.

Widom, Cathy Spatz (2014) "Longterm Consequences of Child Maltreatment" in *Handbook of Child Maltreatment*, eds. J.E. Korbin and R.D. Krugman. The Netherlands: Springer, 224–47.

10 A Case for Political Epistemic Trust

Agnes Tam

10.1 Introduction

Most chapters in this volume analyze *behavioral* trust, that is, trust concerning action. In this chapter, I focus on a different aspect of trust, namely *epistemic* trust. I use the word "epistemic" to denote the broad realm of knowledge, covering claims about the right, the good, and the truth. Epistemologists ask whether and how we can know by taking the word of others. I ask something yet more specific: what are the distinct challenges for members of the public to trust epistemic authorities (e.g. policymakers, politicians, scientists, journalists, doctors, etc.) in our social and political life? And how can they be overcome?

In liberal political theory, epistemic trust plays a limited role. Ideal conceptions of democratic agents rarely include epistemic trust as a virtue. One important reason for this skepticism of epistemic trust has to do with its heightened risk of abuse. Unlike intimate, interpersonal relations characterized by mutual concerns and goodwill, political relations are characterized by conflicts of interests and power. Epistemic authorities, even if they are competent, need not be motivated to meet the epistemic expectations (i.e. to know what is right, what is good, and what is the truth) of the public. Quite the contrary, they are prone to mislead or misinform the public for self-gain (e.g. material and social privileges). As the psychological basis for sincerity is too weak in the power-ridden world, trusting epistemic authorities easily makes us gullible.

Even though political epistemic trust[1] is prone to abuse, few liberal political theorists recommend blanket epistemic distrust. Political knowledge (e.g. tax policies, public health responses) is too complex for ordinary citizens to acquire on our own. Most of us do not have the requisite epistemic competence nor the time to make the relevant inquiries and assess the relevant reasons and evidence. To exercise our political agency properly, we need to rely on the say-so of experts.

Here emerges a widely recognized dilemma of political epistemic trust: we need it, but it is very risky. To resolve the dilemma, a common strategy in liberal political theory is to *cultivate vigilant trust*. This strategy focuses on the trusters and theorizes the conditions, individual or structural, under which they might be more intelligent and less deferential. By cultivating the attitude of epistemic vigilance in trusters and enhancing their capacity for epistemic autonomy, this strategy in practice *intellectualizes* and *constrains* epistemic trust.[2]

In this chapter, my aim is to criticize the strategy of cultivating vigilant trust and call for an alternative strategy of *cultivating trustworthiness*. My critique is based on two main claims. First, I claim that the strategy of cultivating vigilant trust *over-intellectualizes* trust. By making trust overly deliberative, it deprives trust of its epistemic and social benefits. Second, I claim that such an approach exaggerates the risk of abuse. Relying on a flawed psychology of epistemic cooperation, it views epistemic authorities as essentially self-interested agents who tend to exploit the trust placed in them by lying to and misinforming the public for self-gain. Drawing on the recent literature on epistemic normativity and social norms, I show that our everyday epistemic practices are typically governed by the social norm of epistemic trustworthiness, not self-interest. Crucially, this applies to politics as well because epistemic authorities, in virtue of their professional roles, are regulated by the same norm.

Of course, the fact that epistemic trustworthiness is a social norm does not in itself remove all the risks involved in trusting, nor does it dissolve the dilemma of epistemic trust. I will argue, however, that insofar as the risk of improper motives is concerned, it is best addressed not by enabling trusters to be more effective verifiers of trustees' motives, but rather by focusing on trustees' responsiveness to the social norm of epistemic trustworthiness. I end the chapter by suggesting some practical measures to strengthen the social norm of epistemic trustworthiness. Contrary to the common view that liberal institutions *constrain* epistemic trust, I suggest that certain features of liberal democracy in fact cultivate epistemic trustworthiness, thereby indirectly promoting epistemic trust. By assuaging the unwarranted suspicion of epistemic trust, my aim in this chapter is to demonstrate that it is both plausible and desirable to structure our society in a way that promotes political epistemic trust and trustworthiness.

10.2 Cultivating Vigilant Trust

In this section, I will first elaborate on the dilemma of epistemic trust that motivates the strategy of cultivating vigilant trust. I will then detail the strategy of cultivating vigilant trust, before finally arguing that the strategy is suboptimal.

10.2.1 Why Cultivate Vigilant Trust?

As many social epistemologists have argued, human epistemic dependence is profound and inevitable (see, for example, Goldberg 2010; Goldman

1999; Lackey 2008). Throughout our lives, to function properly in society we depend on others in various domains to acquire true beliefs and correct false ones. For example, knowledge of medicine to support our health, knowledge of language to communicate, and knowledge of meteorology to plan our activities. Our cognitive life would be paralyzed if we had to learn each discipline on our own. Our need for epistemic dependence is even greater when it comes to our political life. To function as a political agent, we need political knowledge. As Mark Warren (1999) and Michael Fuerstein (2013) argue, political knowledge is highly complex and cross-disciplinary. To decide on which candidates to vote for, which policy proposals to adopt, or whether or not to join a social movement, democratic citizens often need to know about what justice demands, which values to promote, and as well as facts about history, geography, economics, public health, and so on, that contextualize them. Our cognitive finitude prevents us from making informed decisions by pursuing all the relevant inquiries, assessing all the relevant evidence and reasons, all on our own. That is why almost every society engages in epistemic cooperation to manage the limitations of our cognitive resources. Allen Buchanan calls the common form of epistemic cooperation the "social division of epistemic labor," where individuals and groups occupy distinct roles for a sufficient period of time to develop special expertise (e.g. scientists, teachers, doctors, politicians) (2004, 99). He calls these experts "epistemic authorities," as they are the groups or individuals to whom we "defer as reliable sources of true beliefs" (Buchanan 2004, 103).

While we need to defer to these epistemic authorities as sources of true beliefs, doing so is risky, and particularly so in political life. There are at least two arguments for the heightened risk. One is about the *consequences* of mistrust (Buchanan 2002, 127–40). The harm of mistrust is not just epistemic but deeply moral. Imagine if we were misled by politicians to form xenophobic beliefs or to believe that climate change is a hoax. Mistrust can get people killed. In this paper, I shall not dispute the argument from consequence. What I will dispute is the argument from *psychology*, which states that epistemic trust in politics is too prone to abuse. Here we ought to distinguish the conceptual claim that epistemic trust is inherently risky from the empirical claim that epistemic trust is particularly risky in public life. The conceptual claim is relatively uncontroversial. As Onora O'Neill says, "Since trust must run ahead of proof or control, it is always possible to place it badly" (2014, 179). If our evidence for a truth claim is complete, epistemic trust becomes redundant. In this way, the relative ignorance of the truster is always vulnerable to the trustee's misrepresentation and deception. However, the empirical claim, often made by liberal political theorists, goes further (see generally Allard-Tremblay 2015; Blau 2018; Buchanan 2004; Fuerstein 2013, 185–6; Warren 1999, 311–12). It holds that this vulnerability is prone to abuse. Let's take a closer look.

The idea that epistemic trust is prone to abuse is based on a sociological claim that conflicts of interest pervade the political field, and the psychological claim that humans are primarily self-interested actors. Warren claims that the conflicts of interest found in political relationships "throw the very conditions of trust into question" (Warren 1999, 311). The trusters, that is, members of the public, and the trustees, that is, epistemic authorities, often do not share interests. The epistemic goods that the trusters desire (e.g. truths or relevant information) conflict with the self-interests of the trustees (e.g. material and social privileges derived from misrepresentation and deception). And it is widely believed among liberal political theorists that when such conflicts arise, trustees will be inclined to pursue their own interests at the expense of those of the trusters. Adrian Blau (2018) has recently traced this idea that is common in the writings of Machiavelli, Hobbes, Bentham, and Mill. These liberal thinkers are all wary of deception and manipulation in politics, because they believe that politicians tend to abuse or misuse their power for "private gain" or "factional gain." The "love of party," "high-status," "avarice and ambition," and "self-interest" override the motivations for truth or the common good.

Politicians are not the only ones thought to be self-serving. Other epistemic authorities such as scientists and journalists are also believed to increasingly collude with business interests to misinform the public. To use Buchanan's examples, while members of the public want to know the truth about the value and applications of genomic technology, genomic scientists who collude with the genomic technology industry have an interest in misleading the public to believe that genomic technology is more useful than it is (Buchanan 2004, 128). Physicians often withhold information about their collusion with pharmaceutical companies, misleading the public into believing in the value of overpriced treatments, and that they are selfless promoters of the patients' good (Buchanan 2002, 128–35). As Buchanan explains, epistemic power is an important path to social power. It enables experts to "garner control and reap social rewards" (Buchanan 2004, 104). Experts will be inclined to seek more social power by maintaining their epistemic power. For Buchanan, this explains why epistemic authorities such as teachers, journalists, and scientists were motivated to spread false beliefs about Jews, because they were rewarded, or bribed, with high social status by the Nazis for doing so.

10.2.2 How to Cultivate Vigilant Trust

The ubiquity of conflicts of interest, together with the self-interested reasoning of people in power, renders epistemic trust very risky. As a result, it tends to be discounted or discouraged in liberal political theory. Those who acknowledge and seek to reap the benefits of epistemic trust usually proceed with extreme caution. The strategy of cultivating vigilant trust they adopt tends to have two features: constraining epistemic trust with the attitude of epistemic vigilance; and intellectualizing epistemic trust with the exercise of epistemic autonomy.

Let's first look at the nature and function of the attitude of epistemic vigilance. Allard-Tremblay proposes the idea of "guarded epistemic trust," which he defines as a cautious attitude that "seeks to avert the opportunities for abuse that the political condition makes possible by approaching others' assertions with doubt and with a wary eye, all the while considering them as valid objects of engagement that cannot be summarily dismissed such that they may ultimately lead to a change in beliefs" (2015, 381). We should assume that those with epistemic and social power are prone to corruption, but we should not dismiss their claims outright. Buchanan shares this view and discusses it in further detail. He argues that we should practice "epistemic egalitarianism" in order to constrain but not eliminate epistemic trust (2004, 117). Epistemic egalitarianism is a "widespread" but "not necessarily universal" attitude of basic moral egalitarianism (*ibid.*). It is the willingness of ordinary people to challenge the knowledge claims and credibility of authorities, and it is based on the conviction that everyone is equal, and no one's views are to be dismissed or discounted simply because of their social status (Buchanan 2004, 110). There are two elements here, as I understand it. One is epistemic vigilance: a disposition of alertness to cues of untrustworthiness from the socially identified epistemic authorities or lack of plausibility in their claims. The other is a disposition of equal respect toward everyone's epistemic autonomy, by virtue of a common humanity. We must be willing to think well enough of every individual citizen regardless of social status. These two elements are expressed and nurtured in democratic politics, including "the entitlement of all to participate as equals in the creation of the most important rules of public order" (Buchanan 2004, 118). For example, where there is a widespread epistemic egalitarian attitude, deference to religious, and political demagogues will be limited and it will be more difficult for them to spread false beliefs sustaining the inferior moral status of minorities (Buchanan 2004, 119–20).

In addition to checking the deferential disposition of the trusters with the attitude of epistemic vigilance, cultivating vigilant trust further requires the enabling of a certain degree of epistemic autonomy. Epistemic autonomy is roughly the ability to rely only on one's own cognitive faculties and investigative and inferential powers to accept propositions and judgments. To be sure, maximizing epistemic autonomy is impossible. As explained, epistemic dependence is an inevitable feature of our cognitive life. But a certain degree of epistemic autonomy is still essential to make trust intelligent. To see why, we must first dig a little deeper into what it means for trust to be intelligent.

Trust is intelligent when the reason for trust is *deliberative* as opposed to merely *affective*. Trust is only warranted if it is backed up by an evidentiary assessment of the probability of truth claims or the sincere character of the trustees in each and every case. The mere affective attitude of confidence or normative expectation of trustworthiness is an insufficient epistemic reason to trust. O'Neill, for example, contrasts "unintelligent" accounts of trust that emphasize attitude and affect over judgment and choice (2013, 240). Epistemic trust, to be well-placed, requires evidentiary assessment directed at *specific* claims. This parallels Buchanan's contrast between "status trust" and "merit trust." Status trust is easily misplaced or excessive in Buchanan's view. It refers to the "relaxation of critical attitude," including the disposition of epistemic deference, that is accorded to epistemic authorities "on the basis of their being identified as having a certain status or of being a member of a certain group" and "independently of any evidence-based belief in the competence or integrity" of them as individuals (Buchanan 2002, 134; Buchanan 2004, 111–12). Status trust presumes that the speaker is trustworthy qua status. Merit trust, by contrast, is "individual-performance based" and "conferred on an individual on the basis of an appraisal of her own actions or attributes, so far as they are regarded as exhibiting appropriate qualifications" (Buchanan 2004, 112). In this respect, merit trust implicitly starts from the presumption that the speaker is untrustworthy. Epistemic trust is warranted only if the hearers have sufficient evidence for the probability of the specific claim or, alternatively, that the hearers have the evidence to defeat the assumption that the speaker is lying or deceiving. The hearer must always possess, in each and every case, a reason for thinking the speaker is sincere. The speaker does not, qua speaker or qua expert, warrant trust. You cannot trust a doctor's diagnosis just because her status as a doctor inspires confidence. One is entitled to trust if and only if one is informed of the evidence and arguments for the particular diagnosis, and the credentials and the motivations of the particular doctor.

Intelligent trust is highly demanding in cognitive terms. Institutional measures are therefore put in place to enhance trusters' capacity for epistemic autonomy, such that they can trust more wisely and more easily. Many political theorists argue that liberal democracy plays a role in enhancing the epistemic autonomy of members of the public, thereby reducing the asymmetry between the experts and the public—which might otherwise produce a vulnerability that could easily be exploited by experts (see generally Buchanan 2004; O'Neill 2002, 2014). One important mechanism is the deliberative politics instituted by freedom of speech, freedom of conscience, and freedom of information. The extensive exchange of information through a free media enables the public to make assessments about specific truth claims and the motives of the specific experts. It enhances our "collective capacity for credibility monitoring," which Fuerstein defines as the collective ability to identify reliable and unreliable speakers (2013, 190). The deliberative obligation on office holders, whereby they must give reasons for their claims, provides the public with epistemic reasons and evidence to judge the capacities and motivations of the epistemic authorities. That is because deliberators who repeat themselves in the face of objections, consistently appeal to false premises, employ logical fallacies, or appeal to unjustified sources of evidence can easily be exposed as incompetent and insincere.

In addition to these liberal freedoms, the liberal principle of "careers open to talent," in Buchanan's view, further helps the public to place merit trust in genuine experts, because they have been identified as such by meritocratic hiring policies (2004, 110–13). In other words, as a third party, meritocratic institutions perform the function of credibility-monitoring on behalf of the public. They assign offices and positions to individuals based on objective qualifications rather than social status, and remove those who are incompetent from office. Members of the public do not have to assess the credibility of the experts on their own because the institutions have already done it for them. To use Buchanan's example, the status of physicians in liberal societies is conferred only on individuals who have undergone a rigorous education and training that confers objective qualifications regarding the provision of healthcare and that inculcates a sincere commitment to patients' well-being. But while meritocracy reduces the burden on individuals in the evaluation of experts, it still depends on publicly verifiable evidence to counter the initial presumption of distrust.

10.2.3 Problems of Vigilant Trust

Is cultivating vigilant trust an optimal strategy to resolve the dilemma of epistemic trust? I think not, as it intellectualizes and constrains epistemic trust *too much*. Let me explain.

As we have seen, philosophers such as O'Neill and Buchanan require trust to be "intelligent" or "merited," specifically, for it to be backed up by an evidentiary assessment of the probative value of truth claims or the proper motives of the trustees in each and every case. In epistemology, this conception of epistemic trust is called "evidentialist" as it requires believing that one has the right sorts of evidence for the testimony or that the trusted source is trustworthy.[3] A well-known problem of evidentialist conceptions of trust is that it over-intellectualizes trust. As epistemologist Paul Faulkner puts it,

> *[Requiring evidential reasons] over-intellectualizes our relationship to testimony. We do not always base uptake on the belief that what is told is true, sometimes we merely trust a speaker for the truth. ...*

> *[These reasons miss] a central reason, arguably the central reason, why we trust testimony ... An audience's reason for the uptake of a speaker's testimony can be no more than that the audience believes the speaker, or trusts the speaker for the truth.* (2011, 175–6)

As a phenomenology, epistemic trust is rarely a product of deliberation but fundamentally a matter of having an affective attitude of optimism (Jones 1996) or affective expectation (Faulkner 2011). We simply hope that the trusted will be trustworthy because of our trust. While non-deliberative trust need not be blind, it certainly is more vulnerable to abuse. This explains our reactive attitudes. We feel a sense of betrayal and resentment when our vulnerable trust is abused; on the flipside, we feel a sense of gratification when our vulnerability is met. By contrast, the same reactive attitudes are absent in cases of mere reliance. For example, I can rely on a computer because I predict that it will work well. If the computer turns out to be malfunctioning, I do not resent the computer for betraying me, even though I may feel frustrated. It would be strange if I felt betrayed by a computer, because I could not have expected the computer to be moved by my rendering myself vulnerable. To be sure, the fact that trust is affective does not mean that it is *never* deliberative. When one's trust is shaken, for example, when the truster realizes that she has been betrayed, one will be prompted to re-assess the trustworthiness of the relevant trustee. However, in a relation of trust, these moments of deliberation tend to be rare, possibly limited to the beginning or the end of the relation.

One may wonder: what's wrong with over-intellectualizing trust? Call it "vigilant reliance," if you will. So long as it serves to mitigate the risk of abuse in epistemic cooperation, isn't vigilant reliance a good strategy? My worry is that while the strategy can mitigate the risk, it comes at a great cost.

First, it deprives the *epistemic* benefits of epistemic cooperation. The rationale for enhancing epistemic autonomy is to give some leverage back to citizens, such that we need not live our epistemic lives entirely at the mercy of epistemic authorities. We are better equipped to make intelligent assessments of the merits of the claims as well as their motives. But in passing on the leverage, it passes on the burden as well. Considering the technical, complex, and cross-domain nature of political knowledge, this burden is very high. Liberal theorists are certainly aware of the demandingness. This is why they put in place institutional measures to help with the exercise of epistemic autonomy. But the extent of help that these institutional measures offer is limited. Take credibility-monitoring for example. Unless laypersons are capable of assessing the quality of monitoring systems (e.g. peer reviews, meritocratic hiring policies, qualification standards), the risk of misplaced trust is simply transferred from epistemic authorities to the systems that regulate them. In order to make an intelligent assessment of these regulatory systems, it seems technical and complex knowledge of public policies is still required. Freedom of information exchange certainly makes the *search* for relevant information easier. But it does not make the *understanding* easier, which is what makes intelligent trust demanding and epistemic trust inevitable in the first place.

Second, it deprives the *social* benefits of epistemic trust. To help understand the "social" nature of benefits, imagine a society in which each individual was maximally epistemically autonomous. Each had the intelligence to master every domain of knowledge like a supercomputer. There would be no need to cooperate epistemically. There would also be no risk of being fooled. While these individuals would be epistemically satisfied, we might not want to live in such a society. That is because the individuals in this society would be deprived of the opportunity to connect with one another through epistemic cooperation. When we drop our guard (by not deliberating) and expect that our fellow citizens will not harm us even when they can do so, we enjoy a feeling of social bonding and cohesion that epistemic autonomy cannot provide, even though it can meet the same informational needs. And as pro-social animals, the desire for social bonding through cooperation is fundamental. While behavioral trust is widely considered to be a social glue,[4] it has only recently been recognized that epistemic trust plays the same function.[5] Yet, the strategy of vigilant trust requires us to be on guard far too often and too much. We need to be constantly on alert for cues of untrustworthiness and trust only on sufficient evidence of trustworthiness. I suspect that solidarity between partisans and in social movements will be easily lost, if members are indeed cultivated with dispositions of vigilance and autonomy.

To be sure, there are risks inherent in epistemic cooperation. But in my view, the proper response is not to minimize cooperation but to minimize the risks of cooperation, to improve its conditions. The question is: can the risks of cooperation be reduced without over-intellectualizing trust? I think they can. I turn now to discuss how trust can be wise without being over-intellectualized.

10.3 An Alternative Psychology of Epistemic Trustworthiness

As the preceding discussion has shown, epistemic trust is downplayed in liberal political theory due to a particular psychological view of epistemic trustworthiness and conception of politics. Humans are primarily self-interested. Politics is full of conflicts of interest. Epistemic authorities tend to abuse their power by misinforming and lying to the public for self-gain. Trusting them is very risky. Yet, the public needs to rely on them. This creates the dilemma of epistemic trust. To resolve it, liberals adopt the strategy of cultivating vigilant trust. But as I have argued, this strategy is suboptimal. By over-intellectualizing trust, it removes the social and epistemic benefits of epistemic cooperation. Can we not over-intellectualize trust and still benefit from epistemic cooperation? In the remainder of the chapter, I will show that we can. My central argument is that the psychological view that informs the strategy of vigilant trust overstates the degree and misunderstands the source of risk of epistemic trust. Drawing on the literature of epistemic normativity and social norms, I argue that epistemic trustworthiness is a *social norm*, and that it is operative in everyday as well as political contexts. And when epistemic cooperation is guided by the social norm of epistemic trustworthiness, agents are motivated to conform to the norm and tell the truth sincerely, even when it is against their self-interest to do so. This importantly de-intellectualizes trust. Of course, the fact that epistemic trustworthiness is a social norm does not by itself eliminate all the risks in trusting, nor does it resolve the dilemma. As I will explain, there are different social factors that may undermine the robustness of the social norm of epistemic trustworthiness. The significance of the alternative account of risks is that it opens up the way for an alternative remedy that focuses on social norms.

10.3.1 Social Norms and Motivation for Epistemic Trustworthiness

Epistemologists have long been puzzled by how affective trust can be warranted. Recently, some of them, most notably, Peter Graham (2012, 2015) and Paul Faulkner (2011), turn to the social-scientific literature of social norms for help. Their main idea is this. Social scientists have by and large solved the puzzle of why humans are motivated to cooperate, even against their immediate self-interest, by appealing to the powerful force of social norms. Epistemic cooperation is just a subset of human cooperation. If it can be shown that epistemic cooperation is governed by the social norm of epistemic trustworthiness, then self-interested motives to misinform or lie are overcome. If self-interested motives are overcome, there is no need to make trusters effective verifiers of the motives of the trusted. Let me unpack each of these claims, first by explaining what social norms are.

Graham and Faulkner understand social norms from a broadly rational choice framework.[6] On Graham's formulation, a behavioral regularity R is a social norm when the following three conditions obtain in the population P:

1 Members of P conform to R (and this is common knowledge)
2 Members of P prescribe conforming to R (believe each of us ought to do R) and disapprove of failures (and this is common knowledge)

3 The fact that nearly everyone approves (believes one ought to conform) and disapproves (believes it is wrong not to conform) helps to ensure that nearly everyone conforms (Graham 2015, 251).

Let's see why the three conditions above are jointly necessary and sufficient. Consider paradigmatic examples of social norms: the norms of greetings, gift-giving, mourning, recycling, and paying taxes. In all these instances, condition 1 is obtained. That is, members in the relevant populations conform to a pattern of behavioral regularity. However, how do we distinguish social norms from mere customs such as cleaning our teeth with a brush, using an umbrella in the rain, and eating breakfast in the morning? Condition 1 is also obtained in these customs. As a result, we need condition 2, namely that members believe that each other "ought to do R" for a social norm R. Cristina Bicchieri (2014, 226) helpfully characterize this "ought" in social norms as "normative expectation," a second-order belief that I believe that others believe that I should do R. A normative expectation is to be contrasted with an empirical expectation, that is, a first-order belief that I believe others *will*. While typical customs involve empirical expectations only, typical social norms involve both empirical and normative expectations. The presence of normative expectations explains the motivational power of social norms. They are experienced in the mind of the members as an *obligation*, overriding our personal preferences, desires, or aims. For example, Christians feel that they ought to wear black at funerals. Academics feel that they ought not to interrupt a speaker at conferences. Non-conformity will typically be sanctioned. By contrast, customs are experienced as mere preferences. It is up to you if you wish to use a poncho when it rains or to skip breakfast in the morning.

But why do we need condition 3, namely that the shared normative expectation that each of us ought to do R is what *motivates* mutual conformity to R? Citing Pettit, Graham writes,

> *It is surely not going to be enough for normative status that a regularity commands general conformity and that conformity attracts approval, deviance disapproval. For what if there is no connection between these two facts; what if the approval and disapproval are epiphenomenal, playing no role in ensuring the conformity? In such a case I think it is clear that we would hesitate to regard the regularity as a norm.* (2015, 250)

However, the above passage does not explain why members have to conform because it is the social norm. It merely asserts this. What is missing in Graham's account, I believe, is a distinction between moral norms and social norms, which Bicchieri rightly defends (2006, 20–22); see also Brennan et al. (2013, 213–7). Consider paradigmatic moral norms such as norms against murder, rape, and slavery. In most societies, members share normative expectations that each of us ought not to murder, rape, or enslave others. So, condition 2 is met. But condition 3 is typically missing in moral norms. The reason we refrain from violating these moral norms is not because I think that my peers believe that I shouldn't. Rather, it is because I think it is the wrong thing to do, *independent of peer expectations*. If I refrain from murdering only because my peers think that I should not do so, my behavior cannot merit the label "moral." Moral norms are typically *expectation-independent* whereas social norms are typically *expectation-dependent*. The reason why I reciprocate gifts is because my peers believe that I should; if they do not do so (for instance, perhaps they consider it idiosyncratic or even ostentatious), there is no reason for me to give gifts to them anymore. Similarly, I wear black to funerals because my peers believe that I should; if they believe that I should wear white instead, I will no longer feel that I ought to wear black. This explains why condition 3 is essential for a norm to be a *social* norm.

It is an ongoing controversy as to why shared normative expectations are motivationally powerful, within the rational choice framework (and all the more outside of it). Many social scientists (e.g. Parsons 1937) believe that internalization is key. When people around us routinely approve of conformity and disapprove of non-conformity of a particular act, we gradually develop a desire for the act. Others (e.g. Coleman 1990) reduce it to the (fear of) sanctions entailed by shared normative expectations. More recently, Bicchieri (2006, 52) has argued that shared normative expectations transform utility functions for agents. Philosophers tend to focus on the recognition of the inherent normativity of social norms. This inherent normativity can be cashed out in terms of the structure of group rationality (Gilbert 2013), the values (e.g. group belonging, identification, trust) that social norms express (Anderson 2000; Brennan et al. 2013, 80–81; Scheffler 2018) or its formative process (Tam 2020b, Ch. 4). There are many possibilities here; and they need not be mutually exclusive. For our purposes here, we do not need to settle on one. It suffices to know that social norms are shared normative expectations of conformity, and as such, they are powerful enough to override immediate self-interest.

As Graham (2015) rightly notes, social norms have been widely used in social sciences to explain the dynamics of social cooperation. Social practices such as recycling, queueing, taking part in social movements, dueling, removing genitals, and killing one's daughter to protect family honor all involve significant cost to oneself. While they seem puzzling from the perspective of a self-interested agent, they are not so from the perspective of a member of the relevant norm-community. These practices are governed by shared normative expectations, which are experienced as obligations of group membership. The phenomenon of social norms proves that we are not completely self-interested maximizers nor selfless moral saints, but rather pro-social cooperative animals.

For Graham (and Faulkner), epistemic cooperation is a subset of human cooperation, only with epistemic content and goals. Why a person would be willing to tell the truth when it is not in their own interest is just as puzzling as why they would be willing to do anything against their self-interest for the good of others, such as recycling or queuing. If the latter is not puzzling in light of social norms, then nor is the former. As Graham writes,

> To the extent that we do provide true and relevant information, to the extent that we think we should, and to the extent that our thought that we should partly causes or at least sustains our behavior, provide true and relevant information is a social norm. (2015, 257)

While Graham does not draw on any empirical studies on the social norm of epistemic trustworthiness, Bicchieri et al. (see chapter 1) have demonstrated that trustworthiness is a social norm. Drawing on observations of everyday life, Graham claims that there is widespread conformity to the practice of truth-telling. For example, most people raise their children to be sincere. When strangers ask us for directions, we routinely tell them the relevant information if we have it. Next, he shows that most of us share the normative expectation that each of us should tell the truth. This is evident in our reactive attitudes. We admire those who know a lot and can inform us about what we need to know. We regularly criticize those who deceive or mislead. We feel embarrassed if we mislead others or feel guilty when we lie. Finally, Graham claims that we are moved by the shared normative expectation to tell the truth. For example, when we give directions to a stranger, we do not calculate what is in it for us. We simply do so because we know that is what we ought to do. But this example alone fails to show that epistemic trustworthiness is a social norm, not a moral norm. Is epistemic trustworthiness expectation-dependent? I think so. We do not feel that we ought to be sincere when we are gambling or to carefully deliberate when tweeting. The reason being that the empirical and normative expectations for epistemic trustworthiness in gambling and online communities are weak or non-existent. Based on these empirical observations, we have prima facie reason to believe that epistemic trustworthiness is a social norm in everyday life.

The upshot of the social norm account of epistemic trustworthiness is that it importantly *de-intellectualizes* epistemic trust. Trust is presumptively warranted not because the truster possesses sufficient evidence of the sincere character of the trustee or the probative value of the testimony. Rather, it is because epistemic cooperation has a built-in shared normative expectation of epistemic trustworthiness. And this social norm of epistemic trustworthiness itself raises the probability of the truth claim (Faulkner 2011, 57). The social norm itself is an epistemic reason to believe (*ibid.*, 154). Faulkner puts it as follows:

> ultimately what determines that the attitude of trust provides an epistemic reason is the existence of the causal structures [referring to the social norm of truth-telling] that ensure the attitude of trust can be potential evidence ... Thus, ultimately, the attitude of trust provides an epistemic reason because these are norms of conversational trust, shaping the nature of the reasons we have, for utterance and for belief, in conversations as to the facts. (2011, 159)

10.3.2 The Social Norm of Epistemic Trustworthiness in Politics

Faulkner and Graham's discussions remain at a general and abstract level. We still have to apply their social norm account of epistemic trustworthiness to the specific case with which we are concerned: trust in epistemic authorities in political contexts. Does the power-ridden nature of the political realm prevent the development of the social norm of epistemic trustworthiness? No, it does not.[7] To see this, I want to return to Buchanan's notion of "status trust." Examples of people conferred with status trust are professional politicians, teachers, doctors, journalists, and scientists. As discussed, Buchanan views status trust with suspicion. He believes that status trust is a form of gullibility insofar as we trust someone by virtue of their status, rather than our own vigilant and autonomous assessment of their trustworthiness. However, this is far too simplistic and pessimistic a view of what status in fact embodies. As social scientists March and Olsen (2006) observe, people who work in social and political institutions usually follow a "logic of appropriateness" as opposed to a "logic of consequences." People strive to interpret the social roles they occupy and act according to the norms that govern those roles. And people do so because they come to affirm the values that imbue the institutions within which they work and live, and embrace their social roles as part of their identities. In deliberating over what they should do, these professionals do not ask how they can gain from this; rather, they ask what should someone in this position do? Political theorist Cass Sunstein (1996) argues for a similar view. Social roles are generated by social norms and at the same time generate social norms. As he rightly notes, "social roles: doctor, employee, waiter, law school dean, wife, friend, pet-owner, colleague, student" are "accompanied by a remarkably complex network of appropriate norms" (Sunstein 1996, 921). To use Sunstein's examples, if you are a waiter, you ought not treat your restaurant's patrons the way you treat your friends. If you are a student, you ought not treat a teacher as if she were your co-worker at the local factory.

In my view, epistemic authorities in terms of their social status are similarly regulated by a wide range of role-specific expectations. Consider the example of teachers. They are governed by role-specific expectations. A teacher does not get to do whatever she personally judges to be desirable. The social norm of professionalism, for example, applies to teachers to the extent that students, parents, co-workers, and principals believe that teachers ought to dress appropriately, come to school on time, and excel at their teaching every day. The social norm of care, to give another example, obligates teachers to be encouraging and supportive, to engage with their students, and not to be overly critical or rude. Among these norms is the social norm of truth-telling. Whereas we may not expect a gambler to tell the truth, in ordinary circumstances, we normatively expect that teachers qua teachers will communicate information truthfully, make necessary inquiries if they do not feel competent to inform, and honestly admit their incompetence if something is beyond their area of expertise. We disapprove of a teacher misleading or deceiving her students because of the expectations we have of her as a teacher.

The same applies to the status of doctor. Although doctors occupy a superior epistemic position vis-à-vis their patients, that does not give them free rein to lie and deceive. The status of doctors, and doctor-patient relationships, are also subject to the social norm of truth-telling. In many healthcare industries throughout the world, there are various codes of ethics or even laws (formalized social norms) mandating that honesty and integrity are key virtues of a practitioner. The severe penalty attached to misrepresentation and deception, or to the abuse of conflicts of interest, is evidence of the strength of the normative expectation of truth-telling.

In fact, in most societies, the same normative expectation is attached to journalists, political representatives, scientists, and other epistemic authorities alike as an inherent part of their "status." The normative expectation of truth-telling for experts is much stronger than that for non-experts. We may overlook a racist belief made by a random blogger online. We do this all the time. However, if an academic qua academic publishes an article defending racism, the academic community would not treat this lightly and might even require the journal to remove the article, or call on the academic to apologize or the relevant institution to sanction the academic because she violates the trustworthiness expected of someone responsible for knowledge production. A political leader will not receive respect from her followers if she is found to be a liar. Gandhi and Martin Luther King are revered partly because of their integrity. It is also hard to imagine anyone who would embrace and identify with a public role which expects her to be a manipulator for personal or narrow factional gain.

If these observations are correct, then social status—the professional positions and roles that one occupies—generate and are governed by normative expectations of epistemic trustworthiness, and insofar as normative expectations are widely shared in the relevant professional or wider community, the status issues sufficient reason for those who occupy such roles to be trustworthy. Political epistemic trust is presumptively warranted in those situations.

10.3.3 An Alternative Account of Risks

Of course, not all epistemic authorities are sincere all the time. All I have argued so far is that, to the extent that epistemic authorities are governed by the social norm of epistemic trustworthiness, epistemic trust in authorities is *presumptively* warranted. There are of course risks that can compromise this presumption. The social norm account of epistemic trustworthiness suggests, however, that these risks are not rooted in the self-serving tendency of the expert to exploit their expert power. Rather, risks primarily arise from a failure to respond to the social norm. I will suggest here two common forms the failure might take.

One risk of epistemic untrustworthiness arises from *conflicting social norms*. As explained, social roles are governed by a wide range of normative expectations. These role-specific expectations, however, can sometimes conflict. And the social norm of epistemic trustworthiness may be overridden by competing social norms governing the same role. For example, a teacher in the Jim Crow era can be governed by both the social norm of epistemic trustworthiness and the social norm of racism—the shared normative expectation that whites are superior to non-whites. The racist norm may override the trustworthy norm. According to the social norm of epistemic trustworthiness, teachers feel obligated to meet the informational needs of their students regarding their academic and personal development. However, according to the social norm of racism, teachers may feel obligated to meet the needs of white students before those of blacks. If the social norm of racism overrides the social norm of epistemic trustworthiness, teachers may sacrifice the epistemic needs of black students by instilling false beliefs about their intelligence in order to sustain white privilege and pride. This may well be a superior explanation for the example of the Nazis given by Buchanan. Rather than thinking that Nazi teachers and scientists were self-interested actors who used their epistemic power to gain social power, it is more plausible to think that they were governed by prevailing social norms of racism and patriotism, such that they put the needs of a racially defined German nation above the social norms of truth-telling and justice. Importantly, this changes our diagnosis of the epistemic and social ills of untrustworthiness: in this case, untrustworthiness arises not from our self-serving nature, but rather from flawed elements of our pro-social nature.

So the expectation of epistemic trustworthiness can be overridden by competing expectations attached to the same role. Conflicts can also arise from *competing roles*. To illustrate, let's go back to the healthcare industry case discussed earlier. In Buchanan's account, status trust in physicians is unwarranted because they are self-serving by default. On my social norm account, the source of risk cannot be reduced to the physicians' self-serving nature, but is attributed to divided loyalties. In some healthcare systems, pharmaceutical companies, and healthcare providers (including healthcare organizations as well as professionals) interact frequently. The pharmaceutical companies send gifts, free samples, delegates, and funding for drug research development and continuing medical education. This then creates two potentially conflicting roles for physicians: namely the identity of a not-for-profit healthcare provider; and the identity of a for-profit healthcare provider. If physicians perceive themselves as corporate agents rather than public service providers, they are governed by a completely different set of social norms. The corporate social norms, such as the maximization of profits and efficiency, can override the social norm of truth-telling that usually governs physician–patient relationships or relationships among co-citizens. Physicians might feel obligated to sell a certain product made by the company with which they have a business relationship, or to meet the expectations of those who fund their research team. They feel obliged to serve the expectations of the narrow corporate sector, rather than the patients and the citizens at large.

These are just two possibilities in which the social norm of epistemic trustworthiness is overridden. There are certainly more. The upshot of this alternative diagnosis is that we need not be overly skeptical of epistemic trustworthiness in politics. Epistemic authorities are not inherently corrupt, contrary to the widespread assumption of many liberal political theorists. The risk of improper motives has less to do with self-interest and more to do with competing social forces rooted in norms and roles. This opens up space for an alternative remedy, one that focuses on the trustees and strengthens their responsiveness to the social norm of epistemic trustworthiness. In the final section, I will suggest how institutions of liberal democracy can play a role in this process.

10.4 Conclusion: Toward Cultivating Trustworthiness

In this chapter, I have given an account of the dilemma of epistemic trust as conceived by liberal political theorists. While relying on the epistemic authorities for political knowledge is inevitable, it is also very risky since they are prone to abuse the trust placed in them for self-gain. In order to resolve this dilemma, liberal political theorists have adopted the strategy of cultivating vigilant trust. By enhancing epistemic vigilance and epistemic autonomy, epistemic trust is constrained and intellectualized.

But as I have argued, it constrains and intellectualizes trust too much, defeating the purposes of epistemic cooperation. More importantly, I have argued that we do not need to over-intellectualize trust in order to reap the benefits of epistemic cooperation, because the risk of improper motives has been largely exaggerated. Liberal political theorists have failed to appreciate the fact that epistemic authorities, in virtue of their social roles and professional commitments, are typically governed by the social norm of epistemic trustworthiness, and as such, they are motivated to inform the public, even if it is against their self-interest to do so. This norm can of course be overridden, although when that happens, it is often because of competing social norms or roles, not self-interest. If this argument is right, we need not ensure that trust is wise by intellectualizing it; instead, we can de-intellectualize trust by making the social norm of trustworthiness more robust. In the concluding remarks below, I will show that institutions of liberal democracy can contribute to this end. Contrary to the pre-existing view, liberal democracy does not and should not constrain epistemic trust. Quite the opposite, it can even promote it by cultivating trustworthiness. A point of clarification is in order here. Although I call for more theoretical attention being paid to the strategy of cultivating trustworthiness, I do not suggest that cultivating wise trust is unimportant.[8] All I have argued is that cultivating *vigilant trust*—a strategy that over-intellectualizes trust—is neither necessary nor desirable. If there are other strategies that can make trust wise without over-intellectualizing it, we should explore them.

As explained, a significant source of risk is competing social norms. Very often, the failure to be sincere is rooted not in our selfishness but in our sociality. Our sociality can drive us to do good or evil. In order for epistemic authorities, such as politicians, teachers, scientists, and journalists, to be motivated appropriately, we must be able to counteract perverse motivations originating in bad social norms, such as racist and sexist norms. Liberal institutions, such as those enshrining freedom of conscience, freedom of assembly, and freedom of speech, provide the political conditions for individuals to challenge bad norms. In order to challenge bad norms, the relevant community should be able to destabilize the shared expectation by refusing to act in accordance with it, discussing the harmfulness of norms with their peers, or forming new expectations together about how their shared life should be governed. Bicchieri and Mercier (2014) argue for the importance of open and communal deliberation in changing social norms. The norm of female genital cutting was able to persist in part because it was taboo to bring up the issue in casual conversation, and a specific segment of the population—often women—was not given a public voice. Although many people had private doubts about the value of the practice, they dared not speak up in public. The lack of public deliberation contributed to a state of false consensus, where it was falsely believed that everyone expected girls to be cut. Free and open discussion about everyone's expectations helped to correct this false consensus.

What then is the lesson here for preventing bad cases of status trust? To prevent atrocities like those of Nazi Germany, the best response, in my view, is not to constrain our trust in those positioned to influence our belief-formation. Rather, it is to prevent evil from hijacking our epistemic institutions and practices by treating it at its root. We ought to be vigilant against bad social norms, such as racism and sexism, rather than being vigilant about trust. And we should use our political freedoms to destabilize bad norms through collective action (e.g. social movements, petitions) (Tam 2020a). Epistemic trustworthiness can then thrive alongside these good social norms and function as a source of true beliefs. For example, a political representative can make use of her epistemic and social status to inform her constituents about their political rights and obligations. Leaders of feminist communities can make use of their epistemic and social status to inform their fellow members about how their oppression by men is intimately linked to other axes of oppression, for example, racism, capitalism, cultural imperialism.

Another risk of insincerity arises from conflicting social roles. Recall the example in which physicians occupy the roles of corporate agents and public-service providers. Corporate norms attached to the former may require them to misinform the public to maximize profits, overriding the norm of truth-telling attached to the latter. How can liberal democracy help in this instance? Let me start with a non-epistemic example. In a Swiss town identified as a potential site for a nuclear waste facility, the residents were less willing to accept the facility in response to offers of compensation than they were without compensation. How should we understand this puzzling attitude? Elizabeth Anderson argues, rightly in my view, that the super-ordinate national identity of democratic citizens is the answer. When the Swiss state offered compensation, they essentially framed the question as one of private property and entitlement. It implicitly asked the residents to frame the practical dilemma as: "how much is it worth to me (or we townspeople) to keep my town waste-free?" (Anderson 2000, 197). When they understand themselves as private individuals and the problem as one of business transactions, norms of capitalism shape their deliberation: "Not in my backyard; but maybe in someone else's." By contrast, when the Swiss state asked the residents to accept the facility without compensation, the state addressed the residents as "citizens." It implicitly asked them to frame their practical dilemma as: "what principle for locating the facility should *we* accept, given that we (as Swiss citizens, considered collectively) must process the waste somewhere?" (*ibid.*). Once they understood themselves as solidaristic citizens, norms of solidarity, for example, mutual sacrifice, shaped the deliberation: "This is a national, collective problem; each citizen is responsible for solving it."

How should we apply this lesson to the epistemic trustworthiness of physicians? Appeal to the super-ordinate national identity of democratic citizens. If physicians understand their primary duty as one to the public, rather than to the private healthcare industry that organizes and funds their operations, then norms to the former identity prevail. But so long as the conflicting roles exist, then tension persists. So a more radical solution available to liberal democrats is to establish public healthcare. If healthcare is publicly funded and subject to democratic oversight, physicians will come to understand that they are engaging with the public, their co-citizens, as public servants. They will feel obligated to serve the epistemic needs of their citizens and patients rather than the wishes of the pharmaceutical companies. The conflict will be pre-empted. These are merely my hypotheses though. To what extent the liberal state can create a national identity that everyone can affirm, and whether state agencies can foster the norm of epistemic trustworthiness better than non-state agencies, remain open empirical questions. It is possible that in certain political communities, the bureaucratic culture is so strong that public healthcare fails both patients' epistemic needs and their well-being.

A complete answer to how epistemic trustworthiness in politics can be cultivated would require a huge amount of research. But I hope to have achieved my aim for this chapter: namely to demonstrate that the near-singular focus of theoretical attention toward cultivating vigilant trust is unfortunate. It is based on a flawed psychological account of epistemic cooperation. The social norm account of epistemic trustworthiness explains why political epistemic trust is not overly prone to abuse. If political epistemic trustworthiness is duly cultivated, it can make of us wise agents. And liberal political theory has the resources needed to do so. I hope to have given enough credence to the argument to warrant further development on the politics of epistemic trustworthiness.

Acknowledgment

I would like to thank Sue Donaldson, Jared Houston, Will Kymlicka, and Kevin Vallier for their helpful comments and suggestions which have substantively improved this chapter.

Notes

1. I do not draw a distinction between political and social trust. Common in the trust literature, political trust refers to trust in *government* whereas social trust refers to trust in *society*. The trust relations between epistemic authorities and the public seem to cut across the two spheres. For example, politicians operate in both government and society. For a recent discussion of the distinction, see Vallier (2018, 52–3).
2. Examples of this strategy are abundant. They include: Buchanan (2002, 2004); O'Neill (2002, 2014); Fuerstein (2013); Allard-Tremblay (2015).

3. For a helpful discussion of the distinction between evidentialist and non-evidentialist conceptions of trust, see Origgi (2005).
4. See Vallier (2019, 49–58). Vallier (2019, 52) notes that the same values promoted by *social* trust may not apply to *political* trust.
5. See Graham (2015, 268–9).
6. Two other major frameworks include evolutionary theories and shared agency approaches. Elsewhere, I have defended the superiority of the shared agency approaches because they better explain the justificatory reasons of social norms. See Tam (2020b, Chs. 3 and 4). I will sidestep that debate in this chapter, for I need only show that social norms are motivationally powerful and epistemic trustworthiness is a social norm. Its justification is beside the point.
7. My analysis does not apply to Orwellian societies in which betrayal is the social norm.
8. I thank an anonymous reviewer for pointing this out.

References

Allard-Tremblay, Yann. "Trust and Distrust in the Achievement of Popular Control." *The Monist* 98, no. 4 (October 20, 2015): 375–90.

Anderson, Elizabeth. "Beyond Homo Economicus: New Developments in Theories of Social Norms." *Philosophy & Public Affairs* 29, no. 2 (2000): 170–200.

Bicchieri, Cristina. *The Grammar of Society: The Nature and Dynamics of Social Norms*. Cambridge: Cambridge University Press, 2006.

Bicchieri, Cristina. "Norms, Convention, and the Power of Expectation." In *Philosophy of Social Science: A New Introduction*, edited by Nancy Cartwright and Eleonora Montuschi. Oxford: Oxford University Press, 2014, 208–32.

Bicchieri, Cristina, and Hugo Mercier. "Norms and Beliefs: How Change Occurs?" In *The Complexity of Social Norms*, edited by Maria Xenitiodu and Bruce Edmonds. Berlin: Springer, 2014, 37–54.

Blau, Adrian. "Cognitive Corruption and Deliberative Democracy." *Social Philosophy & Policy* 35, no. 2 (2018): 198–220.

Brennan, Geoffrey, Lina Eriksson, Robert E. Goodin, and Nicholas Southwood. *Explaining Norms*. Oxford: Oxford University Press, 2013.

Buchanan, Allen. "Social Moral Epistemology." *Social Philosophy & Policy* 19, no. 2 (2002): 126–52.

Buchanan, Allen. "Political Liberalism and Social Epistemology." *Philosophy & Public Affairs* 32, no. 2 (2004): 95–130.

Coleman, James. *Foundations of Social Theory*. Cambridge, MA: Harvard University Press, 1990.

Faulkner, Paul. *Knowledge on Trust*. Oxford: Oxford University Press, 2011.

Fuerstein, Michael. "Epistemic Trust and Liberal Justification." *Journal of Political Philosophy* 21, no. 2 (2013): 179–99.

Gilbert, Margaret P. *Joint Commitment: How We Make the Social World*. Oxford: Oxford University Press, 2013.

Goldberg, Sanford. *Relying on Others: An Essay in Epistemology*. Oxford: Oxford University Press, 2010.

Goldman, Alvin I. *Knowledge in a Social World*. Oxford: Oxford University Press, 1999.

Graham, Peter J. "Testimony, Trust and Social Norms." *Abstracta* VI (2012): 92–116.

Graham, Peter J. "Epistemic Normativity and Social Norms." In *Epistemic Evaluation, Purposeful Epistemology*, edited by David Henderson and John Greco. Oxford: Oxford University Press, 2015, 247–73.

Jones, Karen. "Trust as an Affective Attitude." *Ethics* 107, no.1 (1996): 4–25.

Lackey, Jennifer. *Learning from Words*. Oxford: Oxford University Press, 2008.

March, James G., and Johan P. Olsen. "The Logic of Appropriateness." In *Oxford Handbook of Public Policy*, edited by Michael Moran, Martin Rein, and Robert E. Goodin. Oxford: Oxford University Press, 2006, 689–708.

O'Neill, Onora. *A Question of Trust. The BBC Reith Lectures 2002*, Cambridge: Cambridge University Press, 2002.

O'Neill, Onora. "Responses." In *Reading Onora O'Neill*, edited by David Archard, Monique Deveaux, Neil Manson, and Daniel Weinstock. New York: Routledge, 2013.

O'Neill, Onora. "Trust, Trustworthiness, and Accountability." In *Capital Failure: Rebuilding Trust in Financial Services*, edited by Nicholas Morris and David Vines. Oxford: Oxford University Press, 2014, 172–91.

Origgi, Gloria. (2005) "What Does It Mean to Trust in Epistemic Authority?" Columbia University Academic Commons. http://doi.org/10.7916/D80007FR

Parsons, Talcott. *The Structure of Social Action, 2 vols*. New York: McGraw Hill, 1937.

Scheffler, Samuel. "Membership and Political Obligation." *Journal of Political Philosophy* 26, no. 1 (2018): 3–23.

Sunstein, Cass R. "Social Norms and Social Roles." *Columbia Law Review* 96, no. 4 (1996): 903–68.

Tam, Agnes. "Why Moral Reasoning Is Insufficient for Moral Progress." *Journal of Political Philosophy* 28, no. 1 (2020a): 73–96.

Tam, Agnes. *Norms, Reasons, and Moral Progress*. Doctoral thesis, Queen's University, Kingston, Canada, 2020b. Retrieved from http://hdl.handle.net/1974/27804.

Vallier, Kevin. *Must Politics Be War? Restoring Our Trust in the Open Society*. Oxford: Oxford University Press, 2018.

Warren, Mark. "Democratic Theory and Trust." In *Democracy and Trust*, edited by Mark Warren. Cambridge: Cambridge University Press, 1999, 310–45.

Short Bios and Addresses

Cristina Bicchieri

Cristina Bicchieri is the S.J.P. Harvie Chair of Social Thought and Comparative Ethics, and Professor of Philosophy and Psychology at the University of Pennsylvania. She is the director of the Master of Behavioral and Decision Sciences, the Philosophy, Politics and Economics Program, the Behavioral Ethics Lab, and the Center for Social Norms and Behavioral Dynamics. She has published more than 100 articles and several books, among which are *The Grammar of Society: The Nature and Dynamics of Social Norms*, Cambridge University Press, 2006 and *Norms in the Wild: How to Diagnose, Measure and Change Social Norms*, Oxford University Press 2016. She works on social norms measurement and behavioral/field experiments on norm change, cooperation, and fairness on social networks. Her most recent work looks at the role of trendsetters in social change, and how network structures facilitate or impair behavioral changes.

Erte Xiao

Erte Xiao is a professor of economics at Monash University. Her interests focus on applied microeconomics, psychology and economics, experimental economics, and behavioral game theory. Her research has been published in a wide range of journals, including *Games and Economic Behavior, Journal of Public Economics, Management Science, Journal of Economic Behavior and Organization, Public Choice, Synthese, Experimental Economics, Politics, Philosophy, and Economics*, and *Proceedings of the National Academy of Sciences of the United States of America.*

Ryan Muldoon

Ryan Muldoon is an Associate Professor of Philosophy and Director of the Philosophy, Politics, and Economics Program at the University at Buffalo. He is the author of Social Contract Theory for a Diverse

World: Beyond Tolerance. His work addresses questions of how to best leverage diversity, and how informal institutions and social norms work to shape our social lives.

Kevin Vallier

Kevin Vallier is Associate Professor of Philosophy at Bowling Green State University and the author of 4 edited volumes, and forty peer-reviewed articles. His books include *Liberal Politics and Public Faith* (Routledge 2014), *Must Politics Be War* (Oxford UP 2019), and *Trust in a Polarized Age* (Oxford UP 2020).

Christian Bjørnskov

Christian Bjørnskov is professor of economics at the Department of Economics at Aarhus University in Aarhus, Denmark, and affiliated researcher at the Research Institute of Industrial Economics (IFN) in Stockholm. He is also associated with the Centre for Political Studies in Copenhagen and the Institute of Economic Affairs in London. His interests focus on public choice and political economy approaches to different questions, including the importance of informal institutions. His research has been published in a wide range of journals, including *American Journal of Political Science*, *Journal of Development Economics*, *Public Choice*, and *Academy of Management Perspectives*.

Andreas Bergh

Andreas Bergh is associate professor of economics at the Department of Economics at Lund University, Sweden, and affiliated researcher at the Research Institute of Industrial Economics (IFN) in Stockholm. He is also associated with SETS (socio-economic technology studies) at LTH faculty of engineering in Lund. His interests focus on formal and informal institutions, in particular the welfare state and social trust. His research has been published in journals such as *European Economic Review*, *European Sociological Review*, *World Development*, and *Public Choice*. He is the author of *Sweden and the Revival of the Capitalist Welfare State* (Edward Elgar).

Marion Boulicault

Marion Boulicault is a PhD Candidate in Philosophy at the Massachusetts Institute of Technology, and a senior member of the Harvard GenderSci Lab. Starting in 2021, she will be a Lecturer at the University of Adelaide. Her research examines the relationships between social norms and scientific measurement practices. She also has interests in feminist approaches to bioethics and the ethics of technology, and is a Neuroethics Fellow with the Center for Neurotechnology based at the University of Washington.

Prior to her PhD, she completed an MPhil degree in the history and philosophy of science at the University of Cambridge, and worked as a Research Associate at the Environmental Law Institute in Washington D.C.

S. Andrew Schroeder

Andrew Schroeder is an associate professor of philosophy at Claremont McKenna College, where he works on topics in ethics, political philosophy, the philosophy of science, and the philosophy of disability. His current research aims to bring the concepts, tools, and methods of political philosophy to bear on problems traditionally discussed by philosophers of science.

Lacey J. Davidson

Lacey J. Davidson is an Assistant Professor at California Lutheran University. She specializes in philosophy of race, social epistemology, and moral psychology. You can find some of her work in the *Journal of Applied Philosophy*, *Overcoming Epistemic Injustice* (2019), and *Introduction to Implicit Bias* (2020).

Mark Satta

Mark Satta is an Assistant Professor of Philosophy at Wayne State University. He specializes in epistemology, philosophy of language, and applied philosophy of law. His work has been published in *Philosophical Studies*, *Analysis*, *Synthese*, *Episteme*, and *The Buffalo Law Review*, among other venues.

Ted Hinchman

Edward Hinchman is Professor of Philosophy at Florida State University. He works on issues pertaining to both interpersonal and intrapersonal trust, including the reason-givingness of advice, promising and shared intention, the epistemology of testimony, the diachronic rationality of intention, and the role of self-trust in both practical and doxastic judgment.

Alida Liberman

Alida Liberman is an Assistant Professor of Philosophy at Southern Methodist University. She received her PhD from the University of Southern California. Her research focuses on theoretical ethics, practical ethics, and the space in between, as she seeks to understand concepts in ethics both for their own sakes and for how they can help us grapple with real-world problems.

Ira K. Lindsay

Ira K. Lindsay is Senior Lecturer in Finance Law and Ethics at the University of Surrey School of Law where he teaches tax law and property law. Lindsay graduated with a BA in history from Swarthmore College, studied Russian History on a Fulbright Fellowship at the European University of St. Petersburg, received a JD from Yale Law School, and PhD in philosophy from the University of Michigan. After graduating from Yale, he practiced tax law at Cleary Gottlieb Steen & Hamilton in New York City and served as a law clerk to Judge Stephen F. Williams of the US Court of Appeals for the D.C. Circuit. From 2014 to 2016, Lindsay was a postdoctoral fellow at Dartmouth College in the Department of Philosophy and the Political Economy Project. His research interests including taxation, property law, political philosophy, jurisprudence, and comparative law.

Amy Mullin

Amy Mullin is a Professor of Philosophy at the University of Toronto. She has written on topics relating to the responsibilities of both parents and minor children in well-functioning caregiving relationships. Her interests include autonomy, trust, gratitude, and hope.

Simon Scheller

Simon Scheller is a senior lecturer for political science at the Otto-Friedrich University of Bamberg, Germany. He studied Political Science, Philosophy, and Economics at Bayreuth (Germany), Leeds (UK) and Bamberg, where he also received his PhD in late 2017. He was a postdoctoral researcher at the Munich Center for Mathematical Philosophy from 2017 to 2019. His research interests center around formal approaches to political philosophy.

Agnes Tam

Agnes Tam is a Postdoctoral Fellow at the Social Justice Centre of Concordia University (Montreal). Her research focuses on the empirical and normative phenomena of group agency and reasoning, and explores their bearings on ethics and politics.

Index

Note: Page numbers in bold indicate figures and tables.